Angler's Guide to
Jigs and Jigging

Angler's Guide to

Jigs and Jigging

How to Make and Use the World's Deadliest Lure

Kenn Oberrecht

Winchester Press • Tulsa, Oklahoma

Library of Congress Cataloging in Publication Data
Oberrecht, Kenn.
　Angler's guide to jigs and jigging.
　Includes index.
　　1.　Fishing.　2.　Jigs (Fishing lures)　I.　Title.
SH449.O23　　　799.1'2　　　81-23998
ISBN 0-87691-365-6　　　AACR2

Published by Winchester Press
1421 South Sheridan Road
P. O. Box 1260
Tulsa, Oklahoma 74101

Printed in the United States of America

1　2　3　4　5　　86　85　84　83　82

For my young nephew and fishing partner,
Stephen Oberrecht. Despite his father's
attempts to corrupt him by overexposure to
trout flies and to the type of characters who
would angle with such devices and exaggerate
their successes, Steve has learned the two most
important angling maxims: (1) Jigs catch
more fish. (2) Uncles know best.

Acknowledgments

Over the years, many folks have passed on countless valuable fishing tips to me and have shown me new ways to catch fish. Some were friends; others were just friendly chaps I met while fishing. Many of their techniques are covered in the following pages. I thank them for sharing their skills and knowledge with me.

I also wish to thank the tackle manufacturers who have kept me abreast of all the latest innovations and have supplied samples for field testing, evaluation, and photography. For purposes of this book I specifically wish to express gratitude to the following individuals and companies for providing willing assistance, information, illustrations, and photographic samples: Tony Accetta & Son, Inc.; Cliff Shelby, Jim Bagley Bait Co., Inc.; Pete Renkert, Bead Chain Tackle Co.; Blakemore Sales Corp.; Bomber Bait Co.; Bing McClellan, Burke Fishing Lures; Cordell Tackle; Creme Lure Co.; Do-It Corporation; Flambeau Products Corp.; Fle-Fly Mfg., Inc.; Dan Gapen, Gapen's World of Fishin', Inc.; Richard Lee, Lee Precision, Inc.; Lyman Products Corp.; Robert Maserang, M-F Manufacturing Co., Inc.; Tom Mann, Mann's Bait Co.; Mister Twister; O. Mustad & Son (USA), Inc.; Dennis Moyer, Netcraft Co.; D. E. Wintz, Orbex; C. Boyd Pfeiffer, Pfeiffer's Tackle Crafters, Inc.; Glenn Simms, Plano Molding Co.; Sweet's Molds; Jim Vander Mause, Uncle Josh Bait Co.; Weber; Bob Courtright and Dick Worth, Worth Company; Wright & McGill; and Yakima Bait Co.

A special note of thanks is due to my colleague and friend, Boyd Pfeiffer, for all his suggestions, ideas, and most of all, for the fine photographs he provided.

Finally, I would like to acknowledge angler and editor Bob Elman, who knows when to give slack to his fish and his authors.

Contents

Part One
Jigs

Think about the jig for a moment. Create a good mental image. Now imagine the jig resting in the palm of your hand. It can be a large jig or a small one, no matter. It can be dressed with deer hair, synthetic hair, nylon, or marabou, skirted with rubber or vinyl, skewered with any of a number of soft-plastic lures, or tipped with live or cut bait; that doesn't matter either.

What matters is the jig itself. In its various incarnations, it is singularly the most amazing fishing lure ever devised. Now think about *that* for a moment: a bold statement, perhaps, but true, nonetheless. You're skeptical, right?—as well you should be, if you're not yet a confirmed jig fisherman.

Sure, every manufacturer claims his new lure is the greatest fish-catching gizmo to come along since the hook. But that, pardner, is the point. The jig isn't new, and it's not a manufacturer making all the claims about its unparalleled ability to catch fish. The jig has been around, in one form or another, for nearly as long as the fish hook, and the praise being lavished upon it comes from the nation's top angling experts and leading outdoor writers.

Still skeptical? Okay, name one type of lure that has taken as great a variety of fish in fresh and salt water as the jig. Pick any kind of lure that can be adapted to a wider variety of fishing situations and water conditions than the jig. Show me a lure that can be used successfully in as many different terminal riggings. Tell me about one that's easier to cast. Pick any lure that's cheaper to buy. Point out one that's easier to make.

This really isn't fair, is it? I've picked the winner. I'm arguing on the side of the jig, and there's really no argument against it. It's a loaded discussion with the facts in favor of the jig. So let's just leave it at that and go on to find out more about jigs.

But first, let's take one more look at the one resting in the palm of your hand—the sleek, heavy-headed lure that sits there so naturally with its hook turned up, poised, as if ready for battle with anything that dares to take it on. It's truly a marvel of design simplicity. No frills. All business. Fish-catching business.

Now admit it: isn't it the most amazing fishing lure ever devised?

1.  Jigs—The Do-Everything Lures

If a hundred angling experts were surveyed on which type of lure they would pick, were they to be restricted to one kind for all their fishing, the results would be predictably varied. Most of those who concentrate their efforts on bass angling would pick the plastic worm, no doubt. Most trout anglers would opt for flies. And there would be those who would choose plugs, spinnerbaits, spinners, or spoons. But the knowledgeable majority—especially those who fish various types of water for different species—would select the jig as the most versatile, adaptable, do-everything lure ever created. The jig's ability to consistently take freshwater, saltwater, and anadromous species of all sorts goes unchallenged by today's ever-growing legions of lures.

Jigs, in their various designs and weights (from a mere $1/80$ ounce to more than eight ounces) take everything from small brook trout to huge Pacific halibut. On ultralight tackle, the tiniest jigs are excellent substitutes for nymphs favored by trout, char, and related species. Panfish anglers use jigs to fill ice chests and live wells with slab-sided crappies and bluegills. And other freshwater fishermen take both largemouth and smallmouth bass, rock bass, walleye and sauger, pickerel, pike, muskie, and other species in great numbers with the trusty jig.

Jigs are the top choice during the sweltering summer doldrums when they are used to probe the depths, or in the chill of winter when they are fished through the ice or are sent to the bottom in open waters to search for elusive fish. They are suitable for fishing all types of water at all depths during any season.

Off the north Atlantic coast, jigs take their share of big Atlantic cod and pollack. Similar tackle and techniques are used in the Pacific for halibut and lingcod. And just about any other bottom fish that the offshore angler seeks will fall for the jig. Jigs are also trolled or cast on the open ocean for many varieties of marine fishes.

The versatile, do-everything jig in some of its many adaptations.

Inshore anglers use jigs to take tarpon, snook, barracuda, various jacks, and numerous other gamesters. Jigs worked on the flats in southern Florida and in the Bahamas take bonefish and permit. In tidal areas, striped bass, weakfish, and seatrout are among the many gamefish that will attack jigs.

Anglers along the Atlantic and Pacific coasts and on the coastal rivers and their tributaries look forward each spring to shad migrations and the outstanding fishing those runs bring. The number-one lure for these scrappy fish is the shad dart, which takes an estimated 75 percent of all shad caught by anglers. The dart is a productive little jig that will take all manner of freshwater and saltwater gamefish and panfish in addition to the anadromous shad.

In fact, it would be far easier to list the fish that won't take jigs than those which favor this lure.

The U.S. Air Force considers the jig such a universal fish-catching lure that jigs are included in every Air Force survival kit. And from the number of articles on jig fishing beginning to show up in the nation's fishing and outdoor magazines and the record catches being made with jigs, it is obvious that jigs are now gaining the esteem of this country's angling experts and average fishermen as well.

The Evolution Of The Jig

There is really no way to tell how long jigs have been used to catch fish; nor can we attribute the lure's design and development to any one inventor or manufacturer. Jigs, crudely fashioned from available materials (such as bone and shell) were among some of the earliest lures used by primitive man. Nevertheless, the jig's popularity among modern anglers has been slow in growth, often regionally restricted, and fraught with myths and misconceptions. Consequently, the jig has evolved slowly and quietly into one of the greatest fish-catching devices an angler can use.

The jig, as we know it today, can be considered a twentieth-century lure, and until the 1940s it was used mostly by saltwater fishermen. Offshore anglers found the heavy lures ideal for probing great depths and taking a variety of reef species, while surf fishermen used them to reach beyond the combers, often casting into strong winds with their conventional tackle.

It wasn't until after World War II and the widespread acceptance of spinning tackle that scaled-down jigs began finding their way into more tackle boxes. Spinning and spincasting revolutionized fishing in America, allowing smaller, lighter lures to be cast with ease, even by novices. Tackle shops were soon crammed with lures of all sizes, capable of taking the widest possible variety of fishes. Among all these fish attractors were jigs of various weights and designs, but they were often left on the counters and display racks by fishermen enamored of the more complex and expensive lures. Those who were attracted by the jig's simplicity of design and relative low cost soon found that some species of fish could be more readily tempted with jigs than with any other artificial bait. Certainly, a few anglers discovered, also, that some waters were much easier to work with jigs.

In the evolution of jig fishing, many other discoveries were to be made before the lure would gain widespread acceptance by both novice and veteran anglers throughout the country. Fishermen would learn, for example, to use jigs tipped with natural baits to take fish when all else failed. They would learn to use jig heads with pork rinds and soft-plastic baits. They would learn to use multiple-lure jig rigs and jig/plug combinations. They would learn how to explore the depths, bounce the bottom, work the weedbeds, skim the surface, swim the mid-depths, drift the currents, ply the reefs and dropoffs, comb the flats, and scour the bars—all with the simple, effective jig.

While freshwater and saltwater anglers alike would learn new jig-fishing techniques and relearn old ones, the jig would gradually come of age, recognized as the most versatile and productive of all fishing lures. Although the jig, in one form or another, has been catching fish for a long time, it has only begun to claim its rightful position among serious anglers in the last quarter of the twentieth century.

Jigs—Easy To Use, Easy To Own

Jigs are dense and compact lures—heavy, relative to their respective sizes. Consequently, they experience little wind resistance, making them the easiest of all lures to cast with spinning, spincasting, baitcasting, or surf tackle.

Because of these characteristics, jigs can be cast effortlessly and accurately: two important considerations for any serious angler. The fisherman who spends long days in pursuit of his favorite species with artificial lures knows that heavy tackle and bulky lures can cause fatigue. Jigs can keep him tirelessly casting long after other lures would have worn him down and taken the edge of enjoyment off his sport. The accuracy factor, of course, is closely related, because a lure that casts with little effort is one that is more easily controlled.

In short, if the angler can fish harder and longer without tiring and can put his lures on target with greater consistency, the results are quite predictable: he will catch more and bigger fish. Moreover, he will improve his angling skills at a faster pace.

That same compactness that makes the jig shoot through the air like a bullet also allows it to sink like an anchor and work against or with currents with far less drag than other lures experience. On the other hand, the angler can match jig-head weight and design to the right body dressing for a lure that glides slowly to the depths, swims above weedbeds, or skims across the water only inches beneath the surface. No other type of lure offers such versatility and adaptability to varying conditions.

While the novice angler, or even the experienced one who has not yet tried jig fishing, might view the jig, in light of other lures, as a dull and actionless piece of tackle suited only to certain limited and specific types of fishing, nothing could be further from the truth. The fact is, although most jigs have little or no inherent or built-in action, the angler can impart a vast assortment of motions and movements to the jig, or no action at all, whichever meets his needs. No other single lure offers such instant and endless flexibility.

By design, the leadhead jig is far more efficient at hooking fish and avoiding snags than most other lures. Its stationary, upriding hook is usually in the best possible position to connect when a fish strikes. This same feature allows the nose-heavy jig to bounce over obstructions that would certainly hang up most other lures with downriding single or dangling treble hooks. With jigs, you'll spend less time horsing out snags and more time fishing.

All this goes a long way toward making the jig the most effective and productive lure available to the modern angler. Closely related and at least partially responsible for the jig's efficiency and burgeoning popularity is the cost factor. I hesitate to even use the word *inexpensive*. The fact is, jigs are downright, flat out *cheap*.

For the price of a single surface plug or crankbait, you can buy a half-dozen or more assorted jigs. And if you make your own, which is quite easy and requires only a few tools, you can produce several dozen jigs for the price of that single manufactured lure.

What this means, first, is that the average angler can afford to carry far more jigs than other kinds of lures. He can stock a wide assortment of colors, sizes, and designs to match with the various species he fishes for and the ever-changing conditions he faces.

What's even more important to the angler who wants to catch fish consistently is that with jigs he can afford to lose lures. Consequently, he will be more inclined to put his lures amidst the sunken brush, flooded timber, weedbeds, rocks, and other rubble where fish lurk. As the old saying goes, if you aren't getting snags, you aren't fishing where the fish are.

Even the angler who has learned this important maxim and operates accordingly by fishing the snag-strewn waters is usually reluctant to break off an expensive lure when it hopelessly hangs itself on some underwater obstacle. He'll spend precious fishing time trying to work his lure loose, and as often as not will end up breaking it off anyway.

The jig fisherman, on the other hand, will make a reasonable attempt to free his snagged jig, but if he fails, he'll break it off, tie on another, and get back to fishing with little time lost and a minimum of disturbance to his fishing waters.

It's really no wonder that so many of this country's anglers are turning to simple jigs as their do-everything lures.

2.  Modern Jigs: Design, Function, and Adaptation

The current and growing popularity of jigs among anglers everywhere is attributable to several important factors, not the least of which are those mentioned in Chapter 1. Tantamount in importance, though, are the jig's simplicity of design and resultant ease with which the lure is used. Paramount in importance is the lure's function and adaptability.

Basically, there are four types of jigs: leadhead, floating, diamond (also known as tin squid or metal squid), and trolling. Among these basic types are different weights and sizes and numerous variations of design and function, as well as an infinite variety of dressings. In short, the angler can choose lures from the countless possible combinations to fit practically any freshwater or saltwater situation.

Before making intelligent selections, however, the angler must be aware of what is available to him and must understand how to fit a particular jig to any given set of conditions.

Leadhead Jigs

By far, the most popular and widely used jigs are the so-called leadheads (spelled "ledheads" by some dedheads). In some parts of the country, these jigs are known as bucktails, and while this term was once descriptive, in that the jig heads were dressed with deer hair, it is a needlessly confusing term, today, that ought to be dispensed with here and now. Certainly, some leadheads are still tied with deer hair, but that is by no means the only material used. Jigs are tied with a great many different animal hairs, feathers, and synthetic materials. Moreover, the term "bucktail" is also applied to a type of streamer fly, which it aptly de-

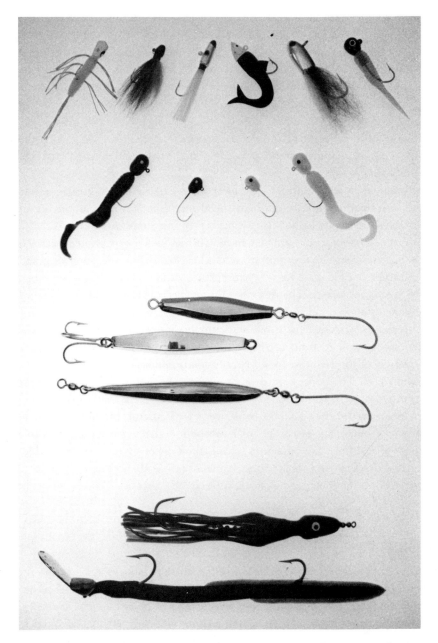

Four basic types of jigs. *Top row,* various styles of leadheads; *next row,* floating jigs; *center,* three diamond jigs or metal squids; *bottom,* two trolling-type jigs.

scribes. Since "leadhead" succinctly describes the jig, and "bucktail" the streamer, I see no need to perpetuate the duplication of terms.

The most common types of leadhead jigs are the roundhead or ball jigs, bullet, lima bean, banana, Erie, and dart. Other popular types include the arrowhead, teardrop, glider or slider, and walleye jig. Additionally, there are other specialty jigs and some regionally popular ones that are noteworthy; among them are the popeye or bugeye jig, gumdrop, rolly polly, open-mouth, horsehead, and various worm and eel jigs. Add to this the vast array of manufacturers' variations and innovations and the list becomes staggering.

Inherent in any leadhead jig's design is a balance which greatly affects the lure's performance and which the angler can use to his advantage in selecting the right jig for his particular fishing situation.

A *standard-balanced* jig is one in which the hook eye is located between the jig's nose and its center of gravity. On a steady retrieve, such a jig will ride slightly nose-up. On a jigging retrieve, the lure will nose-dive when the line is slackened. The roundhead is an example of a standard-balanced jig and is an excellent choice for all-around use.

A *forward-balanced* jig is one with the hook eye located at or very near the nose—well in front of the lure's center of gravity. On the retrieve, this type of jig will nose up sharply, causing the head to protect the hook from snags. The banana jig is one such lure, favored by many anglers for fishing amidst brush, flooded timber, and other likely hangups.

In a *center-balanced* jig, the hook eye is located atop the lure's center of gravity, which causes the jig to ride horizontally when hanging from a taut vertical line. Consequently, this is the type of jig most often used for vertical jigging from boats, docks, piers, and bridges. The rolly polly is an example of a center-balanced jig and one that is a good choice for deep-water jigging.

Roundhead

Roundhead or ball jigs are certainly the most popular of all jigs and are probably used for catching a greater variety of fish than any other. They are commonly available in sizes ranging from $1/32$ ounce to ¾ ounce for most freshwater and light saltwater fishing. Roundhead jigs as small as $1/64$ and even $1/80$ ounce are also available for ultralight fishing, and for larger fish and deeper waters sizes range up to about three ounces.

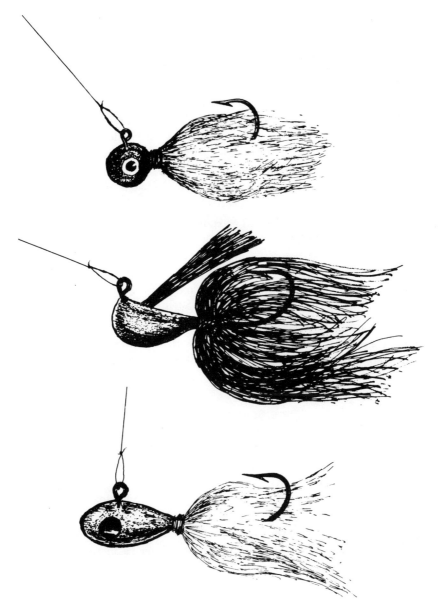

The balance of a leadhead jig, which is determined by the position of the hook's eye in relation to the jig head's center of gravity, greatly affects a lure's performance. *Top,* standard-balanced jig; *center,* forward-balanced jig; *bottom,* center-balanced jig.

The heads are normally cast on light-wire Aberdeen-style hooks which offer a distinct advantage to the angler probing snag-strewn waters. In addition to being inherently snag-resistant, the roundhead with an Aberdeen hook can usually be pulled free if it does get hung up. The pliable wire of the hook will straighten when line tension is gradually and steadily increased. The angler can then bend the hook back to its normal position, dress the point with a hone, and get back to fishing.

Roundhead jigs are commercially available with a wide variety of dressings. This style is also a good choice for the angler who will cast his own jigs, as it is among the easiest to tie. Moreover, plain, undressed roundheads are tops for use with soft-plastic twist-tails—one of the deadliest of all lures for everything from freshwater panfish to saltwater reef species. For such purposes, the heads can be epoxy painted or left in their natural, dull-gray finish.

Bullet

Bullet jigs are widely used in fresh and salt water. They are center-balanced, which makes them good for vertical jigging. Popular sizes for light-tackle fishing are ⅛ and ¼ ounce with Aberdeen hooks in sizes 4 and 2. For saltwater fishing, larger bullet jigs are cast on cadmium-plated and tinned O'Shaughnessy hooks.

Lima Bean

The thin, tapered design of the lima-bean jig (also known as the Upperman, flathead, or oval jig) makes this one ideal for fishing in rocky areas where it is less likely to snag than other lures and other types of jigs. It is also a good jig to use in fast river currents and strong tidal flows.

Lima jigs are normally available in sizes from ⅜ ounce to one ounce or larger, with either Aberdeen or O'Shaughnessy hooks from 1/0 to about 6/0 in size. They also come as either center-balanced or standard-balanced to fit many different needs.

Banana

The banana jig is a versatile lure that has gained widespread popularity in recent years. When tied with hair or nylon it greatly resembles a bait-

Roundhead jig, dressed with chenille-and-tinsel body and marabou tail.

Bullet jig, dressed with bucktail and tinsel.

Lima bean or Upperman jig, dressed with feathers.

fish. Banana jig heads are also favored by many jig-'n'-eel and plastic-worm fishermen.

The shape of the banana jig makes it a good choice for fishing ledges, dropoffs, and other areas where a fast-diving lure is best. Its forward-balance design allows it to bounce over most snags and lets it nose-dive on a slack line.

Common sizes are from ⅛ to ½ ounce for most freshwater applications and 1, 1½, and 2 ounces for saltwater angling. Smaller banana jigs are normally cast on Aberdeen hooks, larger on O'Shaughnessy hooks.

Erie

Named after the Great Lake where it was developed and used primarily for walleye and smallmouth-bass fishing, the Erie jig is another that has gained broad acceptance in recent years.

A good all-around jigging lure in its own right, the Erie's center balance and unusual head design also make it a superb standup jig. When allowed to rest on bottom, the jig's hook will stand at approximately a 45° angle to the bottom, which facilitates an easy hookup when a fish takes it. For that reason, the Erie jig has become a popular one to use with plastic worms and other buoyant, soft-plastic lures.

Erie jigs come in a good assortment of sizes, from ⅛ to ¾ ounce, cast on either Aberdeen or O'Shaughnessy hooks running in sizes from 2 to 4/o.

Dart

The dart jig, or shad dart, as it's more commonly known, is an unusually shaped jig that was originally designed for taking shad on their spawning migrations. Its slanted nose, tapered head, and standard balance impart an exaggerated action when the lure is cast and jigged on the retrieve. When the rod is twitched, the jig rises sharply then drops again on the slackened line. When trolled, the jig planes slightly.

Shad darts are small (usually ⅛ and ¼ ounce) with size 2 or 2/o Aberdeen hooks. They're normally tied with hair or marabou feathers, but can be tied with other materials as well.

They can be cast with light or ultralight spinning tackle for shad and other species. Many shad fishermen also troll them near bottom with extra weight added to the line.

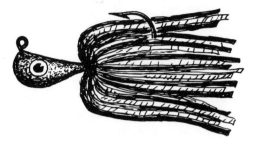

Banana jig, dressed with reversed vinyl skirt.

Erie jig, dressed with living-rubber skirt.

Dart jig, or shad dart, dressed with marabou.

Arrowhead

The slightly flattened, forward taper of the arrowhead jig makes this one adaptable to a variety of tyings as well as use with soft-plastic tails. Its availability in standard or center balance further increases its versatility.

It commonly comes in weights from ¼ to ½ ounce on Aberdeen hooks from size 1/0 to 3/0, but can be found in larger sizes cast on O'Shaughnessy hooks for saltwater use. Arrowhead jigs are often used with plastic grub tails in both fresh and salt water.

Teardrop

The tapered shape of the teardrop jig makes it the most streamlined of the center-balanced jigs. Although it is a good choice for vertical jigging, as other center-balanced jigs are, this one can also be cast and retrieved with long, pumping rod action to impart diving action to the lure.

Normally tied with hair or nylon, it usually comes in weights of ¼ to ⅜ ounce with 1/0 or 2/0 Aberdeen hooks for freshwater and light salt-water fishing.

Glider

Sometimes known as a slider jig, the glider is a center-balanced jig. The topmost side of the head is decidedly flattened, while the underside is rounded. When cast and jigged or worked vertically, the jig has an erratic, tipsy action.

Glider jigs are normally available in weights from ⅛ to ¾ ounce with either Aberdeen or O'Shaughnessy hooks in sizes 1 to 4/0.

These jigs are either tied with hair, feathers, or synthetic materials or are adapted for use with soft-plastic tails and plastic worms.

Walleye

Like the shad dart, the walleye jig is effective on many species other than the one for which it was originally designed. In shape, this jig resembles the arrowhead, but its wedge head is more gradually tapered front and rear.

Normally cast on Aberdeen hooks of sizes 6 to 4/0, walleye jigs are available in a range of weights from $1/32$ to ⅜ ounce. It can be dressed

Arrowhead jig, dressed with soft-plastic grub tail.

Teardrop jig, dressed with nylon.

Glider or slider jig, dressed with soft-plastic twist-tail.

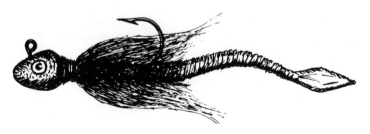

Walleye jig, dressed with Dynel Fishair and plastic worm.

with the usual natural and synthetic materials and is a good choice for use with soft plastics.

Its forward balance makes it an excellent bottom-bumping jig. The walleye jig is a favorite for all-around fishing in fresh water and inshore salt water.

Popeye

The popeye or bugeye jig resembles a roundhead jig with a large collar aft of the head. It gets its name from the eyes protruding from each side of the head which are cast into the jig and are usually painted. In addition to adding appeal to the lure, the eyes also serve as counterbalances which prevent the jig from turning on its side when it is allowed to rest on bottom. The hook is thereby kept upright and ready for the strike.

This is a forward-balanced jig, normally cast on O'Shaughnessy hooks in sizes from 2/0 to 6/0, available in weights from ¼ to one ounce.

Gumdrop

As the name implies, the shape of this jig's head resembles a gumdrop turned on its side. Although the jig can be tied with any of the common natural and synthetic materials, it is favored by coastal fishermen who simply attach soft-plastic shrimp tails to the head.

Since these jigs are used primarily in salt water, they are normally cast on O'Shaughnessy hooks in sizes 5/0 and 6/0. Weights are usually ¾ and one ounce.

Rolly Polly

The rolly polly is an oversized, center-balanced jig that is particularly suited to deep-water jigging. This is a fast-sinking jig that can be tied with hair or feathers, or can be used with soft-plastic tails or vinyl skirts.

The rolly polly comes in weights from $^1/_{16}$ ounce to 1¼ ounces. It is normally cast on Aberdeen hooks from size 4 to size 4/0.

Open-Mouth

The open-mouth jig (variously known as hot lips, ruby lips, and other names) is a big saltwater lure that is quite popular on the east coast. Its

Popeye or bugeye jig, dressed with bucktail.

Gumdrop jig, dressed with soft-plastic shrimp tail.

Rolly polly jig, dressed with Dynel Fishair.

Open-mouth jig, dressed with bucktail and feathers.

size and weight make it ideal for deep-water jigging and working in swift tidal flows.

These jigs are cast on O'Shaughnessy hooks in sizes 5/0 to 7/0 or larger and come in weights of ¾ ounce to 1½ ounces or more.

Although open-mouth jigs are normally tied with hair or synthetic fur, they can be used with soft-plastic tails and plastic skirts as well.

Horsehead

The horsehead jig derives its name from the long, drooping nose, into which is molded a barrel swivel. After the lure is dressed with any of the usual jig-tying materials and the head and molded-in eyes are painted, a small spinner blade is attached to the barrel swivel, usually by means of a split ring.

Horsehead jigs are usually cast on small Aberdeen hooks, sizes 6 to 1, and the jigs normally weigh from $1/16$ to ¼ ounce.

Used primarily in fresh water, the jig is also effective for light saltwater action. It is a favorite in some areas for walleye and smallmouth bass and is also an effective crappie lure.

Floating Jigs

As one might surmise, floating jigs differ greatly from the leadheads, in that they do not sink unless aided by auxiliary weight. Nevertheless, they were designed to be fished near the bottom.

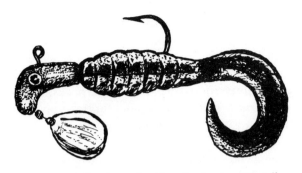

Horsehead jig, dressed with soft-plastic twist-tail.

Although floating jigs are sometimes dressed with the usual tying materials, they are normally used with natural baits, pork rinds, or soft plastics.

The idea behind the floating jig is to present an enticing lure to fish near bottom, but enough above weeds and other potential snags to prevent its getting entangled. This is usually accomplished with one of two popular rigs: the walking-sinker rig, or Gapen's Bait-Walker sinkers.

Walking sinkers have been specially designed to be worked along bottom debris without getting snagged as easily as other sinkers. The walking-sinker rig consists of a walking sinker, barrel swivel, leader, and floating-jig head with dressing of the angler's choice.

Gapen's Bait-Walker sinker is molded directly to a wire arm, similar to those used on spinnerbaits. The fishing line is attached to the eye of the wire arm, and a leader or dropback line is then tied to the barrel swivel on the upper wire of the arm. The floating jig is then tied to the tag end of the leader.

Walking sinkers are commercially available in sizes from about ⅜ ounce to 1½ ounces. Molds are also available for those who wish to cast their own. Gapen's Bait-Walker sinkers come in weights from ¼ ounce to six ounces.

Floating-jig rigs can be deadly, particularly in relatively shallow lakes and ponds from mid-summer to early fall, when such waters are often full of weeds. During colder months, they're often productive because they can be worked deep and slowly, taking fish that are often lethargic when water temperatures are low.

Diamond Jigs

Diamond jigs (also known as metal squids or tin squids) are usually heavily chrome plated or plated with nickel and finely polished to a mirror finish. Some such lures are molded onto single hooks; others have steel rings molded into the bodies to which single or treble hooks are attached. Hookless diamond jigs are also available to which the angler can add his own hooks and tags.

These are dense and compact lures, well-suited to deep-water vertical jigging or casting in a rough surf against strong winds and working in heavy currents. Consequently, they have been favored by saltwater anglers for years.

The fluttering action of a diamond jig is imitative of a wounded baitfish and is quite attractive to such species as bluefish, striped bass, mackerel, cod, pollack, and other marine species. Some models are dead ringers for sand eels, a favorite food of many Atlantic gamefish.

Although the diamond jig has seen most of its action in the salt chuck, it is also an effective lure for freshwater fishes, particularly in its smaller sizes.

Bead Chain Tackle Co. and its subsidiary, Bridgeport Silverware Manufacturing Corp., are major suppliers of diamond jigs and related lures on the east coast.

In addition to being effective jigging and surfcasting lures, diamond jigs also can be deadly trolling lures—used either alone or in conjunction with other lures in multiple rigs.

Trolling Jigs

Although some leadhead and diamond jigs are excellent trolling lures, most are used for casting and jigging. There are other jig-type lures designed primarily for trolling, although some—particularly the smaller ones—are effective casting lures as well.

One such "trolling jig" is the Japanese jig, also known as the Japanese feather or Jap feather. As the name implies, the lure is normally dressed with feathers, but might be skirted with vinyl, too. Unlike leadhead jigs which have heads molded to hooks, the Japanese jig's hook is attached to a wire leader. The head, which has a hole running lengthwise through it, is

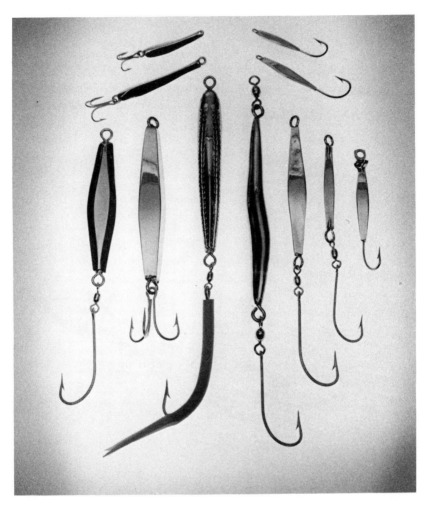

A few of the diamond jigs or metal squids available from Bead Chain Tackle Co.

threaded onto the wire above the hook. When trolled, the lure looks much like a large leadhead jig. When a fish takes the lure, though, the head is free to slide up the leader away from the hook, which makes the hook more difficult for the fish to shake loose.

Another jig-type lure, designed primarily for saltwater trolling and manufactured by Weber Tackle, is the Hoochy Troll. On this lure, a head is molded to a length of stainless-steel beadchain, to which is attached a

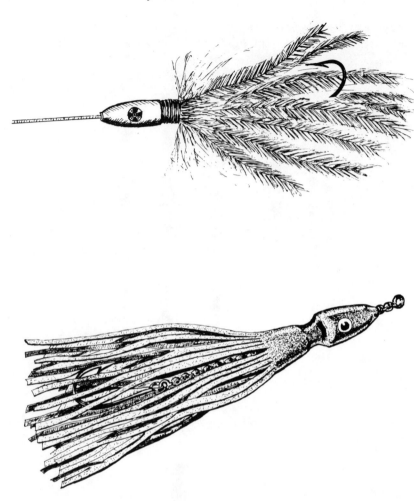

Three jigs designed especially for trolling. *Top*, Japanese jig, or Jap feather; *center*, Weber Hoochy Troll; *bottom*, Burke's Jig-a-Do Spoonhead Eel.

stainless-steel Siwash-style single hook. The soft and pliable squidlike body is made of vinyl. The head of the vinyl body is drawn over the bullet-shaped lead head to form a sleek and durable lure.

Hoochy Trolls come in a wide variety of colors and color combinations, in lengths from five to 14 inches, weights from ½ ounce to six ounces, with hooks from 3/0 to 7/0 in size.

Hoochy Trolls and similar imitations are often tipped with strips of baitfish for added appeal. The smaller models are often cast and jigged much the same as leadhead jigs. The lures are also used for deep-water vertical jigging in salt water and can be effective on larger freshwater species, as well.

The Jig-A-Do Spoonhead Eel is a heavy-duty lure that's in a class by itself. For years it has been a favorite of saltwater fishermen (particularly those pursuing striped bass and bluefish), but with the boom in freshwater striper fishing, it is now taking its share of fish in lakes and impoundments where this species has been stocked.

In the traditional style of a jig-type bait, the Jig-A-Do's upriding hook is weighted, but the metal spoonhead imparts a natural action to the soft eel body. The upriding trailer hook is attached with stainless-steel chain that is molded into the plastic eel body. Hooks are also stainless.

The Jig-A-Do Spoonhead Eel comes in two sizes: the nine-inch, two-ounce model with 7/0 head hook and 6/0 trailer hook; or the 12-inch, 3¼-ounce model with 8/0 head hook and 7/0 trailer hook.

Although these lures are relatively expensive, worn or damaged bodies can be replaced, and spare bodies come either plain or rigged with the trailer hook and chain.

With a basic background in the various types of jigs available to you and a rudimentary understanding of how and where they're used, you should be able to browse through your local tackle shops or the catalogs of mail-order companies and manufacturers and find plenty of jigs to fit your personal needs.

3.  Manufactured Jigs

There are few tackle shops, sporting-goods stores, or discount department stores, these days, that don't carry at least a small assortment of jigs. Certainly, some are heavily stocked, especially with those jigs that are regionally popular. Nevertheless, there are some areas in the country—my own included—where jig selections are far from adequate. Moreover, there are so many manufacturers' variations of jig design and so many different patented designs that no store can possibly carry them all.

For those reasons and others, I thought a sampling of jig manufacturers and their wares might help you determine which jigs will best fit your angling needs. Since you will likely be able to find the most universally popular types of jigs at your local sport shop, and since so many manufacturers include the standard styles in their catalogs, I have avoided listing specifics about those jigs. Instead, what follows are those jigs and related items that are normally of a particular manufacturer's design.

If you can't find these products locally, or if you wish to review the manufacturer's entire line of jigs and other tackle, send for the latest catalog. Complete addresses can be found in the alphabetical directory at the back of the book.

Tony Accetta & Sons, Inc.

In addition to several casting-type jigs tied with traditional materials or dressed with soft-plastic tails, this company offers several trolling-type jigs, primarily for saltwater use.

Rag Mop
Here's one of the most unusual-looking lures on the market today, but one which boasts consistent catches of bluefish, striped bass, king mack-

28

erel, and other marine species. Consisting of a lead head, trailed by a long chain attached to a hook, with strands of nylon woven into the chain, it does more resemble a mop than a fishing lure. Although a bit unwieldly for casting, it is a highly effective trolling lure, and its substantial design and construction make it quite a durable lure for the toothy species. It comes in either six-inch or 13-inch lengths, rigged with single or double hooks. Weight: 1½ oz. Hooks: 6/o or 7/o. Colors: yellow, yellow/green, orange, red/white, blue.

Jim Bagley Bait Co., Inc.

This company markets a varied assortment of lures, among which are a number of soft plastics that can be used with jig heads, including the often-hard-to-find small (2½ inches) plastic worms that are ideal for panfish jigging.

Salty Dog Spoon
This is a lure that's been around for some time but is now enjoying renewed interest among east-coast anglers where it is used for deep-water

No. 37
Illustrated
¼ actual size

No. 34
Illustrated
¼ actual size

Tony Accetta & Son's Rag Mop.

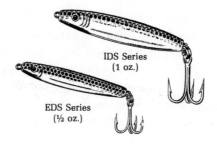

IDS Series
(1 oz.)

EDS Series
(½ oz.)

Bagley's Salty Dog Spoon (metal squid).

jigging. Classed with diamond jigs and metal squids, the Salty Dog Spoon is made of malleable lead so it can be shaped by hand to alter the fluttering action. Weights: ½ oz., 1 oz. Colors: black/white, black/chartreuse, blue/white, red/gold, white.

Salty Dog Grub
This jig-head/grub-tail combination was designed with a balance especially suited to fishing the salt flats and other shallow waters. It comes in a wide assortment of head and tail colors, including "Fire Glo" and glitter finishes. Weight: ¼ oz.

Salty Dog II
The Salty Dog jig head has been combined with reflecting twin tails for a lure that is a top producer of weakfish, snook, red drum (also known as redfish and channel bass), and many other marine species. It is also a good choice for largemouth bass. It is available in the same assortment of colors as the Salty Dog Grub. Weights: $5/16$ oz., 1 oz.

Salty Dog Shrimp
Here's an excellent choice for most inshore marine species. It consists of a jig head and form-fitted shrimp tail made of tough plastic. It is available in the same colors as other Salty Dog jigs. Weights: $5/16$ oz., 1 oz., 2 oz.

Three jig-and-tail combinations from Jim Bagley Bait Co. All are for fresh or salt water and are shown with replacement tails. *Top*, Salty Dog Grub; *center*, Salty Dog II; *bottom*, Salty Dog Shrimp.

Bead Chain Tackle Co.

In addition to their line of superior-quality chain swivels, leaders, trolling weights, and spinners, this company offers a complete assortment of diamond jigs, metal squids, and related lures. These folks have been producing top-quality jigs for nearly half a century. You should own their catalog.

Diamond Jig
This tried and trusty lure, a longtime favorite of surfcasters and deep-water jig fishermen, has a highly polished nickel finish and features heavy steel rings at both ends. It is available with or without treble hook. Weights: from 1 to 16 oz. Hook sizes: 1/0 to 7/0.

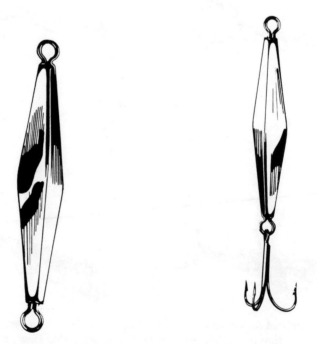

Bead Chain's Diamond Jig, with and without treble hook.

Round Sand Eel

Another favorite of east-coast saltwater anglers, the polished nickel Round Sand Eel can be used in the surf, trolled, or jigged. It comes equipped with swivels at each end and a single O'Shaughnessy hook. By switching the hook from one swivel to the other, the lure's action can be changed. Weights: 3¼ oz. to 8 oz. Hook sizes: 7/0, 8/0.

Wobble Eel

Based on a tin-squid design that has been consistently catching fish for more than forty years, the Wobble Eel has been developed to produce an undulating, wobbling action that makes it a top choice for casting and trolling, but which maintains its abilities to take fish when jigged. Its molded-in features are heavily nickel plated. It trails a single Mustad Bent Limerick hook, dressed with a tube-type tail. Weights: 3 oz., 4 oz. Hook size: 9/0. Tail colors: hot red, hot green, black.

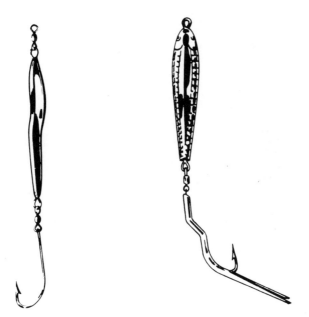

Bead Chain's Round Sand Eel *(left)* and Wobble Eel *(right)*.

Snag-Less Jig

Equipped with a single Mustad O'Shaughnessy hook, this diamond jig is less prone to snags and will hold head-shaking fish better than the treble-hook-equipped jig. The jig can be used bare or dressed with a bait strip, pork rind, or soft-plastic tail. Weights: 1 to 8 oz. Hook sizes: 5/0 to 8/0.

Small Diamond Jig

Here's a diamond jig ideally suited to light-tackle fishing in salt or fresh water, even through the ice. The polished nickel body is molded to a single Mustad O'Shaughnessy hook, which can be dressed with bait, a small pork-rind strip, or plastic twist-tail for added appeal. Weights: ¼ oz., ⅓ oz., ½ oz. Hook sizes: 1/0, 2/0, 3/0.

Diamond Squid

Similar to the diamond jig, this lure's body is molded onto a single O'Shaughnessy hook and is equipped with a nonfouling brass swivel. Weights: 1 to 8 oz. Hook sizes: 1/0 to 9/0.

Slab Jig

The body of this jig features ten sides for maximum light reflection and an action ideal for deep-water jigging. It comes equipped with a single O'Shaughnessy hook. Weights: 3 to 8 oz. Hook sizes: 7/0, 8/0.

Flat Diamond Lure

With the same finish as other diamond jigs, this lure is flattened to cause it to rise when retrieved. Its small size lends it nicely to inshore saltwater and freshwater angling. It comes equipped with a treble hook. Weights: ½ oz. to 2 oz. Hook sizes: 3, 1.

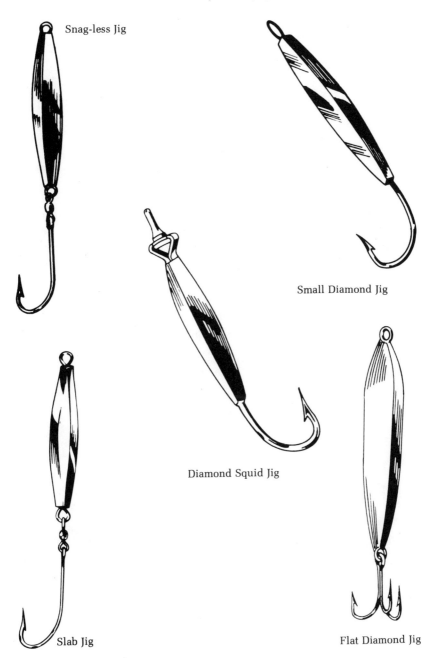

Snag-less Jig

Small Diamond Jig

Diamond Squid Jig

Slab Jig

Flat Diamond Jig

A selection of jigs from Bead Chain Tackle Co.

Vi-Ke Lure

Another brightly finished, nickel-plated jig, the Vi-Ke has an unusual shape that gives it a crazy fluttering action. Because of its wide range of sizes, the lure can be used to fit a great many different conditions and a variety of species. Heavier sizes are ideal for deep jigging. The smallest Vi-Ke lures are great for trout and panfish. Weights: ¼ oz. to 24 oz. Hook sizes: 6 to 7/o.

Blakemore Sales Corp.

For nearly a quarter of a century, this company has been producing a line of horsehead-type jigs known as Road Runners. These jigs come variously dressed with chenille and marabou, plastic worms, plastic twist-tails, and plastic shad bodies.

Road Runner

This horsehead jig is tied with a chenille body, is nylon wound for extra strength, and features a marabou tail. Available in a wide range of

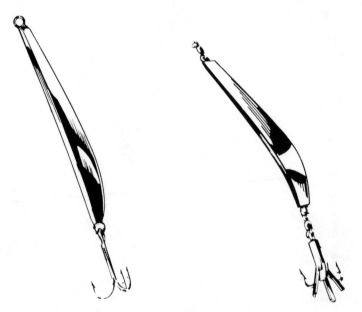

Bead Chain's Vi-Ke Lure *(left)* and Red-Tailed Vi-Ke Lure *(right)*.

colors and color combinations, it is recommended for crappie, white bass, walleye, and trout, as well as inshore marine species. Weights: $^1/_{32}$ oz. to $^1/_4$ oz.

Road Runner With Curly Tail
With the same head and spinner blade featured in the Road Runner, this jig features a soft-plastic twist-tail. In the smaller sizes it's ideal for crappie and other panfish as well as trout; larger sizes are good for large-mouth and smallmouth bass and other freshwater and saltwater gamefish. Weights: $^1/_{32}$ oz. to $^1/_4$ oz.

Shad Series Road Runner
This is the same Road Runner jig head dressed with a soft-plastic shad body. Colors: natural shad, yellow shad, blue shad, chartreuse shad, silver shad, goldfish (except one-ounce size, which is available only in natural and chartreuse shad). Weights: $^1/_{32}$ oz. to 1 oz.

Three of Blakemore's Road Runner series of horsehead-type jigs. *Top*, Road Runner; *center*, Road Runner with Curly Tail; *bottom*, Shad Series Road Runner.

Bomber Bait Co.

Having been in business since the late thirties, this is one of the oldest lure companies in the U.S. today, producing some of the finest-quality and most popular lures on the market, among them several outstanding jigs. Their jig-head finishing process is one of the best, resulting in nearly the most chip-resistant paint job to be found. When you need a jig for rocky areas, especially in salt water, Bomber jigs should fit your requirements.

Bomber also makes another lure that should be in every striper fisherman's tackle box. The Water Dog, though not a jig, is deadly when trolled deep and trailed by a jig, a method discussed more fully in Chapter 8.

Gumpy Jig

The Gumpy is manufactured with a Bomber process that molds the tail right into the head. Coupled with Bomber's chip-resistant finish, this

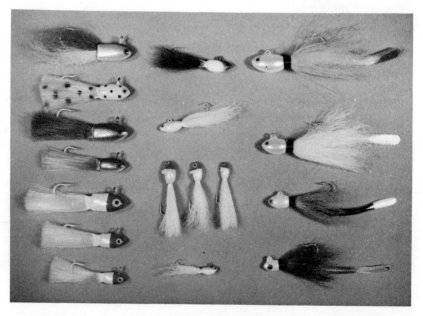

Bomber Bait Co. jigs. *Left column,* various sizes and colors of the Bomber Jig; *right column,* four sizes and colors of Flare Hair Jig; *center,* Gumpy jigs.

makes the Gumpy one of the most durable jigs around. It comes in either nylon or bucktail dressings with either gold Aberdeen or cadmium-plated O'Shaughnessy hooks. Colors: white, black, red head, blue, shad, yellow/black, yellow. Weights: ⅛ oz., ¼ oz., ⅜ oz.

Bomber Jig
Like its smaller cousin, the Bomber Jig has its tail (either nylon or Dynel) molded into the head. Moreover, the lead head is encased in plastic, producing a far more durable finish than a painted head. It comes in a wide array of finishes to fit any need. Hooks are cadmium plated for saltwater use. Weights: ¼ oz. ½ oz., ¾ oz., 1 oz. Hook sizes: 2/0, 3/0, 4/0, 5/0.

Flare Hair Jig
The latest addition to the Bomber line of jigs, the Flare Hair is rather conventional in appearance, except that a Bomber Worm Tail has been added to it for increased appeal. A good jig in its own right for most inshore marine species and freshwater gamefish, it has become quite a hot item for summer striper fishing when trailed on a leader of about 24 inches behind a 1700 series Bomber Water Dog lure. The jig is available in a wide variety of colors and color combinations. Weights: ¼ oz., ½ oz. Hooks sizes: 1/0, 3/0.

Burke Fishing Lures

Burke offers a line of products that should be of interest to any jig fisherman. In addition to a wide selection of plastic worms and twist-tails in various designs and colors, several unique and highly effective jigs and jig-type lures are available.

Wig-Wag Minno
This is one of Burke's specialties and one of the best jigs on the market today. Its unique swimming tail imparts extremely realistic swimming action. Because of the wide range of sizes it comes in, this jig can be used for a great variety of species and can be adapted to numerous fishing situations. The smallest Wig-Wag Minno is deadly on smallmouth bass, trout, and panfish of all sorts and is a good choice for many inshore

saltwater species when ultralight tackle is called for. The ⅜-ounce model is a good choice for largemouth and smallmouth bass, seatrout, snook, and other freshwater and saltwater gamefish. If you're going after big bass, pike, tarpon, stripers, and various reef species, try the larger models. The "Magnum" and "Maxi-Magnum" models are good for deep trolling in fresh water for lake trout and striped bass, and casting for big pike and muskie; in the salt chuck, use them for trolling, surf casting, and deep jigging for stripers, bluefish, snapper, grouper, lingcod, and virtually all large reef species. These jigs come with extra bodies. Both heads and bodies can be purchased separately and in bulk quantities as well. Wig-Wag Minno heads are painted white with black eyes, and more than a dozen different body colors are offered. Smaller models are cast on gold-plated Aberdeen hooks, and larger ones feature heavier forged hooks. Sizes: ⅛ oz. to 2½ oz. Hook sizes: 6 to 8/o.

Split-Tail Eels
These are tough and durable yet supple plastic tails that are ideal for use with plain jig heads or dressed jigs. They also can be used in conjunction with large-eye trailer hooks for fish that are short-striking your jigs. They can be purchased with or without special 4/o trailer hooks. Colors: black, fluorescent red, purple, chartreuse, white, yellow, pearl, silver flake. Size: 4 in.

Squirm Skirt
Here is a soft-plastic skirt with excellent breathing action for dressing jig heads. Two-piece construction includes the Skirt-Lok which slides onto the jig hook and the Squirm Skirt that follows and is locked in position. The skirts are available in thirteen colors. Sizes: 3½ in. diameter, 4¾ in. diameter.

Shifty Shad
In recent years, shad lures have been taking a lot of largemouth bass. Burke's version uses the same jig head as on the Wig-Wag Minno. The soft-plastic body is molded with a dorsal fin and swimming tail. This is an excellent choice where shad are a natural part of your quarry's diet. These lures come assembled (one jig per card) with painted or unpainted heads. Heads and bodies also can be purchased separately and in bulk.

Burke Wig-Wag Minno comes in many sizes and can be used in a variety of fishing situations.

Twin-tail and big eye hook get short strikes!

Stick head of twin-tail on lure hook to keep trailer hook in place.

Slip big eye hook over lure hook.

Stick trailer hook through twin-tail close to "crotch."

Burke Split-Tail Eel and trailer-hook system.

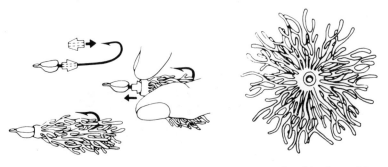

Burke Squirm Skirt has a two-piece construction that locks skirt in position on jig hook.

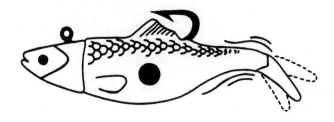

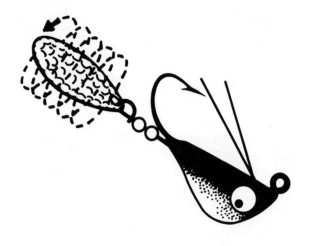

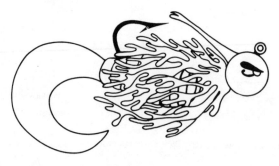

Three speciality lures from Burke Fishing Lures. *Top*, Shifty Shad; *center*, Tail Spin; *bottom*, Arizona Jig.

Colors: silver flash shad, silver shad, gold crawdad, and natural shad.
Sizes: ⅛ oz. (1¾ in. body), ⅜ oz. (2½ in. body), ⅝ oz. (3 in. body), 1¼
oz. (4¼ in. body).

Tail Spin

This heavy, jig-type lure casts like a bullet and sinks like a sash weight,
but also boasts features not found on other jigs. The jig trails a
hammered-finish spinner blade. A pair of stainless whiskers protects the
heavy-duty hook from snags. And for those who like lures that make
noise, the eyes rattle. This is a good choice in heavy cover or for deep-water
jigging over rocky reefs. Colors: shad, green/white, yellow/white, black.
Sizes: ⅜ oz., ⅝ oz.

Arizona Jig

Developed on Lake Powell and designed specifically for deep-water jigging, this jig is made to order for working rocky and snag-strewn waters.
The head and "spike horn" weed guard are molded together to prevent the
head from chipping and the guard from getting out of alignment. The
lure is dressed with the Burke Squirm Skirt and a four-inch Wig-Wag
Worm. The jig is currently available in eight colors. Weight: ½ oz.

Cordell Tackle

Here's a company that has been catering to serious fishermen for more
than twenty years. Not only does Cordell offer one of the largest selections
of jigs for all types of fishing, but it sells unpainted jig heads as well for
those who wish to fashion their own lures.

Cordell manufactures the long-famous line of Doll Fly jigs. The smaller
members of this lure family are some of the best crappie and trout jigs to
be found, while the larger Doll Fly jigs, dressed with natural hair, have
been favorites of walleye and white-bass fishermen for years.

Additionally, the Cordell line includes a number of popping plugs and
swimming lures that are excellent for popper-dropper and trailer-jig rigs,
discussed fully in later chapters.

Cannon Ball Jig

Here's a heavyweight that's made to order for saltwater deep-jigging. All
models are tied with natural hair and are accented with either feathers or

silver Mylar. Two-tone heads are color-coordinated with dressings. The large, round head is molded to a heavy-duty forged hook. Colors: silver-white head/silver Mylar, yellow-white head/silver Mylar, green-white head/green feather, blue-white head/blue feather, red-white head/red feather. Weights: ¾ oz. to 2 oz.

Crazy Leg Jig

This is Cordell's best-selling jig. It consists of a banana head with a nylon weed guard molded in and a bulky body of live-rubber legs that undulate constantly, even when the lure's at rest. A top fish producer in its own right, the Crazy Leg Jig is deadly when used with a pork chunk or pork frog and has become a favorite of largemouth-bass anglers in many parts of the country. It's a natural for fishing the lily pads, weedbeds, and other snag-strewn waters. Colors: white, black, black/chartreuse, brown/orange, yellow, black/yellow, brown. Sizes: ¼ oz., ⅜ oz., ½ oz.

Plasti-Jig Head

This is an unpainted head with molded eyes and a collar barb to hold plastic tails in place. It's ideal for use with small grubs and plastic twist-tails for trout, panfish, and bass, as well as many inshore marine species. Molded on gold-plated Aberdeen hooks, the heads can be left as they are or epoxy painted. Weights: $^1/_{16}$ oz., ⅛ oz., ¼ oz.

Grub Head

This heavier head features a barbed collar for holding plastic grubs, twist-tails, and the like. It is available with or without a molded-in weed guard. The weedless model in heavier weights is a good choice for hunting bass in the weeds and brush. Weights: ⅛ oz. to ½ oz.

Banana Jig Head

This is the same head Cordell uses on its famous Crazy Leg Jig. It is cast on a heavy-duty hook with a moled-in nylon weed guard. Weights: ¼ oz., ⅜ oz., ½ oz.

Creme Lure Co.

Here's where the plastic worm was born. Well, not in Tyler, Texas, where the company is now located, but in Nick Creme's kitchen in Akron,

Cannon Ball Jig

Crazy Leg Jig

Plasti-Jig Head

Grub Head

Banana Jig Head

A few of the many jigs available from Cordell Tackle.

Ohio, in the late forties. Since then, Creme Lure Co. has gone on to manufacture a large line of soft-plastic baits, many of which are well-suited to jig fishing.

In addition to the worms, grubs, and twist-tails that any serious jig fisherman should stock, Creme manufactures a number of lifelike natural imitations of grub worms, hellgrammites, frogs, crawfish, shrimp, and other critters that can be used with jigs.

Killer-Krawdad

This jigging lure is molded of soft plastic and rigged with a keel-weighted jig hook with the hook eye through the tail to give the lure a natural crawfish movement on the retrieve. Colors: tan, smoke, scarlet/green.

Spoiler Shad

Here's Creme's version of the popular shad jig. Rigged on roundhead jigs, the soft-plastic bodies come in two sizes—one for ultralight tackle and panfish, the other for largemouth and striped bass. Colors: pink, pearl, silver, smoke, goldfish. Sizes: 1½ in., 2½ in.

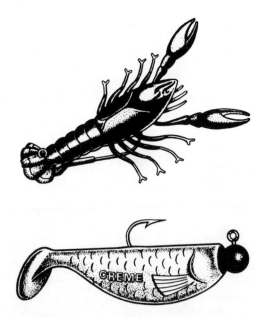

Two soft-plastic baits from Creme Lure Co. *Top,* Killer-Krawdad; *bottom,* Spoiler Shad.

Fle-Fly Mfg., Inc.

Although this company does not offer any particularly unusual jigs, it does manufacture a wide selection of miniature jigs that are ideally suited to fishing for trout and panfish with ultralight tackle.

Niki Spin Fly
A forward-balanced, roundhead jig with a shank tie of chenille and a feather tail, this dynamite little trout and crappie jig is available in no fewer than thirty head-and-body color combinations. Weights: $1/64$ oz., $1/32$ oz., $1/16$ oz., $1/8$ oz.

Niki Spin Worm
Another great trout and panfish lure, the Niki Spin Worm is a split-tail plastic body rigged on a roundhead jig. It comes in twenty-two colors and color combinations. Weights: $1/16$ oz., $1/8$ oz.

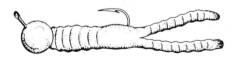

Fle-Fly Mfg., Inc. makes many miniature jigs. *Top,* Niki Spin Fly; *bottom,* Niki Spin Worm.

Gapen's World of Fishin', Inc.

Dan Gapen, the president of this company, is one of the country's expert jig-fishermen. It only stands to reason that his catalog would include a good selection of trout, panfish, and ice-fishing jigs as well as larger jigs meant for bigger fish.

Additionally, Gapen's is a good source for plastic worms and tails, jig heads, and a number of innovative items of interest to jig fishermen.

Ugly Bug

It is, indeed, uuuh-gleeee. But, the hellgrammite, after which this jig was fashioned, isn't one of nature's bright and beautiful creatures either. What the Ugly Bug and the hellgrammite share in common, though, is that fish love to eat them. Although the Ugly Bug was originally designed as a walleye jig, there's scarcely a freshwater gamefish that hasn't fallen for it: largemouth and smallmouth bass, bluegill, crappie, trout, pike, muskie—even sucker, carp, and catfish. The lure consists of an unusual, flattened jig head followed by a soft-plastic body with long, live-rubber legs and tail. It should be worked slowly and can be tipped with bait for added appeal. Colors: white, yellow, black, purple, brown, orange, chartreuse. Weights: $1/16$ oz. to $1/2$ oz.

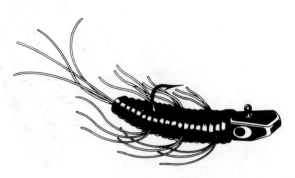

Gapen's Ugly Bug, which imitates a hellgrammite.

Leadheads
These painted jig heads are ready for tying or dressing with soft-plastic tails. Colors: white, yellow, black, purple, green, blue, brown, red. Weights: $^1/16$ oz. to $^3/8$ oz.

Bug Bodies
These are soft-plastic tails to be used with plain jig heads. They come in a suitable variety of colors and sizes to fit most fishing situations. Colors: white, yellow, black, purple, green, blue, brown, orange, red, pink. Sizes: 1 in., 1¼ in., 2 in., 3 in.

Gapen's Leadheads *(left)* and Bug Bodies *(right)*.

Bait-Walker

This innovative walking sinker, used with a floating jig head tipped with bait or rigged with a soft-plastic tail, can be deadly in fresh or salt water. Pick the lighter Bait-Walkers for smaller fish and calmer waters, the heavier ones for bigger fish in strong currents or at great depths. Weights: ¼ oz. to 6 oz.

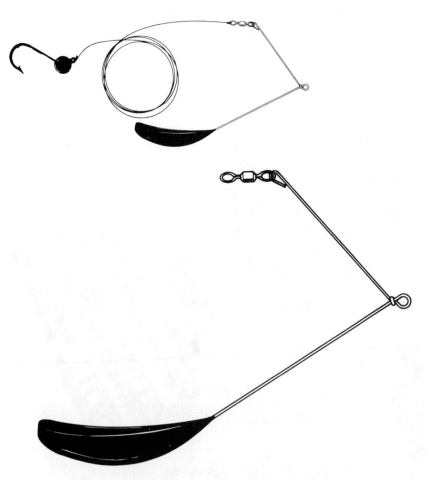

Gapen's Bait-Walker, an innovative walking sinker.

Mann's Bait Co.

Tom Mann started in the lure-making business on a part-time basis by making and selling jigs in his spare time. Today, his company is one of the best-known in the country, offering anglers a full line of top-quality lures. Certainly, jigs are still among the company's offerings, but so are the famous Tom Mann Jelly Worms (super-soft and durable plastic worms, perfect for jig-and-worm fishing), Jelly Wagglers (worms with twist-tails), Sting Ray grubs, Jelly Shad, and Swimmin Grubs. The company also offers crappie jigs and a torpedo-shaped saltwater jig called the Ling-O-Lure.

Swimmin Grub
As the name indicates, this is a soft-plastic grub with a specially designed tail that wiggles on the fall or on the retrieve. It comes either rigged on Mann's leadhead jigs or unrigged for use on heads of the angler's choice. It has been widely field-tested and proven effective on freshwater and salt-water species alike, including largemouth bass, crappie, striped bass, and seatrout. It is available in twelve colors and color combinations. Sizes: 1 in., 2 in., 4 in.

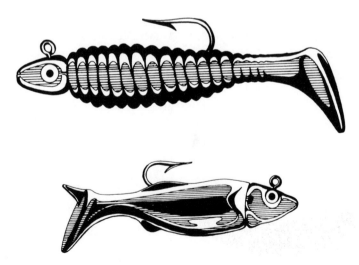

Two soft-plastic, "swimming-tail" lures from Mann's Bait Co. *Bottom,* Jelly Shad; *top,* Swimmin Grub.

Jelly Shad
Made of soft plastic that is both flexible and durable, the Jelly Shad is another of Mann's "swimming-tail" lures. It was designed to imitate the movements of a live baitfish and is extremely effective when rigged with Mann's fish-head jig, although it is also available unrigged for use with other jig heads. It comes in twelve colors and color combinations. Sizes: 1 in., 2 in., 3 in., 4 in.

Mister Twister

Long respected as a manufacturer of top-quality soft-plastic baits, this company also offers an extensive line of jigs, jig heads, and other tackle of importance to the jig fisherman. Among the many products manufactured by Mister Twister are shad-type jigs, bucktail jigs, rubber-leg jigs, weedless jigs, nature jigs (tied in such patterns as crawfish, river darter, perch, shiner minnow, and the like), marabou jigs, crappie jigs, striper jigs, leadheads, floating jig heads, walking sinkers, and much more. If Mister Twister products aren't readily available in your area, you'll certainly want their latest catalog and price list.

Slither
Any knowledgeable fisherman can take one look at this soft-plastic bait and know immediately that it has to be a deadly lure when rigged with a jig or jig head. Not only does it feature the twist tail that has proved to be one of the best fish attractors around, but it also has a slithering plastic dorsal fin of sorts molded to its segmented worm body. Rigged weedless, it is an excellent choice for fishing lily pads and weedbeds. Or use a non-weedless head for casting to cover, bouncing bottom, or swimming at mid-depths in fresh or salt water. Colors: pearl-white, black, purple, blue, smoke, red, grape, STP green, black grape. Sizes: 4 in., 6 in.

"Keeper" Jighead
The key to the "Keeper" Jighead is the pointed, barbed shank attached to the hook eye. Simply push the head of a plastic worm, twist-tail, or other soft-plastic lure onto the shank, slip the jig-hook point into the body of the plastic lure, and you have a perfectly rigged, weedless lure ready to catch fish just about anywhere. Sizes: ⅛ oz., ¼ oz., ⅜ oz.

Floating Jighead

Designed to keep a bait or soft-plastic lure suspended off the bottom when used with a walking sinker, the floating jighead keeps your offering above weeds, rocks, and brush where the fish can see it and take it more easily. Colors: white, black, fluorescent pink, fluorescent red, chartreuse. Hook sizes: 6, 4, 2, 1/0.

Mister Twister Slither.

Mister Twister jig heads. *Top,* "Keeper" Jighead; *bottom,* Floating Jighead.

Eyelet Sinker

This improved walking sinker, with its interchangeable and detachable eyelet, is much better than older models that often caused the loss of rigs when the sinker snagged in rocky areas. If the Eyelet Sinker hangs up, the angler need only give a good pull on his line and the sinker will open to free the rig. The interchangeability allows the angler to replace the sinker and continue fishing with a minimum loss of fishing time. This same feature also allows quick changes from one weight to another. Use it with floating jigs or floating-jig heads rigged with bait or plastic tails. Weights: ⅛ oz., ¼ oz., ⅜ oz., ½ oz.

Floating Bucktail And Marabou Jigs

Tied with natural materials on floating heads, these jigs are designed for use with the Eyelet Sinker. By varying leader length, the jigs can be fished at different distances, from near bottom to as much as five to seven feet above. They are available in the same head colors as the Floating Jig-heads, above, tied with either bucktail or marabou feathers, on No. 4 or No. 2 hooks.

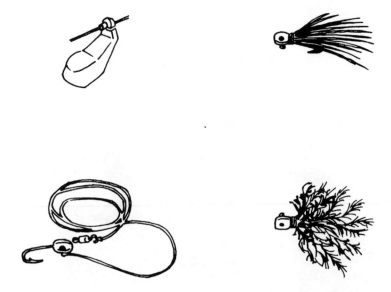

Left, Mister Twister Eyelet Sinker, with interchangeable and detachable eyelet. *Right,* Mister Twister Bucktail and Marabou Jigs, for use with Eyelet Sinker.

Pfeiffer's Tackle Crafters, Inc.

In addition to an excellent selection of jig-making tools and materials, Pfeiffer's also offers an assortment of jig heads for those who don't care to cast their own. The company also carries a line of natural soft-plastic lures that are ideal for use with plain jig heads. Other Pfeiffer products are covered in Chapter 4.

Jig Heads
Pfeiffer's jig heads are made with precision casting equipment for uniformity and balance and all heads are molded on Mustad O'Shaughnessy or Aberdeen hooks. The company currently offers five different styles, but since they are constantly adding to their line of tackle and equipment, it's a good idea to order a catalog each year. Head weights range from ¼ oz. to 1¼ oz., with hook from size 1 to 8/0.

Some jig heads and tying materials available from Pfeiffer's Tackle Crafters.

Soft Plastics

These soft-plastic lures are molded to look and feel natural. Fish have molded-in scales, fins, and eyes. Frogs have detailed legs and bodies. Crayfish have accurately segmented legs and claws. Colors are lifelike. All come unrigged, ready for use with jigs or keel-weighted jig hooks. Minnow sizes: 1⅛ in., 1½ in., 3 in., 4⅛ in. Sucker size: 4½ in. Stone Cat size: 2½ in. Big Eel size: 5 in. Frog size: 2½ in. Crayfish size: 2½ in.

These soft-plastic lures, available from Pfeiffer's Tackle Crafters, can be rigged on jig heads.

Uncle Josh Bait Company

Uncle Josh is the leading manufacturer of pork-rind baits in the United States, offering a wide selection of skirts, strips, and chunks that are ideal for use with jigs and jig heads in fresh and salt water. Although pork rinds have caught about every variety of freshwater fish and many marine species for a number of years, they are currently enjoying renewed popularity with fishermen discovering the versatility and effectiveness of jigs. The jig-and-pork-rind combination is a deadly duo that often outfishes all other baits and lures. Every jig fisherman's tackle box should carry a selection of pork rinds.

Original Pork Frog
Here's a pork bait that's been around for more than fifty years and yet is one of the "latest rages" among southern bass fishermen who work it with

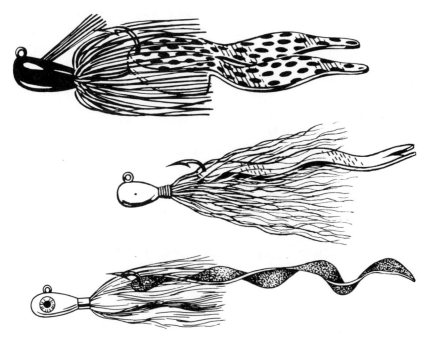

Three jig-and-pork-rind combinations from Uncle Josh Bait Co. *Top,* Original Pork Frog rigged on a weedless living-rubber jig; *center,* Bass Strip on bucktail jig; *bottom,* Ripple Rind on bucktail jig.

a weedless jig. The frog-and-jig combination is also deadly on northern pike, muskie, and—in smaller sizes—panfish. Sizes: Fly Frog, 1¼ in. × ½ in.; Spinning Frog, 1⅞ in. × ¾ in.; Bait Frog, 2½ in. × 1 in.; Jumbo Frog, 3¼ in. × 1⅛ in. Colors: green, red, yellow, black, purple, chartreuse, crawdad brown, white, orange, orange/brown spots. (Fly Frog in green only.)

Black Widow Eel

This is one of the most effective bass baits ever developed. The jig-'n'-eel combination has accounted for many a lunker largemouth in all parts of the United States. The same combination is an effective saltwater lure as well. Sizes: 4 in. × ¼ in., 6 in. × ⅜ in., 9 in. × ⅝ in. Weights: $^1/_{10}$ oz., ⅛ oz., ¼ oz. Colors: white, black, purple (medium size also available in red, blue, and orange).

Bass Strip

This is a tough and active forktailed strip that is great for dressing bucktail jigs for freshwater or saltwater fishing. It will consistently take bass, pike, muskie, bluefish, bonito, weakfish, barracuda, king mackerel, yellowtail, and others. Size: 4 in. × ⅜ in. Colors: white, green, red, yellow, black, blue, purple, chartreuse, crawdad brown, orange.

Striper & Muskie Strip

Here's a strong and lively strip for dressing larger jigs and jig heads, diamond jigs, metal squids, and other such lures for casting or deep jigging. Size: 5¼ in. × ⅝ in. Colors: white, green, red, yellow, black, blue, orange.

Hook Strip

For those short-striking fish, rig your jig with this strip, which has a 3/0 Mustad O'Shaughnessy stainless-steel hook in it. Size: 4 in. × ⅜ in. Colors: white, red, yellow.

Striper Hook Strip

For short-striking stripers, tarpon and other large marine species as well as pike, muskie, and big bass in fresh water, use this strip with its rigged 3/0 stainless-steel hook. Size 5¼ in. × ⅝ in. Colors: white, red, yellow.

Uncle Josh Black Widow Eel

Uncle Josh Striper and Muskie Strip

Uncle Josh Hook Strip

Uncle Josh Striper Hook Strip

Uncle Josh King-Size
Striper Hook

Uncle Josh Spin Tail

Uncle Josh Little "Vee"

Uncle Josh Pork Skirt

Uncle Josh Fly Flicks

A selection of Uncle Josh's skirts, strips, and chunks for use in fresh and salt water.

King-Size Striper Hook Strip
Here's the perfect strip for use with jigs trolled for big gamefish, such as muskie, pike, striped bass, bluefish, and offshore species. It comes rigged with either a 5/0 or 7/0 stainless-steel hook. Size: 4¾ in. × ⅝ in. Colors: white, red, yellow.

Spin Tail
This is a lively tail that is tops for tipping smaller jigs for crappie, smallmouth bass, trout, and other freshwater species, as well as Spanish mackerel, seatrout, snook, barracuda, cobia, and other marine species. Size: 2¼ in. × $5/16$ in. Colors: white, green, red, yellow, black, purple, chartreuse, orange.

Little Vee
Used with small jigs and jig heads, this little pork-rind bait is excellent for most panfish, bass, trout, and inshore saltwater species. Size: ¾ in. × ½ in. Colors: white, yellow.

Fly Flick
This is the smallest pork rind available and is perfect for dressing jigs from $1/32$ oz. to ⅛ oz. for crappie, trout, shad, and small inshore marine species. Size: ½ in. × ⅛ in. Color: white.

Pork Skirt
This thin, dancing rind is cut into a two-inch skirt with ⅛-inch ribbons. Use it on plain jig heads for bass, walleye, weakfish, stripers, bluefish, and other gamefish. Size: 3 in. × ⅝ in. Colors: white, green, red, yellow, black, purple, chartreuse, orange.

Ripple Rind
Made to ripple and undulate seductively, this wafer-thin pork rind will take freshwater and saltwater gamefish of all types and can be used on dressed jigs or plain jig heads. It will ripple on the retrieve or when freefalling. It's a good substitute for the plastic twist-tail and is a lot more durable. Ripple Rinds are available in three standard sizes and two big-game sizes. Standard sizes: 2½ in. × ¼ in., 4 in. × ⅜ in., 5 in. × ½ in. Big-game sizes: 6½ in. × ⅝ in., 8 in. × ¾ in. Colors: white, red, yellow, black, purple, chartreuse, crawdad brown, orange (fewer colors available in big-game sizes).

Weber

Serving anglers for nearly fifty years, this company offers several top-quality items for the jig fisherman, the most famous of which are the Hoochy line of trolling jigs and skirts.

Single And Double Hoochy Tails
These lively plastic skirts are ideal for dressing plain jig heads and come in a suitable variety for a wide range of freshwater and saltwater applications.

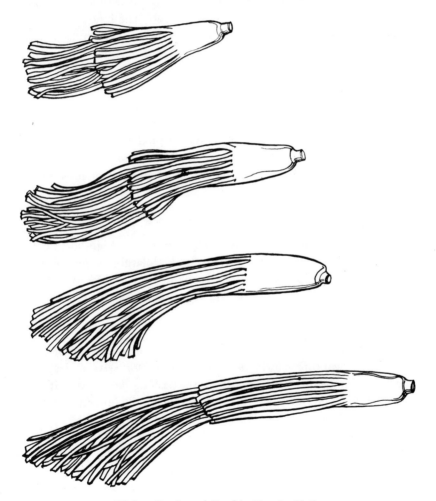

Weber Single and Double Hoochy Tails.

They are made of high-strength vinyl that stays soft and resilient at all water temperatures. They're available in twenty-four colors and color combinations. Sizes: 3 in., 4½ in., 5 in., 7 in., 12 in.

Hoochy Troll

This lifelike, squid-type lure is a favorite for offshore saltwater trolling for numerous big-game species and is equally effective for large freshwater species, particularly Great Lakes salmon. Smaller models are used for casting and jigging for gamefish of all sorts. The tough, pliable sheath and skirt are form-fitted to a lead head, which is rigged with a stainless-steel beadchain and a heavy-duty stainless-steel hook. The lure is available in twenty-four colors and color combinations to fit any angler's needs. Weights: ½ oz. to 6 oz. Sizes: 5 in., 6 in., 7 in., 12 in., 14 in.

Worth Company

In addition to the many top-quality Worth products that have been in wide use for years, this company now offers the Aquacone line of lures that were developed on the west coast and are now finding favor among fishermen everywhere.

Hairy Berry

A unique jigging lure, the Hairy Berry features a high-floating live-rubber tail that produces a tantalizing undulating action with the slightest movement. A snagfree treble-hook jig, it's ideal for working very slowly in dense brush, lily pads, and vegetation. Weight: 5/16 oz.

Bass Berry Jig

Another Aquacone design, this jig also features a snagfree treble hook and is made for working slowly in thick cover or for vertical deep-water jigging. It can be used with or without the flashing tail spinner. It comes equipped with the Aquacone Jig'un skirt that can be quickly changed to another of a different color. Weight: 5/16 oz.

Poly Whopper Jig

Here's a great worming jig for all bass waters and year-round use. It has a high-floating live-rubber skirt molded into the head, rather than tied on,

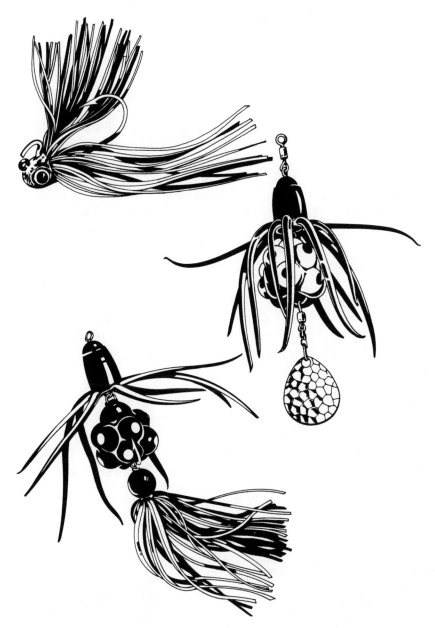

Worth/Aquacone lures were first developed on the west coast, but now are used by fishermen throughout the country. *Top,* Poly Whopper Jig; *bottom left,* Hairy Berry Jig; *bottom right,* Bass Berry Jig.

so it can't come apart. The Aquacone exclusive LUR/LOC head holds the plastic worm securely in place. The jig comes rigged (Texas style) with a Hawg Hackle Swimmer Worm and can be rigged with other worms as well. Weight: ½ oz.

Ice Bugs

Although the Li'l Dipper, Li'l Jigger, and Li'l Imp are billed as ice-fishing lures, these tiny metal jigs are also dandy for warmer-weather fishing for most panfish and trout. All three are available with either nickel-plated or gold-plated body and fluorescent-orange, green, or red belly, all finished with a contrasting dot. They come with or without hackle skirt, same color as the belly. Each is molded on a size-8 Aberdeen hook.

LUR/LOC Glider Jig Heads

The exclusive design of the LUR/LOC head holds plastic worms, twist-tails, and other soft plastics in place, yet permits repeated changing of plastic baits with no trouble. To use, push the curved shaft through the worm or twist-tail, about a quarter-inch from the nose; then gently press the shaft against the hook eye, and rig the plastic bait Texas style for snagfree fishing. Weights: ⅛ oz., ¼ oz., ½ oz. Hook sizes: 1/0 to 4/0.

Worth Ice Bugs. *Left*, Li'l Jigger; *center*, Li'l Dipper; *right*, Li'l Imp.

Left, Worth/Aquacone LUR/LOC Glider Jig Head. *Right*, Worden's Rooster Jig.

Yakima Bait Company

Although this company primarily manufactures spinners, spoons, and trolling lures of various sorts, including the famous Rooster Tail spinner, it offers one jig of unusual design that bears mentioning.

Worden's Rooster Jig
Here's a tiny jig that is dandy for trout and panfish of all types. It is also good for ultralight tackle in saltwater bays and backwaters. It's a well-balanced jig with a hackle skirt tied over a treble hook, and it comes in ten different colors. Weights: $1/32$ oz., $1/16$ oz., $1/8$ oz.

It would be impossible for me to describe, in a single chapter, all the various jigs and related tackle available today. My intention, as I indicated earlier, was to provide a sampling that would familiarize you with some of the products that are currently on the market, and in so doing equip you with some jig-shopping savvy. Here, I have tried to introduce you to some of the important jigs and jig-fishing tackle as well as to a few of my personal favorites.

Even as I'm writing this, and certainly while the book is in production, other new items will be put on the market. Some will be refinements of jigs already in existence; some will surely be gussied-up imitations; a few just might prove to be revolutionary in design, function, and—most important—fish-catching abilities.

Part Two
Making Jigs

The two most obvious reasons for making your own jigs are it saves you money and it's fun. There are other reasons certainly as important, if not more so. If you make your own jigs in quantity, you can keep your tackle box well stocked with a suitable variety to meet all your fishing needs. Moreover, with plenty of inexpensive jigs on hand, you will be less likely to worry about losing a lure from time to time. Consequently, you'll be more inclined to fish closer to brush, flooded timber, lily pads, weedbeds, and other cover that presents snag hazards. With time, you'll get better at making accurate casts to such obstructions and will get hung up with decreasing frequency. Most important, you'll be putting your jigs where the fish are.

Making Jigs—Three Approaches

There are two levels at which you can enter the jig-making process, and three ways to approach this enjoyable and money-saving pastime. You can either buy unfinished molded jig heads and the materials needed to make your finished lures, or you can go all the way and buy the tools and materials required for casting your own jig heads as well.

The simplest approach is to buy a jig-making kit. A number of companies, including Weber and the Worth Co., offer such kits, which are available through some local tackle outlets as well as from various mail-order companies.

This can be an excellent way for the novice to go, because the kits include all the necessary materials and tools to get started, and by following the manufacturer's directions, the angler can learn a good bit about making jigs. Kits normally include a selection of jig heads in a suitable variety of sizes and designs, as well as various natural and synthetic tying materials, a vise, thread, and head cement.

A jig-making kit that includes enough material to make two dozen lures will normally cost you less than what you would pay for the same number of finished jigs, and when you've made your jigs, you will not only have some materials and the vise left, but you will have gained some valuable experience. The typical vise that comes with a jig-making kit isn't the best, but is adequate. It will get you by, but eventually you'll probably want to replace it.

Another approach is to buy your own tools and materials separately. If you are a fly tyer, you already have the tools and probably most of the materials on hand. Even if you're not, you might prefer to shop around for a good vise, bobbin, fly-tying scissors, and a selection of materials that will fit your needs. Then all that remains is to lay in a supply of jig heads and paints. The greatest advantage to this approach is that you will get better tools than those supplied with the kits, and you will get only those materials needed for tying the kinds of jigs that fit *your* kind of fishing. And if you buy in bulk quantities—perhaps in a joint effort with a fishing partner or two—you will recognize even greater savings.

The third approach is to cast your own jig heads, thereby eliminating the need to purchase them elsewhere. Although your initial investment will be greater, the long-run savings will be significant. And, again, if you have a partner or two to share expenses, you'll save even more. A fifteen-dollar jig mold might seem a substantial investment when compared to the cost of jig heads purchased in bulk, but if that cost is

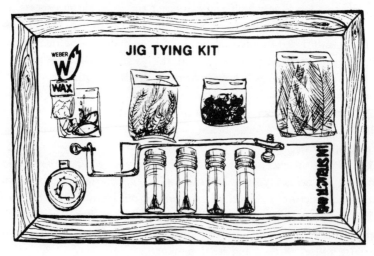

Weber Jig-Tying Kit.

Worth Jig-Tying Kit.

shared by three anglers, one person's share is only five dollars, and very likely you'll save that much during your first casting session. Moreover, the mold, and other tools, will, with proper care, outlast its owner.

The Cursory View and Beyond

The purpose of this section is to introduce you to the basic tools, materials, and techniques for casting your own jig heads, painting and tying the heads, and molding soft plastics for use with jig heads. Space does not permit any more than a cursory view of these topics, but one that is nevertheless adequate—something to get you started.

If you care to delve more deeply into any of these areas, you'll find a number of books to help you. For example, you'll gain a good bit of savvy about tying jigs by studying fly-tying manuals and applying the various techniques to the tying of jigs. Of the several manuals I own, my favorites are *Western Trout Fly Tying Manual*, by Jack H. Dennis, Jr., published by Snake River Books in Jackson Hole, Wyoming; and *Popular Fly Patterns*, by Terry Hellekson, published by Peregrine Smith, Inc. of Salt Lake City, Utah. Dennis's book is a large-format paperback with excellent step-by-step photographs for each pattern covered. Hellekson's book is a large-format hardbound volume, consisting mainly of fly "recipes" accompanied by exquisite pen-and-ink illustrations.

In my rather extensive angling library, one of the most valuable of books, in terms of practical and useful information, is C. Boyd Pfeiffer's *Tackle Craft*. This book is a must for any angler who is inclined toward making his own tackle and accessories. Instructions throughout are clear and are augmented by excellent photography. The book is loaded with helpful tips.

In his book, Pfeiffer is able to delve more deeply into the molding of leadhead jigs and soft plastics. He even includes a chapter on making molds, from block aluminum or plaster of Paris, for casting lead and molding plastic.

The book is available hardbound or in paper covers. If you can't find it at a local bookstore, have the dealer order you a copy. Or you can mail-order it at a slightly cheaper price from the Pfeiffer's Tackle Crafters catalog. It is certainly a worthwhile addition to any do-it-yourself angler's library, and one that will pay for itself many times over.

4. Casting Leadheads

Casting lead jig heads is about the easiest of all lure-making processes. What's more, the angler can make leadhead jigs that are every bit as good and as professional-looking as those produced by manufacturers.

The tools required are relatively inexpensive and are quite easy to use. Moreover, they can also be put to work casting sinkers and spinnerbait heads. So your initial investment could lead to substantial savings every fishing season to come.

Tools and Materials

There are only a few specialized tools you'll need for casting leadhead jigs, and several others you probably already own. You'll need some sort of melting pot, possibly a ladle, and one or more molds—depending on how many styles and sizes of jigs you want to cast.

If you will be using a common cast-iron melting pot, you'll need a heat source, which can be the kitchen range, a camp stove, or a heavy-duty hotplate. You may prefer, however, to invest in an electric melting pot which has its own heat source self-contained.

Other tools and accessories you should have on hand include a pair of heavy gloves, safety glasses or goggles, side-cutting wire cutters, pliers, a file, file brush, an old tablespoon, and a tin can. You may wish to have a sharp pocketknife on hand, and an ingot mold is a handy and inexpensive item, though not essential.

The only materials required for this phase of jig-making are lead or lead alloy and jig hooks.

71

Basic tools for casting leadheads include a cast-iron melting pot, ladle, pliers, wire cutters, heavy-duty gloves, and one or more jig molds. *(Photo by C. Boyd Pfeiffer.)*

Cast-iron pots and ladles require a reliable heat source, such as the kitchen range. *(Photo by C. Boyd Pfeiffer.)*

Melting Pots

Cast-iron melting pots and ladles are available at some hardware stores and plumbing-supply outlets. They also can be mail-ordered from several tackle suppliers, including Do-It Corporation, Netcraft, and Pfeiffer's Tackle Crafters. I have also seen them at some secondhand stores.

This is certainly the most economical melting equipment available, and a pot with a 15- to 20-pound capacity should be adequate for most purposes.

If you use a kitchen range for heating the pot, be sure to keep your work area uncluttered and make sure the only people in the kitchen are those helping with the casting chores. Be sure to do your casting when there are no young children about. You should also cover nearby counter-tops with scraps of plywood or other material to protect the surfaces from possible burns.

With a camp stove or heavy-duty hotplate as the heat source, you are free to do your casting in a safer, more convenient area, such as a garage, basement, or workshop. In good weather you can even do the job outdoors, on a patio, porch, or deck.

Cast-iron pots and some electric melters require the use of a long-handled ladle for dipping molten lead and pouring it into the mold. Most are equipped with narrow pouring spouts that allow the lead to be poured in a fine stream into the mold sprues or gates (holes in the top of the mold).

Both Netcraft and Pfeiffer's carry small, relatively inexpensive electric melting pots that will handle from four to six pounds of lead, depending on the model. These pots are adequate for casting jig heads in small quantities and will fit most anglers' needs.

Lee Precision, Inc. offers two small electric melters, each with a four-pound capacity. One features a 275-watt heating element; the other has a 500-watt unit, capable of melting four pounds of lead in less than 15 minutes.

Both Lee and Lyman manufacture large-capacity, bottom-pouring electric melters with calibrated thermostat controls. The Lee Production Pot IV will melt 10 pounds of lead in about 20 minutes. It also features a four-inch clearance beneath the spout to accommodate most jig molds. Lyman's Mould Master XX has a 20-pound capacity for the angler or club in need of the ability to cast many jig heads rapidly.

For casting jig heads in small quantities, Lee Precision offers an inexpensive pot and ladle.

Lee Production Pot IV *(left)* and Lyman Mould Master XX *(right)* both have calibrated thermostat controls and bottom-pouring feature.

Jig Molds

Although there are professional-type molds available for casting jigs of all sizes and designs, most anglers prefer the less expensive and more practical molds. While professional molds are precision-machined and produce perfect or near-perfect castings every time, they are single-cavity molds that aren't suited to the amateur's casting procedures.

For the sport fisherman, there are two types of molds most readily available: pinned molds and hinged-and-handled molds. While the pinned molds are less expensive, they are a bit more difficult to use than the hinged-and-handled types. Each produces good-quality jig heads, so the choice between the two is a matter of personal preference. With either type, you should be able to cast plenty of jigs to meet your needs by simply following the manufacturer's directions.

I personally prefer the hinged-and-handled molds, and the best I've found are made by Do-It Corporation. They can be bought directly from the manufacturer or from a number of tackle suppliers, including Netcraft and Pfeiffer's. Although these molds are a bit more expensive than the pinned molds, they are still cheap and produce jigs for pennies apiece. They're quicker and easier to use, and, consequently, they save time, which for most of us is as important as saving money.

Most jig molds have from one to eight cavities, depending upon the

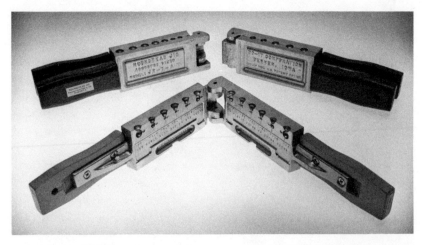

Author's personal choice in jig molds is the hinged-and-handled type made by Do-It Corporation.

size of the head—the larger the head, the fewer cavities possible. Some molds are made for casting a single size head, while others will turn out several different sizes. By studying the offerings of mold manufacturers and mail-order suppliers, in light of your own angling needs, you should be able to easily determine which mold or molds best fit your requirements. Most anglers should find that they can get by with fewer than a half-dozen molds.

If you have trouble finding molds locally, you'll find good selections in catalogs from Do-It Corporation, Netcraft, Pfeiffer's Tackle Crafters, and Sweet's Molds.

Selecting The Right Molds

Nobody can tell you which molds to buy. Only your personal needs and preferences will guide you there. But a few pointers should help.

You should first decide which jig-head designs best fit your requirements: roundhead, banana, dart, Erie, etc. Then determine how many different sizes you'll need to keep on hand. If you normally only use a few different sizes of jigs for all your fishing, you can get by with fewer molds and molds that cast only from one to perhaps four sizes at a time. If, like most anglers, however, you use a wide variety of sizes, you'll find the molds that cast the greatest variety of sizes will save time in the long run. You should know, though, that the smaller jigs are a bit more difficult to cast than larger ones and require more patience.

Where you do most of your fishing is another important consideration. If you fish mainly or only in fresh water, the molds that call for the light-wire Aberdeen-style hooks will be best. These hooks are also good for many inshore saltwater fishing situations, especially for the smaller species. For heavier saltwater use, the more substantial O'Shaughnessy hooks are best, and you'll need molds designed for these. There is some overlapping of application in both types of jig molds.

Collar design is another important consideration. The collar is the area immediately behind the head of the jig, and collars might differ from one design to another, or, as in the case of the popular roundhead jig, you might have a choice of several different collar designs or no collar at all.

Collarless heads are preferred by some anglers and are best for tying certain kinds of jigs, such as the traditional roundhead crappie jigs and shad darts. Collarless-head molds are also available in other designs and are best when a minimum of material will be used to tie the jigs. Some anglers also prefer the collarless jig for use with live or natural baits.

The *plain collar* is a simple lead sheath molded to the hook shank during the casting process. This is perhaps the most common type of collar and is preferred by many anglers as an all-around design. It is best suited to tying jigs with any of the traditional materials but can be used also with soft plastics, although the barbed collar is a better choice for that purpose.

The *barbed collar* was designed specifically for holding plastic twist-tails, grubs, worms, and the like and is the best choice for such purposes. This type of head can be used for conventional tying by simply bending the barb into the collar with pliers or filing it down. So if you need a

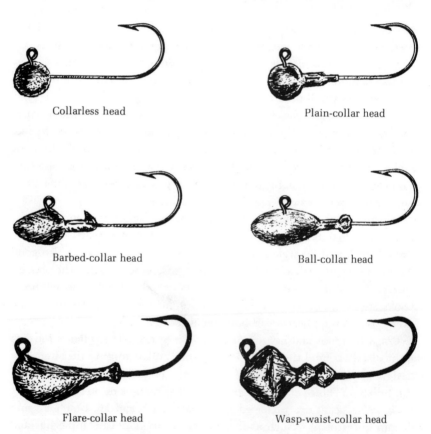

Collarless head   Plain-collar head

Barbed-collar head   Ball-collar head

Flare-collar head   Wasp-waist-collar head

The collar, the area immediately behind the jig head, comes in various designs, each with its particular advantages.

single mold to cast heads for soft plastics as well as for tying, this is a good choice.

The *ball collar* is similar to the plain collar, except that the trailing end of the collar is slightly enlarged and ball-shaped. Since the ball end helps to prevent thread wrappings from slipping off the collar, this is a good choice for inexperienced tyers. The ball also slightly flares the tying material for a fuller body that tends to pulsate in the water more than others. This collar will also hold soft plastics better than the plain collar will.

The *flare collar* causes the tying material to flare out from the jig head when the thread wrap is tightened. It also helps keep the tying material in place and will do a reasonably good job of securing soft plastics in place.

The *wasp-waist collar* was designed specifically for holding plastic shrimp tails and grubs in place and is an excellent choice for the angler who does a lot of fishing with soft plastics. Heads with this type of collar also can be tied conventionally and the collar will help secure the tying materials.

Hooks

Most freshwater-type jigs are molded on Aberdeen hooks. These hooks are made of relatively soft wire that will straighten and pull free from most snags; then they can be rebent with pliers, resharpened, and used again at once. These hooks come gold plated or bronzed. The gold hooks are best for most purposes, as they tend to resist corrosion better than bronzed hooks do. If you're concerned about the bright appearance of gold, bronzed hooks might be a better choice for you.

O'Shaughnessy hooks are stronger than Aberdeen hooks and won't bend to work a snag loose. Some are available either gold plated or bronzed, but most are cadmium plated and tinned to resist saltwater corrosion.

When extra strength is needed, the forged and cadmium/tin-plated O'Shaughnessy hooks are a good choice. For a bit more money, Mustad now offers super-strong and corrosion-resistant stainless-steel O'Shaughnessy jig hooks in sizes 8 to 8/o.

O. Mustad & Son, Inc. and Wright & McGill Co. (Eagle Claw brand) are the largest manufacturers of hooks. Their jig hooks are widely available, but if you can't find a particular type of jig hook locally or through mail-order sources, you can write the companies directly for ordering information or the addresses of nearby dealers.

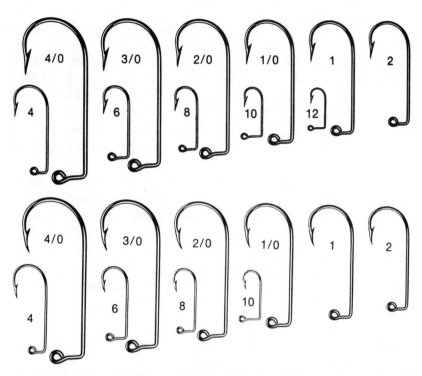

O. Mustad & Son, Inc. offers two types of Aberdeen-style jig hooks. *Top,* standard Aberdeen jig hooks available bronzed, gold-plated, or tinned; *bottom,* these hooks feature bent-in points and are available bronzed or gold-plated.

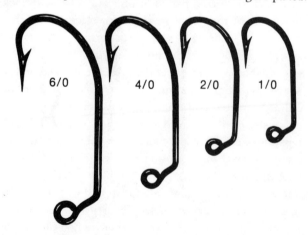

These Mustad O'Shaughnessy-style jig hooks are made from stainless steel for saltwater use.

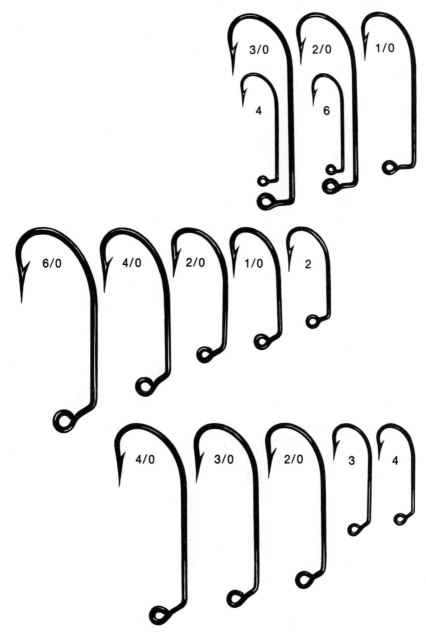

Mustad O'Shaughnessy-style jig hooks. *Top,* cadmium-plated and tinned for corrosion resistance; *center,* cadmium-plated and tinned, and forged for extra strength; *bottom,* cadmium-plated, tinned, and forged, with extra long shanks.

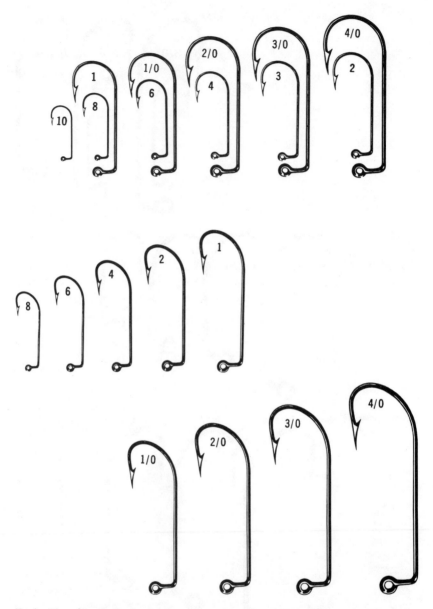

Eagle Claw brand jig hooks from Wright & McGill Co. *Top,* Aberdeen-style hooks, available either bronzed or gold-plated and made of regular or heavy wire; *center and bottom,* O'Shaughnessy-style hooks, available in bronze finish for freshwater use (e.g., worm heads) or cadmium-plated and tinned for saltwater use.

Lead and Alloys

Mold manufacturers generally recommend the use of pure or soft lead, especially for casting small jigs. Pure lead flows better than the harder alloys, which allows it to quickly fill the mold cavities and make smooth castings. The harder alloys tend to solidify more rapidly and will sometimes clog the mold sprues or gates, causing incomplete castings to result.

Commercial pig lead is 99.6 percent pure and is available in lead ingots or pigs from some industrial metal suppliers, plumbing-supply outlets, and a few hardware stores. Pure or reasonably pure lead (in the form of lead pipe, cable sheathing, sheet lead, and the like) is often available at lower prices from scrap-metal suppliers and junk yards. In these forms, lead is usually about 98 percent pure and is perfectly adequate for casting jigs of all sizes.

One distinct advantage to some harder alloys is that they are cheaper than pure lead and are often more readily available in scrap form. Indeed, some can be found free for the asking. Automotive wheel weights are one example of such scrap lead. This alloy (90 percent lead, 9 percent antimony, and 1 percent tin) is available at most automotive service stations and tire suppliers where wheel balancing is done. At some smaller outlets you might find them free for the asking or mighty cheap, but larger tire companies invariably charge for salvaged weights. So you'll have to check around for the best prices.

When wheel weights are melted down, a substantial amount of slag will rise to the top, along with the steel clips that are attached to them. Be sure to skim these wastes away before pouring the molten alloy, and certainly consider this waste when comparing the cost of wheel weights to other scrap lead.

Lead salvaged from automotive and industrial storage batteries is another scrap alloy that is 90 percent pure. In hardness and character, it is much like wheel-weight alloy and can be used accordingly for casting all but the smallest of jigs.

Linotype metal is another form of scrap lead that is suitable for casting large jigs, but is a bit difficult to come by these days. Harder than wheel weights and battery lead, and consequently more difficult to cast, this alloy is 82 percent lead, 15 percent antimony, and 3 percent tin.

Despite mold manufacturers' recommendations and what you might have read elsewhere, you could face some difficulty locating pure pig lead, and when you do, you might not like the price. Lead isn't as widely used

Types of lead and lead alloy suitable for casting jigs include several sizes of cable sheathing *(top)*, sheet lead *(center)*, wheel weights *(bottom left)*, as well as salvaged decoy keel weights, damaged fishing sinkers, a five-pound ingot of pure lead, and even air-gun pellets salvaged from a target trap.

by plumbers as it once was, so isn't as readily stocked in all areas. And, like everything else, it costs more than it used to.

Since prices will vary greatly from source to source, and since any prices mentioned here will have increased by the time you read this, I can't really give you an idea of what lead will cost you in its various forms; nor can I tell you exactly what your jigs will cost you. You'll have to determine that on your own.

What I can do is provide some prices that I got recently from various sources, as a means of offering you a comparison base and a few examples of how prices do, indeed, vary. Since I have always scrounged most of my own lead, the quotes I got came as no small shock. One would think we were striking the coin of the realm from the stuff instead of tying it to a line and heaving it into a convenient body of water.

Your best bet for finding lead for casting jig heads is to do as I do—scrounge it, beg it, borrow it, and stop just short of stealing it. And if you've never done it before, you should start the way I did when I made my survey for the purpose of discussion here. I acted as if I had no lead on hand and needed the best quality and best price, or some suitable compromise.

The Yellow Pages of the telephone directory provide a good starting point. There you can check such headings as Sporting Goods—Retail; Fishing Tackle—Retail; Fishing Tackle—Wholesale & Manufacturers; Fishermen's Supplies (Commercial Fishing); Marine Equipment & Supplies; Guns & Gunsmiths; Hardware—Retail; Plumbing Fixtures & Supplies—Retail; Plumbing Fixtures & Supplies—Wholesale & Manufacturers; Batteries—Storage—Wholesale & Manufacturers; Surplus Merchandise; Tire Dealers—Retail; Tire Dealers—Used; Steel Distributors & Warehouses. Also don't overlook any listings under Scrap Metals as well as Junk Dealers.

All of these will not necessarily prove to be sources for lead, but by checking as many as possible, you should turn up several good prospects. If you have gun clubs or shooting clubs in your area, contact them, as many of them are engaged in lead scrounging, too, for casting bullets. Any muzzleloader club should be a good source of information about local outlets for pure lead.

I started my own survey by calling the largest sporting-goods dealer in town. He offered to sell me all the sinkers, decoy anchors, and downrigger weights I wanted, but had no raw lead on hand. None of the fishing-tackle retailers I phoned carried lead, nor did any of the commercial-fishing or marine suppliers, which surprised me, since commercial trollers use pure-lead "cannon balls" on their trolling lines.

It turned out that the few commercial fishermen who cast their own weights buy their lead from a local hardware store that carries lead in five-pound ingots and charges 65 cents a pound. The only other source of pure lead ingots I found was a plumbing-supply store that sells five-pound ingots for $4.50 each, which works out to an incredible 90 cents a pound. I wrote that source off.

My best source for pure or nearly pure lead turned out to be a scrap-metal dealer who assured me he had a large supply of cable sheathing and sheet lead on hand, the latter "very pure" in his words. His price of 40 cents a pound was only twice as much as I paid for pure lead the last time I laid in a supply a few years back.

My search for the harder alloys proved to be equally varied in results. The largest tire dealer in town wanted 38 cents a pound for discarded wheel weights. Considering the steel clips and slag that have to be removed, and the alloy's hardness, I'd be better off buying the sheet lead from the scrap dealer. Remember, the idea is to find the best quality for the best price, and wheel weights ought to be far cheaper than 98-percent-pure lead.

Another tire dealer wanted 40 cents a pound for wheel weights—if you can believe that—and most of the smaller dealers wanted similar prices when they had quantities on hand. One dealer in a town about thirty miles from where I live said he'd sell me wheel weights for 25 cents a pound, and I made a note to stop by next time I was down his way, as it became obvious to me that people just aren't giving wheel weights away any more, and my years-old supply is dwindling.

I found one local battery manufacturer who told me he had a pile of used batteries I could haul off for 12 cents a pound, which might sound like a bargain, but probably isn't. If you can get battery lead at a price cheaper than wheel weights, don't buy the latter. But if you have to salvage the lead yourself, you could lose on the deal. It's my guess that lead can comprise no more than half the dry weight of a battery—though I've never checked this. If batteries cost you 12 cents a pound, then the lead salvaged must be 24 cents a pound or more. And you must consider the time spent tearing the batteries apart to get to the lead and the time and fuel spent hauling the scraps to a disposal site.

All in all, lead isn't nearly as cheap as it was only a few years ago, but it's still a bargain for the angler casting his own jig heads. Even if I had no choice but to pay the highest price I was quoted (90 cents a pound for pure lead) I could still cast about sixty quarter-ounce jigs per pound, even allowing for waste, which is minimal with pure lead. That's only 1½ cents worth of lead per head.

Of course, I would be using the scrap lead that I found for 40 cents a pound, which, for my purposes, is every bit as good as the most expensive lead. Depending upon the type of jig being cast, the kind of hooks used, source of hooks and quantity purchased, hooks will range in price from about 1.8 to 2.6 cents apiece, with an average of about two cents each. With 40 cents worth of lead and $1.20 worth of hooks, I would end up with five dozen jig heads at a cost of $1.60, or just over 2½ cents apiece. To buy that same number of finished heads I would have to pay about $12.00, or 20 cents a head.

You can see that it doesn't take many pounds of lead, melted and molded into jig heads, to pay for the melting pot and molds you'll need. And after you've saved enough to pay for your tools, you'll continue using them to turn out your own lures for mere pennies apiece.

Of course, the cheaper the lead is, the cheaper your jig heads will be, and if you can find free lead, your only cost will be for hooks and whatever materials you use for finishing the lures. If you learn to scrounge and stay alert, you'll find free or mighty cheap lead from time to time, as I did when I was making my phone survey.

On the chance that he might have some suggestions, I phoned my good friend, Larry Breniman, a local gun dealer and avid shooter and hunter. I thought he might lead me to a source, but he turned out to be the source. He told me he and a buddy had collected wheel weights for several years when they could get them for nothing, and he had five 10-gallon milk cans full of them—more than he would use in a lifetime of casting bullets. "Take as many as you want," he said.

But it's not just the big finds that matter. Every little scrap of lead is useful, and you must keep this in mind. You have to develop the scrounger's attitude that every piece of lead you find is so many fishing lures when it's melted down and molded to hooks.

To illustrate, not so long ago I headed out early one morning to dig some clams on a good minus tide. On my way to my favorite flats, I crossed some rocky rubble that is normally under water on the high tide. On the mud between two rather large rocks I found an eight-ounce bank sinker with its eye broken. It had obviously become snagged between the two rocks, and when the angler put the pressure on his line, the sinker eye gave way; it was obviously cast of very soft lead, possibly pure stuff. Into my pocket it went, and I noted mentally that it would make about five dozen ⅛-ounce crappie jigs or shad darts for next season. I hadn't just found another hunk of lead. I had discovered sixty fishing lures right there in the mud and rubble of low tide.

Obviously, whenever you come across pure lead, cable sheathing, sheet lead, or lead pipe at a good price, you should take advantage of it and stock up. But don't overlook the harder alloys when they're available cheap. Just remember the limitations of the latter, and keep the various kinds of lead separate and identified. Mark the ingots with a scratch awl or other pointed instrument, identifying each appropriately. A simple marking system I use is to scratch a single line or slash in each ingot of pure or nearly pure lead, two lines for ingots made of wheel weights or battery lead, and three lines for linotype metal.

If you use any of the alloys, you will have to experiment with them and your own molds to determine the limitations, which will vary according to jig size, jig style, and mold design. You might find, for example, that in some molds you can cast jigs of ⅛ ounce or even smaller with one of the harder alloys, whereas with some molds you might have to use pure lead for any jigs smaller than ¼ ounce to get perfect castings every time.

After any casting session you can either pour leftover lead or alloy into an ingot mold and mark the ingots as mentioned, or simply let the lead cool and harden in your melting pot. If you use one of the bottom-pouring electric melting pots, however, it is best to drain leftover lead into an ingot mold, as the nozzle will leak when the lead is reheated for your next casting session if you don't.

At any rate, try not to melt much more lead than you'll need for any session, since repeated melting and cooling will cause even pure lead to harden somewhat, making it difficult to pour properly for perfect castings.

Incidentally, if you're looking for a good, inexpensive ingot mold, Pfeiffer's Tackle Crafters is a source for the Palmer mold that has three cavities for making one-pound ingots. Lee Precision also offers one that makes two one-pound and two half-pound ingots in a single pouring. The Lee ingot mold imprints the name "Lee" on the one-pound ingots and the fraction "½" on the half-pound ingots. By casting only pure lead in the half-pound cavities and harder alloy in the one-pound cavities, your ingots

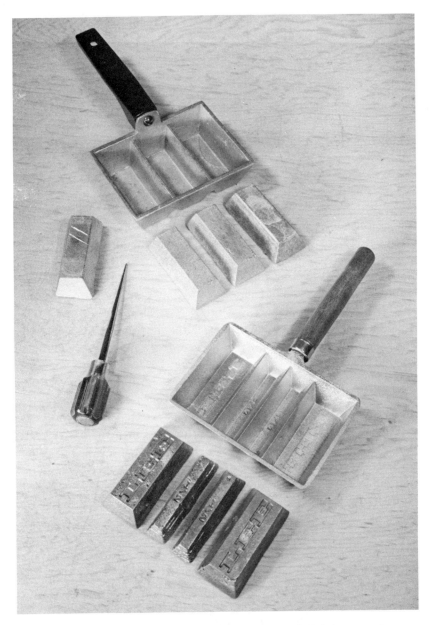

Palmer three-cavity ingot mold *(top)* produces ingots of slightly more than one pound that can be identified with marks made by a scratch awl. Lee ingot mold *(bottom)* has two one-pound and two half-pound cavities that imprint during casting for easy identification.

will be marked automatically, making it easy to keep the different types of lead separate without additional markings.

Casting Jig Heads

Casting jig heads is so simple that step-by-step instructions are really unnecessary. In fact, most anglers can look at a jig mold and melting pot and determine on their own what steps to follow. This section, then, is meant only to augment what you already know and help you solve any problems you might encounter along the way.

Without question, the most important part of casting jig heads is safety, which mainly amounts to using common sense. Molten lead is hazardous material and should be treated with the utmost care and caution. Obviously, it can cause serious burns if mishandled. Other sources of burns are the melting pot, a hot ladle, a hot mold, and even the finished jig heads themselves.

Moisture is another danger to contend with when casting lead. When molten lead comes in contact with water, it will spatter and pop violently, which can lead to serious injury. So always make sure all your tools and any lead that will be used are completely dry. To that end, it is important to store your molds and lead in a dry place and to check them before casting jigs. You can eliminate any residual moisture by spreading out your lead and open molds on a bench or countertop before you begin any casting session and blowing warm air over them with an electric hair dryer.

Protect your eyes by wearing safety glasses or goggles. Some people wear full face shields to afford even greater protection from the possibility of spattering lead. Since hands are most vulnerable, wear heavy gloves during the entire casting process.

As lead and lead alloys melt, they release slightly toxic fumes, so you should make sure that your casting area is well ventilated. If you suffer from any sort of respiratory ailment, be sure to check with your physician before working with molten lead and alloys.

If you will be using a cast-iron pot and the kitchen range, camp stove, or heavy-duty hotplate, fill the pot about three-fourths full or less with lead and set your heat source for medium-high or high heat. Adjust the setting, as required, until the lead melts properly. Remember the settings used to melt the lead and to retain the proper temperature, and use these in the future.

If you're using one of the electric melting pots, follow the manufacturer's directions for melting and casting. While the lead is melting, set out all your casting tools and materials in an orderly fashion. If you'll be casting a large quantity of jig heads, make sure you have a sufficient supply of lead and the proper hooks ready and nearby. You might also want to cover the enameled surface of the kitchen range with heavy-duty aluminum foil to protect it from dripping or splattering lead.

The first secret to success in casting molten lead is to make sure the lead is hot enough. The time it takes for lead to reach the proper temperature will vary with the types and capacities of pots and amounts of lead being melted. The best way to judge its readiness is to watch the color changes the lead undergoes as it melts and reaches its proper pouring temperature. When the lead has melted to a uniform liquid consistency and its surface has taken on a purplish-golden color, it's ready.

Before pouring (with all but the bottom-pouring pots) you'll need to remove the slag (impurities) that have risen to the surface during melting. Use an old tablespoon to skim it away, and deposit it in a tin can that you can keep nearby for this purpose. A reminder: make sure the tin can's interior is completely dry.

The second secret to successful casting is to have the mold sufficiently warm. As hot lead touches a cold mold, the molten metal will cool too quickly and will produce imperfect castings or might clog the mold sprues, especially the smaller ones. A warm mold allows the lead to flow freely into the cavities, filling them to capacity before it begins to solidify.

Although some anglers warm their molds over open flames, I can't recommend this procedure, as overheating can damage the mold. The best way I know of to heat a mold is to make the first pourings without hooks. Let the first pouring cool in the mold for two or three minutes. Open the mold and remove the solidified-but-hookless heads and repeat the process. After the second pouring, your mold should be warm enough.

Arrange the jig hooks (of proper size and design, as recommended by the mold manufacturer) in the mold, being careful to seat each one correctly in its cavity. Close the mold, and you're ready to pour. If the particular mold you are using permits the hooks to protrude from the

When wheel weights are melted down, they produce a lot of slag that will rise to the top with the steel clips. Use an old tablespoon to remove these wastes to a nearby tin can.

bottom, be careful not to set the mold down in such a way as to jar or move the hooks.

Even if your mold is equipped with wooden handles, wear heavy gloves to protect your hands from possible splattering of molten lead and the radiant heat from the pot which can become uncomfortable. If your mold has metal handles, by all means, wear insulated chef's mittens to keep from burning your hands.

Bottom-pouring pots have small nozzles designed to discharge molten lead in a very fine stream. If you're pouring from one of the smaller spouted electric pots or are dipping lead from a cast-iron pot with a ladle, make sure you pour the lead slowly, in a fine stream. Start at one end of the mold and fill one cavity completely before going on to fill the next. Cavities should be filled all the way into the mold sprue, just short of the sprue rim.

Set the mold aside (on a hot pad to protect workbench or counter surfaces) and allow it to cool for several minutes.

You should always be careful to keep lead from overflowing the sprues. But on the chance that some lead might find its way to the mold hinges,

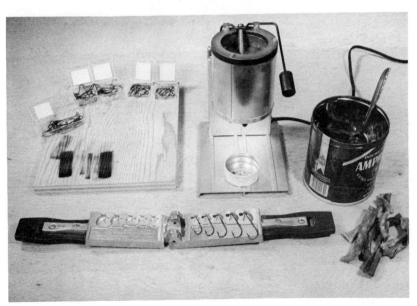

Before casting your jig heads, arrange and carefully seat the hooks in the warmed mold.

Filling mold from a bottom-pouring pot. Pour lead in a fine, uninterrupted stream, entirely filling each cavity to the top of the sprue or gate.

always check them before opening the mold. If there is any lead on the hinges, use a pair of pliers to gently pry it away. Don't ever force the mold open if the hinges are clogged with lead. You could damage the mold by doing so.

Remember that the jig heads will still be hot, so remove them with care. If any tend to stick to the molds, don't bang the mold to release them, as this, too, could damage the mold. Instead, use pliers to grip the hooks and gently work the heads loose.

Fill the mold with hooks, and you're ready to cast another batch. Keep watch on your lead supply and add more as required. Remember to allow the lead to heat fully before pouring, and if your mold cools down while the lead melts, be sure to warm it again as before.

When your jigs are cool enough to handle, you will need to remove the sprues (the lead that filled the pouring gates of the mold and which will be attached to the heads). Use side-cutting wire cutters for this. Then smooth out any excess lead remaining there and along the seams with a file.

Molten lead being poured into mold from a cast-iron ladle. *(Photo by C. Boyd Pfeiffer.)*

With most modern molds, you should have little or no problem with flash—excess lead that leaks around the castings at the seams. Small amounts can be trimmed away with a sharp pocketknife and polished with a file. If flash is severe, check to make sure your hooks are properly seated in the mold and that nothing is interfering with the closing of the mold.

For any of several reasons, castings sometimes come out of the mold malformed or incomplete, particularly the smaller ones. Such imperfections can be caused by lead that has not been sufficiently heated, so double-check your procedure here. If your problems persist, try melting a smaller amount of lead. Fill your pot to half capacity and see if that doesn't heat the lead better and faster.

Also, molds that are too cool will have a similar effect. If you have warmed your mold by making the first two pourings without hooks, you might need to make three or four such pourings instead. If that solves your problem, make the same number of mold-warming pourings at any future casting session.

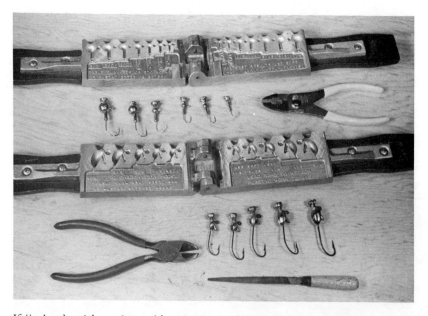

If jig heads stick to the mold, grip the hooks with pliers and gently work the head away from the mold. Once jig heads have cooled, remove sprues (the lead that collects in the pouring gate of the mold) and file smooth any rough surfaces.

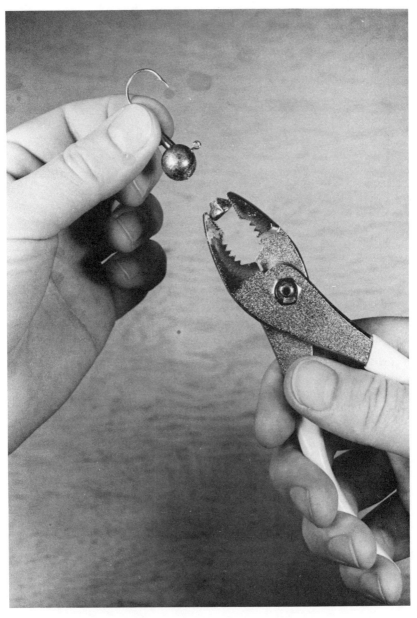

If you use pure or very soft lead, sprues on most heads can be quickly and cleanly removed with pliers. Simply grip the sprue and twist off. Often, the break will be so clean that no filing is required.

Remember, too, that the lead being poured into the mold must flow steadily in a very fine stream. If your ladle has a broad spout that produces too wide a stream, use a file to make a narrow notch in the spout. This should produce the fine stream required.

You can also use a small file or hobbyist's router (such as the Moto-Tool) to slightly enlarge the opening in the pouring gate. This will allow the lead to flow more quickly into the cavity, assuring complete castings. Be careful to remove only a small amount of metal from the problem gate; then check it by pouring a casting.

If you continue having problems with imperfect castings, it could be the material you are using—especially if you are casting with one of the harder alloys. If you have been using linotype material, try switching to wheel weights. If you have been using wheel weights or battery lead, you might need pure lead to solve your problem.

With some experimentation, you'll learn the limitations of your tools and the casting materials available to you. You'll know when you must use pure or soft lead and when you can get by with one of the harder alloys.

After your casting session, allow your molds to cool. Then put a drop of oil in the hinges and store them in a dry place.

Your jig heads are now ready for painting or storage. Any heads that will be used unpainted can be stored in any convenient manner. Those you plan to pain should be stored only briefly, in a dry area and in airtight containers.

5.  Painting and Tying Jigs

Whether you cast your own jig heads or buy them, what you then do with them depends on your personal preferences and the type of fishing that interests you. You might just fill a drawer or tray in a tackle box with unpainted jig heads for use with plastic worms, grubs, and twist-tails. Or you might paint and tie all your jig heads into bucktail jigs or crappie jigs. Most likely, you'll put your jig heads to a variety of uses, calling for several different types of preparation.

Heads that will be left unpainted and used that way can be stored in any fashion that suits you, although storage in a dry area is preferable, if not always possible. Heads that will be painted should be stored unpainted for as brief a period as possible and should be packaged in some sort of airtight container. Plastic bags are best for such storage, and air should be forced out of the bags before sealing them. Pack the bags with small quantities of jig heads, leaving as few air pockets as possible; be careful to keep hook points from puncturing the bags. Ziploc sandwich bags are ideal for such purposes.

Your best bet is to paint your jig heads immediately or soon after casting them, because lead left unpainted and exposed to air will oxidize, leaving a white powdery residue on the lead surfaces to which paint will not adequately adhere.

Jig heads that will be tied into various patterns with traditional tying materials can be painted before or after tying, depending upon your personal preference. The advantages of each practice are best determined by the angler's needs and inclinations.

When you tie jigs with unpainted heads, you can paint the heads in colors that match or contrast the tying materials and can then paint over the thread wrap behind the head to provide the necessary protective sealing.

If you use prepainted heads you can select tying materials that match or contrast the head colors, and you have the option of using threads of any color that suit you. The thread wrap can then be sealed with clear head cement.

Since I usually tie jigs when the mood moves me, or when I feel a need for diversion, or when the fishing season is bearing down on me and I need to restock my jig supply, I normally do my tying weeks (sometimes months) after I have cast the heads. For that reason, I paint my jig heads as soon after casting as possible so that I have a supply to work on at my leisure.

Although I often have unpainted heads in my tackle box for use with the soft plastics, I also try to paint those now when time permits. I like to have an assortment of matching and contrasting heads for use with plastic twist-tails and grubs, and I've taken to painting my worming heads in colors that match the plastic worms I normally use.

Painting Jig Heads

The paint on jig heads chips and scratches rather easily when the lures are bounced over rocks or dragged over gravel and sand. Poorly painted heads are even more susceptible to such damage. For that reason, you should take care and precautions in the selection of paints and the methods of application to assure a reasonably damage-resistant finish.

Some of the processes used by commercial jig manufacturers produce extremely tough and durable finishes. (I've already mentioned the jigs made by Bomber Bait Co. as being some of the toughest available.) But even these jigs will succumb to the rigors and abuse of hard fishing. So you aren't likely to ever come up with a completely damageproof finish. If you do, let me know, so I can invest in your process and get rich.

What you can do, though, is prepare and paint your jig heads for optimum durability. And when some of your favorite fish producers become battle-scarred veterans, run them through the shop again for a facelift.

Neutralizing and Base-Coat Painting

Before applying any paint, dip the jig heads in vinegar to neutralize them so the paint will adhere better. The vinegar also helps to clean away oily fingerprints and the like. Then rinse the heads in running water and

Unless you plan to paint jig heads with a neutral base coat, neutralize them by immersing them in vinegar. Set them on paper towels to dry, and store them in airtight containers until you're ready to paint them.

spread them on paper towels to dry. You can speed the drying process by blowing warm air over them with an electric hair dryer.

Next comes the important base coat that not only primes the jig head for the finish coats but also enriches many finish colors, particularly the lighter ones.

Regardless of what color the head will be finished in, use white for the base coat. White is easily covered by black, purple, blue, and other dark colors, and it improves final coats of white, yellow, silver, and other light

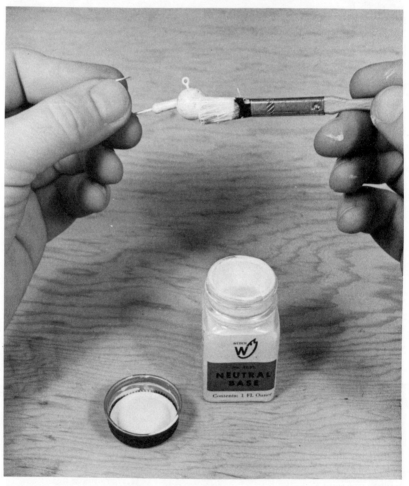

You can combine the neutralizing and base-coating operations by using neutral-base paint, available from Netcraft.

colors. If your final coat will be lacquer, make sure the base coat is also lacquer, as lacquer applied over an enamel base coat will soften the enamel, causing it to merge with the lacquer.

You can combine the neutralizing and base-coat painting by using Netcraft's Neutral Base Coat—a white primer formulated specifically for jigs. It can be covered with lacquer, enamel, or epoxy paint.

Once the base coat dries, you can go on to finish-paint your jig heads or put them away for later painting. Once base-coated, the heads will be sealed and will not oxidize.

Painting Methods and Types of Paint

Because of the jig head's compactness, it is well suited to any of three basic painting methods: brushing, dipping, or spraying. Which method to use is largely a matter of personal choice, but can be influenced by the availability of suitable finishes. Generally, you'll find lacquers available in a wider array of colors than enamels, and some special-purpose finishes might be available only in aerosol spray cans.

No matter what type of paint you use, always follow the manufacturer's directions for surface preparation, application, thinning, and cleanup.

Whichever method you choose, you will get the best results if you apply several thin coats rather than one heavy coat. Heavier coats tend to run and drip and take longer to dry adequately. A buildup of several thinner coats is also more durable than a single layer.

Lacquers are usually thinner than enamels and can normally be applied as they come, right out of the can or jar. If thinning is required, use lacquer thinner only.

For best results, enamels should be thinned to a consistency similar to that of lightweight motor oil. Oil-base enamels should be thinned with paint thinner, mineral spirits, or turpentine. Water-base enamels should not be used for painting jig heads.

Naturally, aerosol paints and enamels are used as they come. If you plan to use a spray gun, however, you will need to thin most paints according to the spray-gun manufacturer's recommendations.

Another reason for thinning the paints you use is that the jigs will have to be hung to dry. Thicker paints that take longer to dry will form a drop at the nose of the jig that will harden as the paint dries, distorting the shape of the jig.

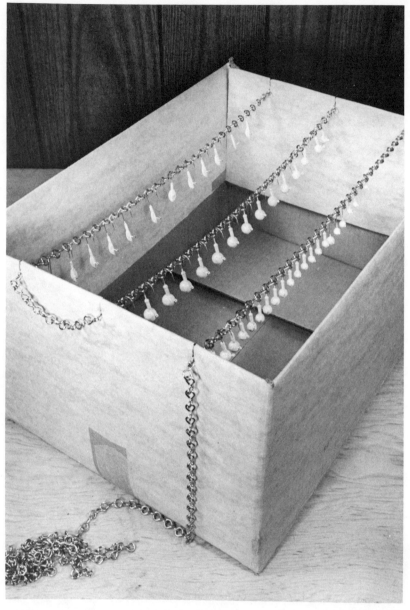

You can make a jig-drying-and-painting box with a length of light chain and a cardboard box. Cut slits in the sides of the box and anchor chain in slits. Hang jigs from chain to dry.

A cardboard box is handy for drying jig heads and confining any messy dripping, and it is easily discarded afterward. Although you can fashion hangers out of wire or string, a length of light chain or perforated pipe strap is best for keeping the jigs from touching while they dry.

Simply stretch one or several lengths of chain or pipe strap across the open top of the cardboard box and attach to the box sides with tape. As you finish brush-painting or dipping your jigs, just hang them from the chain or strap to dry.

If you plan to spray-paint your heads, turn the box on its side and hang the jigs from a single length of chain or pipe strap that is positioned near the top of the box opening. After the first coat dries, turn the jigs and spray another coat, assuring that all sides of the heads get an even coating. Apply as many coats as necessary to provide a deep and durable finish. If you have a large quantity of heads to spray, you might wish to set up several spray-painting boxes.

If you plan to spray-paint your jig heads, simply turn the box on its side and you have a perfect spray-painting box. After spraying all surfaces you can reach, carefully invert the box, leaving the jig heads hanging in place, and spray any unpainted surfaces.

Lacquers dry faster than enamels, sometimes allowing a second coating within minutes of the first. Enamels, on the other hand, usually require fewer coats for a good, even finish.

Obviously, paint stores and paint departments of discount stores are good sources of jig paints, but you'll also find selections of lacquers and enamels (in jars, cans, and aerosol sprays) in most hobby shops, as well as in the hobby and automotive departments at most discount stores.

Buy your paints in small quantities at first, until you determine which types and colors are best for your purposes. The one-ounce jars of auto touch-up paint and model-maker's paint are excellent for starters. If you like to carry a large assortment of jigs of various colors, you might find these paints best anyway. When you find one or several paints that you use more than any others, you'll save money by purchasing them in half-pint or pint cans.

Jig heads that are to be used with plastic worms, twist-tails, grubs, and other soft plastics should be painted with a white base coat and then finished with epoxy paint. Ordinary lacquers and enamels will react chemically with soft plastics, causing the paint to soften and smear. This problem is eliminated with epoxy paints.

Enamels, lacquers, and epoxy paints are available from a variety of sources and can be brushed on, sprayed, or applied by dipping.

One objection many anglers have had to epoxy paints is that they come in two containers (pigment and hardener) and must be mixed before they're applied. Any leftovers then have to be discarded, which often leads to waste, especially when only a few jig heads require painting.

This problem has been solved by a one-step aerosol spray epoxy that is now available from Netcraft. Although aerosol paints are more expensive than bottled or canned paints, the convenience and elimination of waste associated with the spray epoxy makes it a good choice when such a paint is required.

Paint Colors

Modern lacquers and enamels are available in just about any color or hue you can imagine. What's more, you can buy special pearl finishes, fluorescents, and luminescent paints. You can opt for a glossy, satin, or dull finish, although a high gloss is usually preferable for finishing most fishing lures. I doubt that the degree of gloss matters as much to fish as to fishermen.

The best advice I can give you is to experiment with the colors that strike your fancy, but be sure to keep at least several of the most basic colors on hand and carry a good supply of jigs and jig heads in these colors.

Although I have experimented with plenty of different colors, I now paint most of my jig heads in one of these basic colors, and I use a few other colors that have worked for me under certain conditions.

If I had to recommend the most important paint colors—those which are the most widely used and are the easiest to adapt to a variety of tying materials and soft plastics—my vote would go to white, yellow, red, and black, not necessarily in that order. Next, I would pick purple, blue, chartreuse, and fluorescent orange as personal favorites for certain circumstances.

Plastic Coating for Extra Durability

If you fish the jetties, breakwaters, rocky ledges, rip-rap, or any other areas that are hard on jig finishes, you might prefer to coat some of your jig heads with plastic, which isn't as difficult a process as some might think.

Plasti-Dip International manufactures a thick liquid plastic that is ideal

For an extra-durable finish, coat your jig heads with plastic. You can make a handy dipping tool out of a bent wire or a piece of dowel rod with a screw eye inserted into one end for holding the jigs and another in the opposite end for hanging in your workshop. Author's "dipstick" has a small alligator clip attached to one end for holding jig heads.

for dipping jig heads. This is the stuff pliers and other tools are dipped in to plastic-coat the handles. Look for it at your local hardware store or order it from Netcraft.

To use, prepare the jig heads as you would for painting, including the application of a base coat of white. Since the tall, narrow can that Plasti-Dip comes in is made for dipping and is filled only to within an inch of the top to prevent overflowing, you might need to suspend your jigs from something during dipping to keep from getting the sticky stuff on your fingers. A bent wire works fine; use a large paper clip. I made a small dipping tool from a scrap of dowel rod to which I attached a small alligator clip with a wood screw.

Plasti-Dip is really tough material that will take just about all the abuse you can give it. It's so tough, in fact, that cleaning and freeing the hook eye can be quite a chore. After trying several ways, I settled on using an X-Acto knife to first cut around the hook shank, immediately below the eye. Then I just peel the coating away from the eye, using the point of the knife to pick away the more tenacious bits.

Currently, Plasti-Dip comes in only four colors, but the four most important jig colors: white, yellow, red, and black. For coating over jigs already painted another color, it is also available in a clear finish.

The Eyes Have It

Commercially manufactured jigs come with or without eyes, and preferences for eyed jigs will vary from one angler to the next. If you make your own jigs, the decision whether or not to add eyes is yours, but keep in mind that eyes are sometimes important to the predator species feeding on forage fish. Eyes are sometimes very prominent in forage species and are even disproportionately large in the young of most species of fish.

If you will be making and using jigs that resemble some sort of forage fish, I recommend putting eyes on the painted heads. I don't think, however, that eyes are important or even desirable on jigs made to represent most insect life; nor are they needed on worming jigs.

Eyes are easy to add to any jig head after all other painting has been done and the heads are completely dry. As with any other painting, remember not to use lacquer over enamel. And if the heads will be used with soft plastics, use epoxy paint for the eyes.

The eyes are no more than dots that can be applied with the heads of various sizes of nails and straight pins. For the largest dots, use large box nails. For smaller dots, use finishing nails, brads, or straight pins. Some mail-order companies also offer special applicator bottles designed specifically for adding eyes to lures.

When you're adding eyes to your jigs, lay out all your painted heads on their sides and put the eyes on one side only. When the paint has dried, turn the heads over and add the eyes to the other side. To prevent running, use unthinned paints for applying eyes.

Most painted eyes consist of two dots—a larger outside circle at the center of which is a dark pupil. The colors to use are largely up to you, but you should pick those that contrast nicely with the colors of the jig heads as well as with the dark pupil.

Since I stick to pretty basic colors for most of my jig heads, I only use a few different colors for the eyes. On heads painted dark colors, I usually use white, yellow, silver, or gold for the first dot. On heads of lighter colors, I use one of the same colors as well as red, making sure the color contrasts with the jig head. For example, on a white head I might use any of the above-mentioned colors except white; on a yellow head, I would

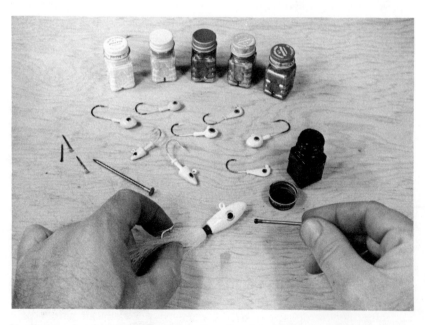

Use the heads of nails and straight pins of various sizes to apply eyes to your painted heads.

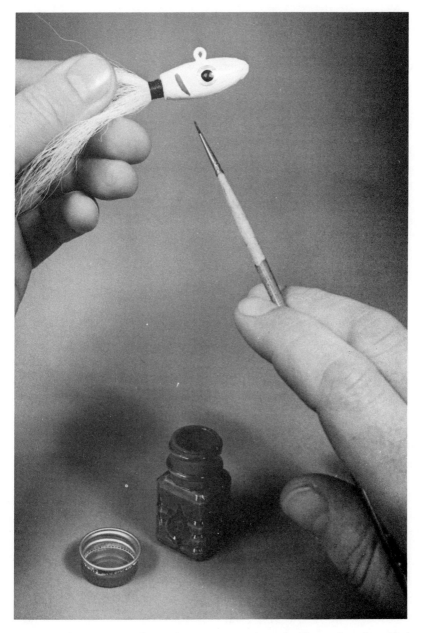

On jigs tied to represent forage fish, you can paint red gill openings for added attraction.

pick any but yellow. My preference runs to red on most of the light-colored heads.

I keep things simple by using black for all the pupils. Of course, you can experiment with any dark color, but I think black gets the job done as well as anything else.

A Slash of Red for Attraction

Red seems to be a turn-on color for many gamefish, and I like to add a bit of red to many of my jig heads. On those jigs I use to represent forage fish, I often put a small diagonal or curved slash on each side, behind the eyes, where the gills would be. I sometimes put a slash or two on the "chin" of the jig.

Much convincing research as been done on the ability of fish to determine and distinguish colors. And red being the color of blood is probably one reason that the color is attractive to fish.

Tying Jigs

The experienced fly tyer needs no instructions on tying jigs, but to those who have never attempted to tie flies or jigs, it might seem at first a mysterious and difficult art. Nothing could be further from fact, as jig tying is quite a simple craft, requiring only a few specialized tools.

Certainly, the successful tying of many fly patterns calls for a fair share of manual dexterity, patience, and a knowledge of some specialized techniques. But jigs, for the most part, are simple lures that even the novice will find easy to tie. Moreover, there are only a few standard patterns you will need to know to get started. After that, you can stay with those patterns, experiment with some of your own designs, or delve deeply into the art by studying some of the better tying manuals.

Jig-Tying Tools

The only fly-tying tool that is absolutely essential is some sort of vise for holding the jig head during tying. Any of the fly-tying vises will do a great job, but you can also get by in a pinch with a small workshop vise.

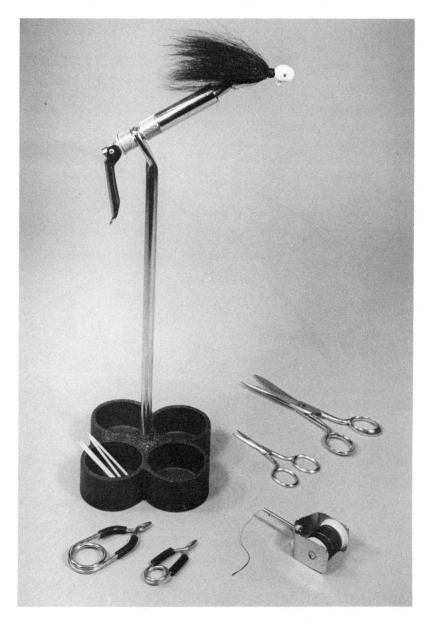

Basic jig-tying tools include a fly-tying vise, scissors, a bobbin, hackle pliers (for tying hackled patterns), and toothpicks for applying head cement.

Since fly-tying vises are not all that expensive, though, you would do well to invest in one, as they make the tying job easy.

You can get by without a bobbin, but bobbins are so cheap and handy, you ought to buy one. One of the modern bobbins will prove a real aid to tying.

You'll need scissors for cutting and trimming the various tying materials and for clipping thread. A pair of household scissors will do, but the smaller ones are better for delicate work. If there's a sewing box around the house, you might find a pair of embroidery scissors there that will do a dandy job at the tying bench. Or you can buy fly-tyer's scissors. If you buy scissors, make sure the thumb and finger holes are large enough to fit comfortably. The thumb hole should fit loosely down to the first knuckle. The finger hole should fit between the first and second knuckles. Many

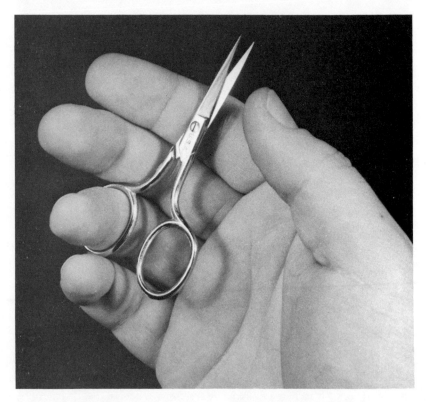

Many tyers like to keep their scissors in hand, attached to the ring finger, during the entire tying process.

tyers like to keep scissors in hand during the entire tying process, and they'll slip them onto the thumb and ring finger instead of the usual forefinger. Make sure your scissors fit whichever fingers you'll normally use. That might sound like a petty consideration, but it is important to any tyer who wants to work quickly and produce in quantity.

Some patterns call for hackles, and if you plan to tie these you'll surely want hackle pliers. If you have no immediate need for such patterns, you can put off the purchase of hackle pliers until later.

Although there are a few other items you might find a need for in the future—as you become more proficient and want to experiment with more patterns—these are all the tools you need to start with and might well be all you'll ever need.

Jig-Tying Materials

To list all the natural and synthetic materials that are suitable for tying jigs would take far too much space. There are some basic materials you should know about and should keep on hand for the patterns you tie most frequently.

No matter what other materials you use, you will need fly-tying thread. Rod-wrapping thread also does a good job. Size 3/0 is fine for tying small jigs and sizes *A* to *E* are good for medium to large jigs. Black, white, red, and yellow are colors you should stock as standard. Beyond those four, chose from the dozen or so different colors normally available to best fit your personal needs.

You can buy prewaxed thread, which is quicker and simpler to use, or you can buy plain thread that you'll need to wax as you tie your jigs. If the latter is your choice, you'll need thread wax, which can be purchased in handy slotted dispensers.

For finishing off your thread wraps, pick up a small bottle of head cement, and keep a supply of toothpicks on hand for applying it.

The term "bucktail," as applied to a type of jig, has come to embrace a large variety of materials. Certainly, the traditional deer hair is one, but so-called bucktails are also tied with other natural hairs, synthetic fibers, and even feathers. So it seems the term applies more to the way the jig is tied than to what it is tied with.

Nevertheless, a supply of bucktail is handy to have on hand. Tails are available in natural white or dyed any of a number of colors. I stock bucktails in natural, black, red, yellow, and orange. You'll also find them available in blue, green, purple, and several fluorescent colors. They usually come as whole tails or in cheaper pieces.

Next, I'll recommend Dynel Fishair as an excellent synthetic. It's easy to use and is very lively in the water. If you have any trouble finding it locally, try Netcraft or Pfeiffer's Tackle Crafters. It comes in about ten different colors, and I suggest you order one of the sampler packs that includes all colors and can be had for a couple of dollars.

For tying sleek nylon jigs, you'll need a supply of bulk nylon. I keep a few nylon jigs in my tackle box for saltwater fishing, and I tie quite a few shad darts each year with nylon. I stock bulk nylon in the most productive colors: white and yellow.

Naturally, if you plan to tie marabou jigs, you'll need some marabou feathers. Here, again, choice of colors is broad and largely up to the individual.

If you will be stocking your tackle box with any patterns that call for hackles, you'll want to keep a supply of hackles on hand. Good basic colors are black, white, yellow, and grizzly.

Basic jig-tying materials. *Top row,* dyed and natural bucktail, calf tail, and various colors of Dynel Fishair; *center row,* chenille, marabou feathers, and hackles; *bottom row,* living rubber, bulk nylon, yarn, tinsel, and thread.

For tying crappie jigs and some other patterns, you'll need chenille, which usually comes rolled on cards in a variety of colors. White and yellow are the most popular colors, but black and red are others that can be considered standard. Chartreuse is another color that is popular with crappie fishermen.

You might also want to have on hand a spool each of flat silver and flat gold tinsel. Tinsel can be used to add sparkle to crappie-jig bodies or can be tied in strands into bucktail and other hair and feather jigs.

These are some of the basic materials, any of which you'll find at a local fly-tying shop and at many tackle shops and discount stores. A number of mail-order companies also sell fly-tying supplies.

A trip to any fly-tying shop or a few minutes of browsing through a fly tyer's catalog will introduce you to dozens of different materials and a variety of sizes, colors, quantities, and grades. Many of these can be put to use by the angler who ties his own jigs.

Tying the Bucktail Jig

The most popular and widely used of all jigs is the bucktail. That is one reason I chose to include directions for tying it. Another reason is that the tying method is basic. Jigs of all sorts can be tied by following these same steps: nylon jigs, Fishair jigs, feather jigs, marabou jigs, and others.

After securing the jig head in a vise, follow these simple steps:

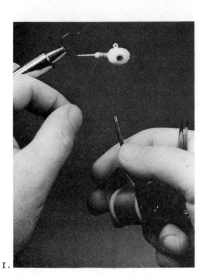

1.

Step 1.
Hold the tag end of the tying thread against the jig collar and make several wraps over it to secure it to the collar. Then use scissors to snip off the tag end near the wrap.

Step 2.
Continue wrapping the thread down the length of the collar, one layer deep. As you reverse directions to wrap the second layer back toward the head, add a small amount of bucktail along the collar and wrap over it with the thread. Continue adding small amounts around the collar until the collar is completely skirted.

Step 3.
Make several more tight thread wraps around the bucktail-covered collar. Then use scissors to trim the excess hair away in front of the wrap.

2.

Step 4.
Continue wrapping the collar until the forward ends of the bucktail have been concealed. Then tie off the wrapping with several half-hitches.

Step 5.
Apply several good dabs of head cement to the wrappings to secure them and to keep the half-hitches from coming undone.

3.

In those five quick-and-easy steps you'll finish your bucktail jig. All that's left to do is take it fishing.

There are other ways of adding the hair to the jig, but this is the method most easily learned by beginners. Also, it's the best method for making two-color tails and for tying in long hackle feathers or strands of tinsel.

5.

Finished bucktail jig, ready to catch a fish.

It works equally as well with a variety of other materials. One that might give you a few problems, though, is bulk nylon strands. They tend to slip out easily, so after making the first thread wrap down the collar, dab a bit of head cement on the thread. Then continue dabbing cement on the thread and nylon as you wrap. If your problems persist, try dipping the ends of the nylon in head cement to help them adhere. Finish the wrappings off with an ample amount of cement to keep the tail in place.

Head design is the tyer's choice, but I recommend beginners start with collared heads. Some experienced tyers prefer collarless models, which are easy enough to switch to after the basic techniques are mastered.

Tying the Chenille-Body Crappie Jig

The traditional crappie jig is among the most popular of jigs used in fresh water for all varieties of panfish and trout as well as for crappies. Larger versions are effective lures for other gamefish in fresh and salt water.

My primary reason for including instructions on tying this jig is to show the techniques for tying the chenille body. I am including directions for a tinsel overwrap for the sake of discussion, though this is an optional material.

For this jig, use a collarless roundhead design of ⅛ ounce or smaller for panfish and trout. For larger fish, use heads of ¼ ounce or heavier.

After clamping the jig head in the vise, follow these steps:

Step 1.
With the tag end of the thread held against the hook shank, just behind the head, wrap the thread several times, and snip off the tag end of the thread with scissors.

Step 2.
Continue wrapping the thread down the length of the hook, stopping just before the bend. Here, add a small amount of marabou feathers and wrap them tightly.

2.

Step 3.
Wrap the thread back up the hook shank to the head. Here, wrap in one end of a piece of chenille and let the bobbin hang with its weight holding the thread wrap in place.

Step 4.
Now tightly wrap the chenille down the hook shank to where the feathers were tied in. Overwrap the chenille with several tight wraps of thread, down to where the chenille wrap ended.

Step 5.
Wrap in the end of a piece of tinsel; then wrap the thread back up the hook shank to the head. Let the bobbin hang.

3.

5.

6.

Step 6.

Now carefully wrap the chenille up the hook shank in tight spirals that touch one another, forming a bulky body the length of the hook shank. At the head, tie off the chenille with several wraps of thread and trim away any excess chenille with scissors.

Step 7.

Wind the tinsel up the shank, over the chenille, in tight but separated spirals. Tie off with several wraps of thread, and trim the excess tinsel away with scissors.

7.

Step 8.

Finish by making several more wraps of thread around the shank, just behind the head. Tie off with half-hitches, and dab a few drops of head cement onto the thread wrap after cutting the thread free.

Finished crappie jig, ready to tie onto a light line and tempt crappies, as well as smallmouth bass, trout, and marine panfish.

For best results, use thick, fluffy chenille for these jigs. You can use the same techniques for making chenille bodies on other types of jigs as well. On larger jigs, you might have to build up the body with several layers of chenille.

Marabou is the material most often used for crappie-jig tails, but bucktail, Fishair, and other materials are also suitable.

Tying the Woolly-Worm Jig

I don't know of any company that offers a finished woolly-worm jig. I tie it and use it for only one reason: it catches fish. I'm including it here to illustrate the method for tying in hackle.

As a fly, the woolly worm is a favorite western pattern that has seen plenty of action elsewhere as well. It's one of the most popular flies in the Yellowstone Park area and annually accounts for both large quantities of fish and large fish.

In some of the bigger rivers, the fly is weighted heavily for working the depths and currents. In the same type of water the woolly-worm jig will prove every bit as effective, if not superior.

In most respects, this jig is similar to the chenille-body crappie jig. Use a collarless roundhead design in weights of ⅛ ounce and smaller. Black chenille is an excellent choice for body material, but brown and green are other good colors to try. In fact, the whole array of chenille colors is at your disposal, so try whatever colors interest you.

With black chenille, I prefer grizzly hackle over all others, and with other colors I normally use grizzly, black, or white hackle.

Tails are usually red wool, but I sometimes use chartreuse or fluorescent orange. And I paint the heads to match the color of the chenille.

Here's how this one goes together:

Step 1.
After securing the jig head in a vise, hold the tag end of the thread against the hook shank, just behind the head, wrap the thread several times around the shank, and snip off the tag end with scissors.

Step 2.
Continue wrapping the thread down the length of the hook, stopping just before the bend. Here, wrap in a small double strand of wool yarn. Then wrap the thread back up the shaft of the hook to the head.

2.

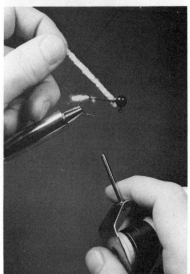

Step 3.
Wrap in a piece of chenille with the thread. Now tightly wrap the chenille down the hook shank to where the wool tail was tied in. Overwrap the chenille with several tight wraps of thread, down to where the chenille wrap ended.

Step 4.
Select a large hackle—at least three times as long as the hook shank. Tie it in with the hackles pointing forward. Then wrap the thread back up to the head.

3.

4.

6.

Step 5.
Carefully start the chenille wrap with one turn around the hook shank behind the hackle.

Step 6.
Make the next and all subsequent wraps of the chenille in front of the hackle, and continue wrapping it up the length of the shank. Wrap it off behind the head and snip away the excess with scissors.

Step 7.
Clamp hackle pliers to the end of the hackle, and wrap the hackle up the length of the chenille body in evenly spaced spirals. Tie off the hackle with several wraps of thread, and trim away excess hackle.

7.

Step 8.
Continue wrapping thread just behind the head until hackle and
chenille ends are concealed. Tie off
with several half-hitches. Cut the
thread and secure with a drop or
two of head cement.

Finished woolly worm jig, a top
producer of trout and other gamefish
and panfish everywhere.

Tying the Living Rubber Jig

Jigs with bulky bodies of live rubber have become extremely popular for
use with soft-plastic tails, plastic worms, and pork-rind lures. The jigs
can be made most easily by slipping a skirt made of the so-called living
rubber onto the jig collar, but you'll find it much cheaper to buy living
rubber in bulk and to tie the jigs with permanent skirts.

Living rubber comes in long, wide strips that have been preslit into
many strands, with narrow, regular, and wide strand widths available.
The material also comes in a variety of colors, with black and white being
among the most popular.

For tying this jig, you'll need a small spool of fine, soft wire, instead of
the usual tying thread. Here's how it goes together:

2.

4.

5.

Step 1.
Cut living rubber into strips about twice as long as you want the finished lure to be.

Step 2.
Lay the strips along and around the jig collar, and secure them in the middle with a tight wrap of wire, allowing an equal amount of rubber to extend from each side of the wire.

Step 3.
Twist the ends of the wire together tightly about three or four turns.

Step 4.
Trim away excess wire with wire cutters and bend the twisted end around the collar.

Finished living-rubber jig can be used as is or dressed with pork rind or plastic twist-tail for taking the wariest of bass.

Step 5.
Stretch the living rubber away from the lure body, and cut the tip ends away with scissors to release the individual strands.

Step 6.
Remove the jig from the vise and hold it nose up. Use scissors to trim the strands to their desired length.

Although you can use any collared jig head for this tie, the ball collar is best, as it will keep the skirt from sliding off if the wire should loosen during use.

To make multicolored skirts, simply use two or more different colors of living rubber. You'll find the material available in bulk from Netcraft and from Limit Manufacturing.

For weedless lures, buy weedless jig heads with molded-in weed guards from Cordell, Mister Twister, or Limit Manufacturing.

Other Jig Patterns

A fat volume could be written on tying various patterns of jigs without even scratching the surface of the infinite possibilities. These basic patterns should get you started and should enable you to look at various jigs and determine how they were tied.

Examples of just a few of the jigs you can make by using the techniques discussed in this chapter. *(Photo by C. Boyd Pfeiffer.)*

If you enjoy tying your own jigs and would like to have more techniques at your disposal, I suggest you look at several of the better fly-tying manuals and perhaps even sign up for a fly-tying course if one is available in your area. Such exposure to fly-tying techniques will make you an excellent jig tyer in short order.

You don't have to be a professional to tie professional-looking jigs. These are just a few homemade jigs that will rival the best store-bought models. *(Photo by C. Boyd Pfeiffer.)*

6.  Molding Soft Plastics

If you have to be told that the development of the plastic worm has revolutionized bass fishing in America, you as well should be informed that Ford is no longer making Edsels and Ike isn't president anymore.

Not only have new tackle and techniques grown out of the plastic-worm boom, but new soft-plastic lures have evolved as well. What's more, the soft-plastics have taken nearly all freshwater gamefish and countless varieties of marine fishes.

If the sixties was the decade of the plastic worm—the period when the counterfeit worm caught on as the number-one bass lure in the country—the seventies had to be the decade of the worm's cousins: twist-tails, grubs, shrimp, eels, frogs, salamanders, and even plastic fish with molded-in swimming tails. The eighties certainly promises more of the same, plus some new developments that will be pounced on by fish and fishermen.

The silent partner in this plastic revolution has been the unobtrusive, unadorned, unmistakenly unbeatable leadhead jig. Not only is the jig-and-worm a deadly duo, but jig heads are essential additions to the makeup of most of the other popular soft plastics. The plastic grub, for example, is just another hunk of pliable plastic until it's married to a jig head.

Just as the leadhead jig was at first used exclusively by saltwater anglers and later gained widespread popularity among freshwater fishermen, the soft plastics were first developed for fishing fresh water but are now among the most effective of saltwater lures as well.

Surely, there's no place in America where the soft plastics are difficult to find. They're stocked by tackle shops everywhere and can be found at most discount stores and in most mail-order catalogs. So the reason for molding your own is certainly not to make them more easily obtainable. The only reason is to save money. Enjoyment, for some, might be another reason, though I personally don't find the job all that much fun.

As I write this, six-inch worms are selling for 25 cents or more apiece; some are as high as 50 cents. A four-inch twist-tail sells for about 30 cents. By buying in bulk quantities you can get the 30-cent lures down to about 20 cents each. But by pouring your own you can drastically reduce your costs.

Once you have made your initial investment in melting pots and molds, you can make your own worms and twist-tails for less than a nickel apiece, at today's prices. The larger lures, naturally, are going to cost a bit more to make, and the smaller ones will be cheaper yet. At any rate, you should be able to make your own at about one-fifth the cost of store-bought lures, or possibly even less.

Tools for Molding Soft Plastics

As with the casting of lead jig heads, to mold soft-plastic lures you'll need a source of heat, a melting pot (possibly two), and molds as the most basic of instruments. You'll need an old tablespoon, wooden paint paddles, or other improvised stirring tools; since these get quite messy during the molding process, you might prefer something disposable.

If you only have a few molds, you might want to keep a shallow baking pan of water nearby for quick cooling of the molded lures. An electric hair dryer is handy, too, for quickly drying the wet molds.

If you have a problem overrunning the mold cavities, a bit of thin plastic "flash" will adhere to the edges of your lures. You'll need something for trimming that away. It can be cut away with scissors or an X-Acto knife with a rounded blade.

Melting Pots

The pots sold for melting and molding plastic are nothing more than small-capacity saucepans, equipped with pouring spouts and capable of holding about two or three cups of liquid—the sort normally used in the kitchen for melting butter, baker's chocolate, and the like in small amounts. Such pots are available from Limit Manufacturing Corp.; M-F Manufacturing Co., Inc.; and Pfeiffer's Tackle Crafters. You will also find suitable pots at most discount and department stores.

If you buy a pot from the housewares department of a local store, make sure it is equipped with a narrow pouring spout, as the molten plastic must be poured in a very fine stream. If the pouring spout on your pot is too wide, crimp it with pliers until it is narrow enough.

To facilitate pouring, the pot should never be filled beyond the halfway point. Consequently, these small pots are only adequate for pouring plastic lures in small batches. For larger operations, you might wish to do as some anglers do and keep a larger pot of heated plastic on a nearby burner set on low heat to replenish the smaller pouring pot.

The tools and materials needed to mold soft-plastic lures: melting pot, heat source, molds, spoon, liquid plastic, color additive, lubricant, and paper towels.

With such pots you'll need a heat source, and I'm going to recommend either an electric kitchen range or an electric hotplate. Although some fishermen use gas ranges or camp stoves, there is some danger in such a practice, as plastic is a flammable material. If you choose to use an open flame as a heat source, be very careful about wiping any dripping plastic away from the outside of your melting and pouring pots. For safety's sake, keep a dry-chemical fire extinguisher nearby.

If you'll be making your lures in the kitchen, be sure to cover countertops, the range top, and other surfaces to protect them from dripping plastic. Use scraps of plywood or sheets of paper to cover countertops. Aluminum foil is best for protecting the range top.

Some anglers use newspapers for covering counters and work surfaces, but freezer paper or plain brown wrapping paper is better, as the ink on newspaper tends to smear and can ruin your lighter-colored lures.

As with the casting of jig heads, an electric hotplate offers the advantage of removing the operation from the kitchen into a more suitable area, such as a workshop, garage, or basement. Even here, though, you should spread freezer paper or wrapping paper on a workbench, table top, or other surfaces that might get splattered with the liquid plastic.

I only know of one electric melting pot designed for molding soft-plastic lures. This melter, sold by Limit Manufacturing, is identical to the large electric production pots used for melting and casting lead, except that this one is equipped with a special heating element and thermostat control specifically designed for the lower temperature required for plastic, which at 350 degrees Fahrenheit is about 300 degrees lower than that required for lead.

If you already own an electric range or electric hotplate, you're in business. If you use natural gas in your kitchen, though, I am going to recommend that you use a hotplate or electric melter. If you plan to mold plastic lures in large quantities, a two-burner hotplate is better than a single-burner model. If you have to purchase a hotplate, though, you should weigh its advantages against those of the electric melter. The hotplate can be used for other purposes, and if you have such uses in mind, it will be the more versatile instrument. If you need only something for melting and pouring plastic, however, the electric melter might prove the better buy and the more efficient tool. It costs more than a good, two-burner hotplate, but it eliminates the need to purchase melting and pouring pots. Moreover, the small, bottom-pouring nozzle creates a fine and steady stream that makes pouring easier.

Were it not for the fact that I already owned a hotplate, I would have invested in the electric melter.

Molds

Although there are aluminum molds available for use in a process which' requires heating the mold and adding unheated liquid plastic to them, the most popular molds are made of rubber or plastic and are designed to have the heated plastic poured into them, much like the casting of lead jig heads.

One reason the rubber and plastic molds are more popular is that their cavities are more rounded, providing a better-detailed lure. To that end, there are also some low-cost injection-molding outfits offered by Limit Manufacturing and Netcraft that make completely rounded and fully detailed lures.

The traditional flattened side of the homemade soft-plastic lure is one objection raised by anglers, but it's my guess that it makes precious little difference to the fish, since, after all, what we're engaged in is the presentation of an illusion rather than an exact duplicate of something in nature. If you'll argue this point with me, then please first explain to me what it is that those hideous-looking spinnerbaits are supposed to be duplicating. Certainly, nothing on this planet. Yet no one can deny their proven fish-catching abilities. I hardly think that any creature that will engulf a spinnerbait—or any of a number of other lures, for that matter— is going to snoot its nose at a plastic worm, simply because it's slightly flat on the bottom.

Most of the molds available have from one to three cavities, although some used for making smaller lures might have as many as four to eight or more. And there are molds available for just about any sort of lure you can imagine and possibly a few that are beyond your wildest mind-wanderings.

Because of the relatively small capacity of most molds and the curing time for the molded lures, it's hardly practical to set up a molding operation with only a single mold. With several molds, you can pour perhaps a dozen or more lures quickly, allowing them to cure and cool while you heat up and color more plastic for the next pouring.

The molds I use most are for plastic worms and twist-tails of several sizes. And since I normally stock the same colors in both types of lures, I'm able to set up a fairly smooth and productive operation.

Materials for Molding Soft Plastics

The basic materials for molding soft-plastic lures are the plastic and the coloring agents. Other additives are available, as well, to fit a variety of needs. You'll want to keep a roll of paper towels handy during the molding operation, and plastic sandwich bags are best for storing your finished lures.

Plastic and Additives

Although plastic is available in block form in a variety of colors and color densities, I prefer the liquid plastic that must have a coloring agent added to it. This type of plastic offers anglers the opportunity to experiment with the coloring of his lures and to control the degree of transparency desired.

The milky-white liquid plastic used for molding lures is available from several sources, including Limit Manufacturing and M-F Manufacturing. It commonly comes in pint, quart, and gallon bottles and can be purchased in bulk quantities, normally in five-gallon cans. Unless you're purchasing for a club or are combining efforts with several fishing buddies, you won't likely need to purchase the material in bulk quantities. For starters, buy a quart and judge your needs based on how fast you use up that quantity. One quart is enough to make nearly 200 six-inch worms. The material will last indefinitely on the shelf and can be reused even after it has been heated.

When heated, the plastic turns clear and becomes thick and syrupy. At this point, color additives should be used. You'll find about two dozen colors available, and since these can be added to the plastic in varying quantities, the possible range of colors is infinite.

A little bit of color goes a long way (one ounce will color about a gallon of plastic) so use it sparingly. Use only a drop or two at first and add more if you need it.

If you prefer a tougher, more durable plastic for your lures, you can add plastic hardener. For softer, more pliable worms, plastic softener is available. You can also give your lures sparkle by adding silver or gold glitter to the heated plastic.

Finished worms should be lubricated to keep them from sticking together. Plastic softener is excellent for this purpose, or you can use scented worm oil. The scented oils are available from M-F Manufacturing and Mann's Bait Co.

Molding Soft Plastics

Like casting jig heads, molding soft plastics is really simple. Although working temperatures are considerably lower with plastic than with lead and potential hazards are consequently reduced, you're still working with hot liquid that can cause a nasty burn if you're careless with it. So exercise caution at all times.

Basically, working with plastic is no more difficult than working with lead, but it can be a bit trickier until you get the hang of it. Since the molds differ in design and principle, you'll have to develop a knack for pouring hot plastic. Mostly, it amounts to pouring with a smooth, steady motion that maintains a fine stream of plastic and fills the mold to the rim without overflowing. You'll probably make some mistakes at first, but you'll improve with only a little practice and should be pouring perfect or near-perfect lures by the end of your first session.

Before beginning any molding session, gather all your tools and materials together in an orderly fashion. Make sure your molds are completely dry, as the hot plastic will pop and spatter if it touches water, which can lead to injury at worst and imperfect lures at best.

Here are the simple steps to molding your soft-plastic lures:

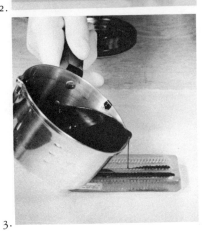

Step 1.
Pour the liquid plastic into the melting pot. Remember that a mere ounce will make about a half-dozen six-inch worms; one cup is enough for about four dozen. Place pot on electric range or hotplate burner on a medium setting and heat, stirring frequently.

Step 2.
When plastic turns clear and is the consistency of white corn syrup, add the color of your choice very sparingly until the desired shade is achieved. Stir thoroughly. (Note: Some fluorescent colors do a better job when added to the liquid plastic prior to heating. Follow manufacturer's directions.)

Step 3.
For most efficient operation, have several molds lined up and ready. Pour plastic into mold cavities in a fine, steady stream until cavities are full and almost ready to brim over. For best results, pour from the tail (or shallowest part of cavity) to the head (or deepest part of cavity).

Step 4.
Allow lures to cool in molds for about three minutes. Run a finger across the tail end of the lure until an edge turns up and can be grasped. Gently lift the lure from the mold and lay it out on clean freezer paper or plain wrapping paper to completely cool.

After you have filled all mold cavities (Step 3), use a paper towel to wipe any dripping plastic away from the pouring spout and outside of the pan. Plastic that dribbles down the side of the pan is a source of fire when an open flame is used for heating the plastic, and when an electric range or hotplate is used, the dribbling plastic will scorch and smoke.

Do not return the pan of plastic to the burner after you have filled all your mold cavities. Instead, set it aside on a hot pad while you remove the lures from the molds and get ready for your next pour. The plastic will cool a bit and will likely have to be reheated, but that's better than putting it on the burner where it will likely get too hot and can scorch, ruining the rest of the batch.

Some anglers like to speed up the cooling of the lures by placing the filled molds in a shallow pan of cold water. The problem I've had with this method is that by the time I get the molds dry and ready for the next pouring, I've taken more time than I would without the water bath. If you have someone helping you though, you might well be able to save time this way. While one person reheats the plastic, the other can wipe the mold cavities out with paper towels, then blow-dry them with an electric hair dryer.

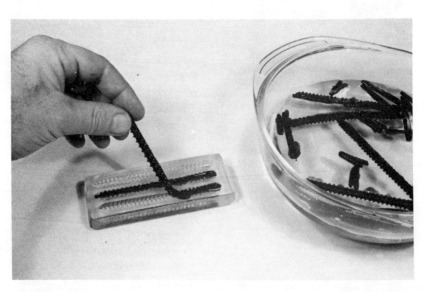

Carefully remove finished lures from the mold and spread them on freezer paper or immerse them in a pan of water to cool.

I do use a pan of water in my own operation, but for cooling the lures after they come out of the mold. Then, when my molding session is over, I spread all the lures on paper towels and leave them there overnight to air dry completely.

Injection-Molding Process

Not long ago, injection-molding equipment was so expensive as to be prohibitive for the angler. At a cost of several thousand dollars, the gear was strictly for manufacturing in large quantities. Thanks to the little Super-SPORT injector and molds sold by Limit Manufacturing and Netcraft, the average angler can now injection-mold his soft plastics at home.

The process calls for all the usual tools and materials, except for the molds used in the above procedure. Instead, you'll need to purchase special molds and the plastic injector.

The special two-piece molds are made of unbreakable plastic and fea-

Super-SPORT injection-molding system consists of a reservoir and plunger and mold halves held together with plastic C-clamps. The reservoir and mold interiors should be lubricated with PAM prior to use.

ture integral aligning pins that assure completely rounded and fully detailed lures. These are single-cavity molds, so you should have several to
produce lures in quantity.

The injection-molding process differs only in the molds and pouring
method. Other steps for heating, coloring, hardening, or softening the
plastic are the same as described above.

The mold manufacturer does recommend lubricating the molds and
injector with vegetable oil prior to making lures. The most convenient
lubricant for this is an aerosol spray coating, such as Pam.

After spraying the mold halves, assemble the molds with the special
C-clamps provided. Then spray the injector reservoir and plunger with
the same lubricant, but do not assemble the injector.

To injection-mold a lure, follow these steps:

Step 1.
Fill reservoir of injector to within
about a half-inch of the top with
heated plastic.

Step 2.
While holding reservoir in place on
work surface with one hand, insert
the injector plunger into the reservoir with the other hand.

1.

Step 3.
Carefully lift the assembled injector
and invert it; then set it on your
work surface, resting upright on
the flat base of the plunger.

3.

4.

Step 4.
Slowly push reservoir down onto the plunger until hot plastic begins running out of the up-pointing nozzle to force out any air in the reservoir.

Step 5.
Set the assembled and lubricated mold in place on the injector with the small hole at the tail end of the mold fitted over the nozzle. (The larger hole in the head end of the mold is an overflow vent.)

Step 6.
With both hands on the mold for stability, press the mold down firmly on the injector until the mold fills with plastic and the vent hole in the top of the mold fills completely. (Be sure vent cup is completely filled to allow for shrinkage during the curing process.)

Step 7.
Remove mold from injector and set aside in upright position to cool. (Do not lay mold on its side, as hot plastic will leak out.)

Injection molding produces fully rounded lures, as perfect in every detail as any commercially produced lures.

If you have several molds ready for injecting, simply repeat the process with them. You will be able to get several lures out of one batch before the reservoir needs to be refilled.

Although I haven't had any mishaps yet, the injector could be overturned; if a hand is in the way, a bad burn could result. For that reason I wear rubber gloves. While these thin gloves don't afford the protection of heavier gloves, they're easier to work with. And in the event that I do manage to spill hot plastic on a gloved hand, I can yank the gloves off quickly and prevent serious injury.

When the reservoir is nearly empty, allow the remaining plastic to set up. Then you can remove the solid mass with the aid of a bent paper clip and the unit is ready for refilling. Do the same at the end of your molding session, and keep the plastic plug which can be melted down next time.

When your lures have cooled, remove them from the molds and cut away the overflow excess at each end with an X-Acto knife or razor blade.

Storing Soft-Plastic Lures

Soft plastic will react with many other types of plastic, most paints, and other finishes. Moreover, colors of the lures will run if different-colored lures are stored together. So these lures must be separated by color and should only be stored in tackle boxes with so-called "wormproof" trays or drawers, or in plastic bags.

You can use an X-Acto knife to trim any flash from your finished plastic lures.

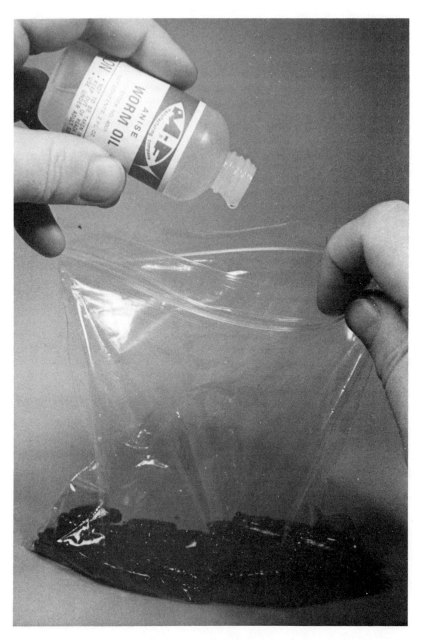

Store your soft-plastic lures in plastic bags, and lubricate them with plastic softener or worm oil.

Since you will probably be making your lures in large quantities to see you through the fishing season, it's doubtful that you'll be storing them all in your tackle box. So keep some plastic food-storage bags on hand for this purpose. I like the Ziploc sandwich bags for this. With these small bags I not only separate all my soft plastics by color, but in any bag I store only one type and one size lure.

The new lures will be dry and will tend to stick together, so they should be lubricated either with plastic softener or one of the scented oils. I prefer to use the scented oil, not so much as a fish attractor but rather as a way of masking the human scent. This is particularly important with soft plastics that fish sometimes approach slowly and pick up gently, which enables them to quickly detect objectionable scents and discard the lure before the hook can be set.

Molding Multicolored Lures

It's possible to mold plastic lures of more than one color, if you're so inclined. Frankly, you couldn't pay me to. Not only is it more work, but multicolored plastics create a storage problem, since black worms with red tails cannot be stored with black worms with yellow tails. The colors will run. For my purposes, it's just too much of a nuisance.

But I do realize that there are some anglers who will swear by their

You can also produce multi-colored lures, such as this soft-plastic minnow with a dark back and light undersides.

chartreuse worms with fluorescent-orange tails and purple stripes. And the molding of more than one color at a time is possible. What it takes is simultaneous preparation of the colors to be used, which calls for extra melting pots. The job is a lot easier, too, if you have someone to help, because the secret to success is pouring the second color immediately after the first one has been poured.

If you want to pour a plastic minnow or frog body with a darker back and lighter underside (as in nature), prepare the two batches of plastic in separate pouring pots and add the color as described earlier. Follow the normal pouring procedures, using the darker plastic first, but fill the cavities only about half or two-thirds full. Then immediately follow that by filling the cavities with the lighter plastic. The two pourings will meld, forming a bond, provided that the second pouring was made while the first was still hot liquid.

To put a lengthwise stripe down the back of a plastic worm, the technique is similar, except that the first pouring should not be as extensive. For example, if you want a yellow worm with a red stripe the length of its back, pour the red plastic first, in a very fine stream, the length of the cavity. Follow that immediately with yellow plastic that fills the cavity entirely.

To make worms and twist-tails with bodies and tails of two different colors, the technique is a bit different. To put a red tail on a black lure, for example, start with the red plastic. Pour the tail section until the cavity is full there, and follow that immediately with the black plastic, filling the rest of the cavity. It's best to have both pots near the molds and ready to pour. This is where a partner comes in handy.

If your lures come apart where the two colors meet, you have let the first pouring cool too long before making the second pouring. One should follow the other as if a single pouring were being made.

You can even make multicolored plastic lures with the Super-SPORT injection-molding outfit. The manufacturer supplies complete instructions for the procedure with the purchase of the equipment.

Recycling Damaged Lures, Scraps, and Mistakes

Certainly, the cash savings is motivation enough for most of us to mold our own soft plastics. But there are additional savings to be made in the form of salvaged lures damaged while fishing.

On a typical day of bass fishing, my wife and I will return to the dock with perhaps a couple dozen damaged twist-tails and plastic worms. Of course, an eight-inch worm with the head damaged can be pinched back to a six- or seven-incher, but the damaged head is no longer usable. A worm or twist-tail with the aft half torn away on a premature strike is equally useless. In the past, all these remnants went into the trash can. Now they're saved to be recycled into new lures.

I let all the damaged plastics accumulate during the fishing season. I separate them by colors and store them in plastic bags. Then, during the off-season, when I'm molding new soft-plastic lures, they go into the pot with the fresh plastic. When I'm molding black plastic lures, the damaged ones of that color from last season get melted down at the same time.

Before storing your damaged lures, it's a good idea to rinse away any sand, dirt, and other debris they might have picked up while in use. Let them dry on paper towels overnight, and pack them away next day.

Also, mistakes made during the molding process, as well as scraps trimmed from the new lures, can be melted down and used again. I store the scraps, by color, with my damaged lures.

So in addition to the initial savings we recognize by making our lures instead of buying them, we also save by salvaging all our damaged lures, thus reducing our per-lure price, probably by another penny or two on the average.

Part Three
Jig Rigs

In Parts I and II you were introduced to the various types of jigs, the purposes of their designs, their applications, the products of various manufacturers, and the tools and techniques for making your own jigs. With Part III we begin a nuts-and-bolts discussion of jig use that is continued in Part IV with specific applications in various environments for a number of popular freshwater and saltwater fishes.

By now you are aware of the full range of jigs and jig-type lures that are available to you. Chances are, you have already bought or made a good supply and have begun to stock your tackle box. Now it's time to learn the various ways to rig them to fit the circumstances you'll face on the water.

Every bit as important as picking the right jig for any particular situation or species is the ability to present it properly or enticingly. Certainly, in most instances you need do no more than simply tie the jig to the end of your fishing line and start fishing with it, but even then, the way you tie it is important. Moreover, there are times when more specialized rigs are called for.

If you're an experienced jig fisherman, chances are you already use some of the knots and terminal rigs covered in the next chapter. You have very likely already made good catches with some of my favorite jig rigs. And you've probably learned to use jigs in conjunction with other lures, pork rinds, and natural or live baits. You have certainly mastered the techniques that are popular in your part of the country and could, no doubt, show me some ways to fish jigs that I've never tried. I think, too, that you might find a tip or two in the coming chapters that you can put to use on your favorite waters.

If you haven't done much jig fishing, though, and are just now discovering the wonders of these great lures, the following chapters should prove extremely important to you, because here is where you'll learn how to catch fish with jigs.

We are getting, as they say, down to the nitty gritty. Pay attention. You'll be tested on this material—every time you take rod in hand and set out to catch fish.

7.  Jig Knots and Terminal Rigging

As most of us learn, sooner or later, the average angler need not be able to tie a hundred different knots in order to attach something to a fishing line that will catch fish. We can get by quite adequately with the ability to tie perhaps a dozen different knots to cover all possible needs. As regards jig fishing, four simple knots will see you through, whether you merely want to attach a jig to a line or make up a more complex terminal rig for specialized purposes.

Loops, Snaps, and Swivels

Since in most cases leadhead jigs have little or no built-in action, the angler must impart it by the way he retrieves the lure. There are some exceptions, of course, and certainly there are times when a straight, steady retrieve is best. But for the most part, jigs must be jigged—or at least twitched, bounced, or in some other way made to move enticingly. For that reason, knots that are pulled down tightly against the tying eye of the lure, thus impairing the jig's action, are normally considered less desirable than looser connections that improve the action and take advantage of the jig's balance.

The loose connection can take the shape of either a loop knot or a lure snap. And here is a point of some controversy. Some jig fishermen contend that snaps are extra hardware that will cause the fish to shun the jig. They argue that a loop knot is always the better choice.

I will not argue the point. Instead, I'll leave the decision to you. I will, however, tell you that I use both loop knots and snaps. And when I assume it makes little difference to the particular kind of fish I'm after, I always opt for the snap, as it allows me to change lures rapidly. It also makes it easier to change lures in cold weather when numb fingers are troubled by knot-tying.

With larger jigs used for big fish, I truly doubt that the use of a snap makes any difference. The jigs will catch fish with or without snaps. With some smaller jigs used for certain species, though, I suspect that a loop knot is better, and I usually use one then. For example, when I'm fishing

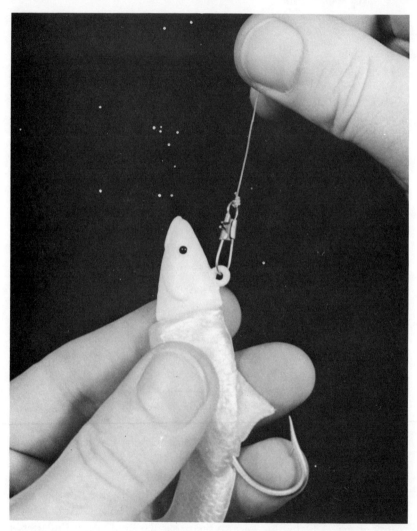

You can use simple lure snaps with most jigs.

for trout in the low and clear waters of late summer and early autumn, I never use a snap. Then, these wary fish will shy away from lines and leaders that are too heavy, and surely a shiny snap will put them off.

On the other hand, there are times when the snaps make no difference, even when used with the tiniest of jigs. One morning earlier this year, my wife and I were on our way out for a morning of bass fishing on our favorite lake. As our boat neared the creek mouth we planned to fish first, we saw vast schools of big bluegills ahead, virtually churning the water to a froth. We first happened on such schools several years ago and have since searched them out, usually finding them only in the early spring and late fall. This was early summer, and we weren't prepared for the encounter. We each had the usual three spinning rods rigged with jigs of various sizes and designs—all bass-weight gear. We also had our ultralight outfits along, but these were rigged with spinnnerbaits.

As I cut the throttle on the outboard and lowered the electric motor into the water, my wife unsnapped the spinnerbaits and snapped tiny jigs onto our lines. We eased down on the first school under the low hum of the electric motor, then drifted and cast to the hungry bluegills.

Before making it to the creek mouth and our day of bass fishing, we had boated 123 bluegills, 88 of which were filleting size. All were caught on tiny jigs, and none seemed to object to the presence of a lure snap. In fact, it was a rare cast that failed to get a strike. And as often as not, the jig would be hit two or three times before a fish was hooked.

I do not recommend using a snap swivel on a simple jig rig; that is unnecessary hardware. The simple, ordinary snap (without the swivel attached) is smaller, lighter, and cheaper. If you're going after big fish, however, use only the locking-type snaps, as others can pop open under the strain of a powerful fish. Other than that, use your own discretion. If you want the convenience of quick-and-easy lure changes, use snaps. But if you suspect the snap is keeping you from getting strikes, retie with a loop knot.

Palomar Knot

Several years ago I tested a number of different knots, searching for a simple, easy-to-tie knot that proved better than all others for use with monofilament line. The Palomar knot shook out on top. This is an extremely strong knot that can be tied quickly, even in cold weather, with numb fingers.

Since it cinches down tight to whatever it's tied to, I don't recommend it for tying directly to the jig but rather to a snap, or in some rigs to a swivel. It's also a useful knot for other purposes, such as tying hooks and small lures. Its one drawback is that it cannot be used with large lures that won't fit through the loop created during tying. Otherwise, it's a good all-purpose knot, and an ideal one for tying snaps to lines.

In the accompanying illustrations, a larger-than-normal snap and extra-heavy line are used for clarity. Here's how to tie the Palomar knot:

Step 1.
Double several inches of line back against itself to form a loop.

Step 2.
Slip the loop through the eye of the snap.

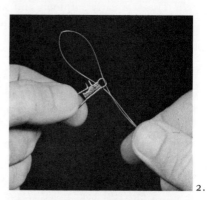

Step 3.
Make a simple overhand knot in the doubled line.

2.

Step 4.
Slip the snap through the loop and bring the loop up beyond the eye of the snap.

Step 5.
Clasping the snap between the thumb and forefinger of one hand and the doubled line between the thumb and forefinger of the other, slowly pull the knot tight with a steady, even tension.

3.

Step 6.
Trim the tag end of the line next to the knot, and the snap is ready to attach to a jig.

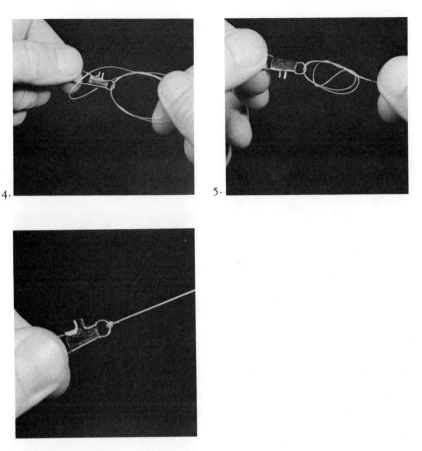

4.

5.

Palomar knot, tied to a lure snap.

Double Improved Clinch Knot

In my knot tests, the double improved clinch knot proved second only to the Palomar knot, and since it is not limited in use as the Palomar knot is, this is the one to use for tying a line to a lure in various jig-and-plug and other combinations. It is also the knot to use in making terminal rigs where the Palomar cannot be employed.

Tie the double improved clinch knot as follows:

2.

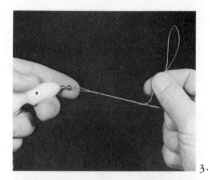

3.

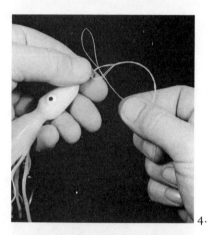

4.

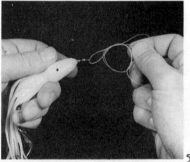

5.

Step 1.
Double several inches of line back against itself to form a loop.

Step 2.
Slip the loop through the eye of the lure or swivel.

Step 3.
Bring the loop up against the doubled line and make at least five turns around the line.

Step 4.
Push the end loop through the loop created in front of the lure's or swivels's tying eye.

Step 5.
Pass the end loop back through the large loop near the five twists you made earlier.

Step 6.
With steady, even tension, slowly pull the knot tight, and snip excess line away near the knot.

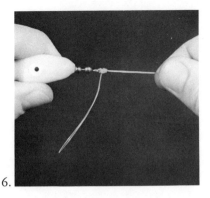 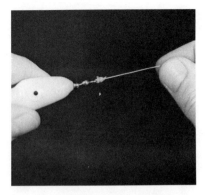

6.

Finished double improved clinch knot
tied to a Weber Hoochy Troll.

Simple End Loop

There are a number of end loops described in angling literature, many of which are appropriate for tying jigs to fishing lines. Some are difficult to tie and impossible to describe. Others simply don't work with jigs.

Any loop that can be tied with a jig on the line and that won't slip after it's tied will do the job. If you have a favorite loop knot that meets these criteria, by all means, use it. If not, here's the one I use:

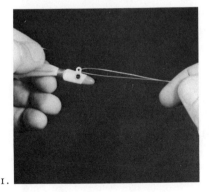

1.

Step 1.
Slip the line through the jig's eye and double the line back against itself, about six to eight inches.

Step 2.
Holding the doubled line between the thumb and forefinger of one hand and the jig with the other hand, bring the jig back toward the hand holding the line, cross it over the doubled line, and wrap it once, as if tying a simple overhand knot.

Step 3.
Then wrap it again, making three wraps in all.

Step 4.
To complete the loop knot, pinch the doubled line between the thumb and forefinger of one hand and the jig in the other. Pull your hands away from one another and the wraps will tighten to form an end loop. (Note: Work the knot down toward the jig eye as you tighten it to keep the loop fairly small.)

Step 5.
Snip the excess line away near the knot.

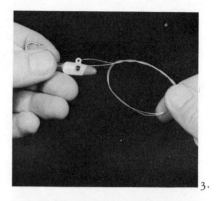

3.

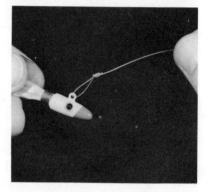

Simple end loop, tied to a jig.

Some anglers tie this knot with only one wrap. Although this sometimes works with light lines that will reach the breaking point before the knot slips, with lines of eight-pound test and heavier, the extra wraps are necessary to keep the knot from slipping and cinching down against the jig eye. I use the three wraps no matter what weight line I'm tying.

Simple Droppers

Droppers are used in many different terminal rigs. They can take the form of dropper loops or dropper lines, depending on the type of rig being made or the angler's preference.

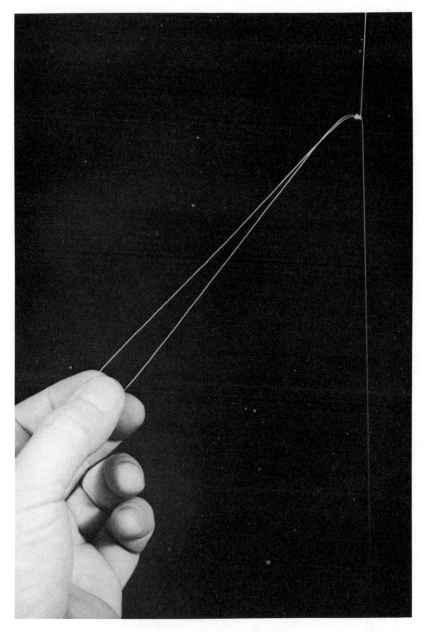

You can use the same techniques employed in tying the simple end loop to tie droppers into your line.

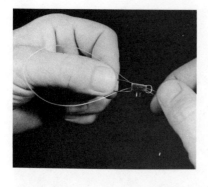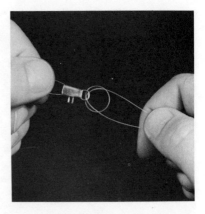

Attaching a snap to a dropper loop: *Left*, step 1; *right*, step 2.

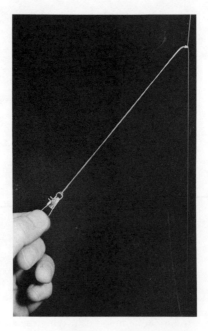

Snap attached to dropper loop.

As with the end loop, if you have a favorite technique for tying drop-pers, use it. If not, you can tie one or more droppers into your line by using the same techniques described for tying the simple end loop, except that you'll not attach a jig to the line before tying.

To tie a dropper loop into your line, instead of doubling back only six or eight inches of line against itself, double back two or three feet. Tie the loop, as described above. When the loop is finished, you should have about 24 inches or more of line hanging down from the dropper loop.

You can tie additional loops into your line in the same manner, and to these you can attach jigs by means of leaders or snaps.

To attach a snap to a dropper, simply slip the loop through the eye of the snap; then pass the snap back through the loop and pull tight.

If you want a dropper line instead of a loop, just snip one end of the loop near the knot. A jig or weight can then be tied directly to the dropper line, depending upon your needs.

Vertical-Jigging Rig

Vertical jigging is sometimes called deep jigging, though the technique need not be restricted to deep waters. To be sure, the method is quite popular in offshore salt water where anglers seek various and abundant reef species, but it is also a way of fishing from a dock, pier, bridge, or boat in fresh or salt water of any depth.

Sometimes anglers use vertical-jigging techniques from a boat at an-chor or one that is drifting with a current or perhaps moving under the power of a sculling oar or electric trolling motor.

Often, the only rigging required is a jig heavy enough to probe the depths. But when small jigs or multiple-jig rigs are called for, additional weight might be required. Terminal rigging that works well here in-cludes one or more short dropper lines or loops, a sinker, and possibly a barrel swivel and leader material.

The simplest of such rigs consists of droppers tied into your fishing line, with an end loop tied to the tag end of the line. Jigs are attached to the droppers and a dipsey-style sinker is attached to the end loop.

When the sinker bounces bottom on a taut line, the jigs are kept just above bottom where they are most easily taken by the quarry.

Although the dipsey sinker, because of its rounded surfaces, is less

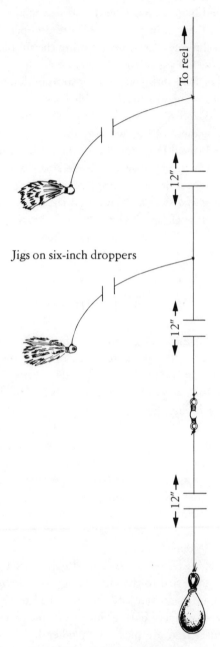

To reel

12"

Jigs on six-inch droppers

12"

12"

Breakaway vertical-jigging rig.

susceptible to snags than most other styles, it will still hang up, especially in rocky and other snag-strewn waters. For this reason, I prefer a slightly different rig.

After tying the droppers to my line, I tie a barrel swivel to the tag end of the line with a Palomar knot. Then I tie a short leader to the other eye of the swivel with a double improved clinch knot, using leader material that tests lighter than my fishing line. The end of the leader gets a loop knot tied into it and a dipsey sinker attached. This rig allows me the versatility of quick weight changes to accommodate various currents, but offers the added advantage of a breakaway weight line. When the sinker hangs up and can't be pulled free, I simply break it off and tie on another sinker while the rest of the rig remains intact.

Winneconne Rig for Shad Darts

I was first introduced to the Winneconne rig some years ago in Wisconsin where walleye fishermen use it primarily with Rebels, Rapalas, and other swimming lures, spinners, and spoons. It is an excellent rig to use when trolling shad darts where some additional weight is needed to reach fishing depths. The only materials you'll need for each Winneconne rig are a three-way swivel, a dipsey sinker, leader material, and a dart jig.

Tie the tag end of your fishing line to one eye of the swivel with a

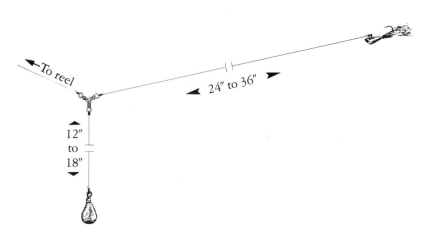

Winneconne rig for shad darts.

Palomar knot. To another eye of the swivel, tie a 24- to 36-inch or longer leader with a double improved clinch knot. Tie the shad dart to the end of the leader with an end loop. Now tie a dropper of about 12 to 18 inches to the remaining swivel eye. For the dropper, use material that tests lighter than your fishing line. To the end of the dropper, tie an end loop and attach a dipsey sinker to it.

This rig offers several advantages over other rigs used for trolling. Because of the shad dart's design, it planes slightly when retrieved or trolled. While the heavier dipsey sinker runs near or along bottom, the jig will plane a foot or more above it, depending on leader length and trolling speed.

If more or less weight is required, the dipsey sinker is quickly and easily exchanged for another with no need to retie; just slip it off the end loop in the dropper. As with the vertical-jigging rig, this too is a breakaway rig that will allow you to break off a snagged sinker without losing the rest of your tackle.

Floating-Jig Rigs

Floating-jig heads are among the most effective fish-catching innovations to have come along in a good while, and I'm certain we will be seeing much wider use of floating-jig rigs in the years to come. Properly rigged, floating jigs will take gamefish in just about any type of water. What's more, the rigs are designed to get down deep, where the fish most often are.

The idea behind floating-jig rigs is to get the weight down to the bottom where it can be worked with the jig, attached to a leader, trailing behind and above the weight. All the rigs described below are relatively snag-resistant and can be worked where other rigs and lures would hang up frequently.

Floating heads can be used with bait, soft plastics, or pork rinds, or they can be tied with bucktail, marabou, and other traditional tying materials.

Walking-Sinker Rig

The design of walking sinkers allows them to be worked along the bottom, over rocks, logs, ledges, and the like, without snagging as other types of sinkers would. Walking sinkers will get hung up from time to time, and they aren't a good choice for use in dense vegetation.

Walking sinkers are available from a number of mail-order sources. If you want to make your own, molds are also available from Do-It Corporation. If you prefer a breakaway-type sinker, use the Mister Twister eyelet sinkers that were developed for that purpose.

The walking-sinker rig is quite easily assembled. Start by sliding the sinker onto your fishing line; then attach a barrel swivel to the tag end of the line with a Palomar knot. To the other eye of the swivel, tie a leader of 18 to 36 inches with a double improved clinch knot. Tie the jig head to the other end of the leader with an end loop.

When the sinker rests on bottom, the buoyant jig head will be suspended above it. When the rig is worked along the bottom with short twitches and jerks, the jig will dart toward the bottom and will rise again. Strikes come at any time during the retrieve and are often violent, especially when the jig has been floating motionless for a few seconds.

When the pickup is more gentle, as is often the case with a jig-and-bait combination, the walking sinker will function the same as an egg sinker or sliding worm sinker: if slack line is given, the fish can move with the bait, without feeling the drag of the sinker.

This is an ideal rig for use in ponds and lakes as well as in the calm backwaters of saltwater bays and estuaries.

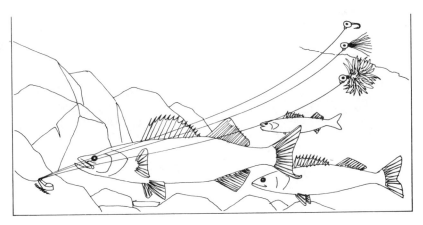

Mister Twister walking sinker and floating jigs.

Bait-Walker Rig

Gapen's Bait-Walker sinkers, rigged with floating jigs, are deadly in all types of water, and they come in a wide enough variety of weights to fit any situation. The lighter Bait-Walkers are good for fishing ponds, lakes, and small streams, while the larger ones are well-suited to fishing the heavy currents of large rivers and strong tidal flows. The heaviest models can be used for deep-water jigging.

The Bait-Walker should be tied to the tag end of your fishing line. To the barrel swivel on the upper arm of the sinker you can then attach a 24- to 36-inch leader. Tie the floating jig to the leader with an end loop, and the rig is ready for fishing.

Like the walking-sinker rig, the Bait-Walker rig can be worked along the bottom with short twitches and jerks. It is also especially deadly when

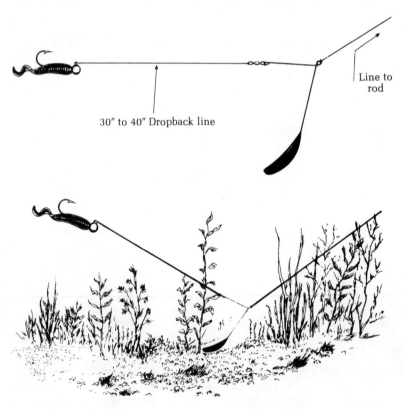

Line to
rod

30″ to 40″ Dropback line

Gapen's Bait-Walker sinker, rigged with floating jig.

crawled along the bottom very slowly, particularly when the jig is tipped with bait.

Bait-Walkers can also be rigged for trolling, either with floating jigs or leadhead jigs that are lighter in weight than the sinkers. They can be used as well with shad darts, but the breakaway Winneconne rig is a better choice where frequent snags create problems.

Jig-Drifting Rigs

Drift fishing is a technique that was developed on the streams of the Pacific Northwest where Pacific salmon and steelhead make their spawning migrations. The technique found its way to the Great Lakes states when these anadromous species were planted there.

While drift fishing has become a popular method among salmon and steelhead anglers, and a few old river rats who fish for other species as well, the method isn't as widely used as it might be. It's an excellent way to work just about any river current and to cover any potential spot thoroughly. The floating jig head is well-suited to drift fishing, but, I suspect, is seldom used for that purpose.

In drift fishing, the angler casts his rig diagonally upstream and allows it to sink to the bottom where it is carried along by the current. The amount of weight used in the rig is determined by the swiftness of the current. The weight should bounce bottom about every foot or two. If it drags along the bottom, the weight is too heavy; if it touches bottom only occasionally, it's too light.

During the drift, the angler keeps a taut line. He allows the rig to drift downstream and sweep past him, at which time he terminates the drift, reels in, and makes another cast. By casting to various parts of the pool, the angler is able to drift his lure or bait over all potential fish-holding areas.

The purpose of drift fishing is to get your bait or lure to the bottom and keep it near the bottom throughout the drift. Of course, you will want a rig that allows a snagged sinker to break away or pull free. There are several ways to accomplish this.

One way is to make a rig similar to the Winneconne rig, using a three-way swivel. Tie the swivel to your fishing line with a Palomar knot. Tie 18 to 36 inches of leader material to another eye of the swivel with a double improved clinch knot and attach the floating jig with an end loop.

To the remaining eye, tie a short length of monofilament. To this dropper, pinch on enough No. 3/o or larger split-shot to get your rig to the bottom, but not so many as to impair the drift. You'll simply have to experiment with a few casts to determine how much weight to use. Weight requirements will differ with current velocity and water depth.

You can cut down on the hardware by making a similar rig, but substituting a small split ring for the three-way swivel. Tie the split ring to your fishing line and attach the leader and dropper as above.

A third alternative is to tie a dropper into your fishing line, leaving about two feet or more of the line extended beyond the dropper. Then tie the floating jig to the tag end of the line with an end loop and attach the split-shot to the dropper.

When, during a drift, your split-shot gets wedged between rocks or otherwise snagged, a steady pull on the line will cause the sinkers to slide off the dropper, freeing the rest of the rig. Then you need only pinch on more split-shot and resume fishing.

Another rig that is ideally suited to big waters and heavy currents calls for pencil-lead sinkers that are attached to lengths of surgical tubing. In

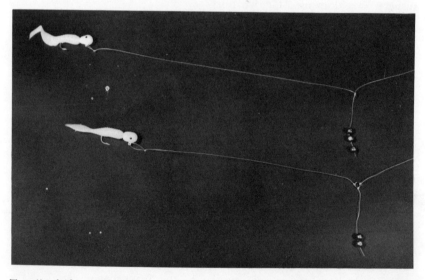

Two jig-drifting rigs. *Top* rig consists of a dropper tied into the line with split-shot attached; floating jig is then attached via an end loop. *Bottom* rig employs a split ring to which a dropper is tied and split-shot attached; light leader is then tied to split ring and has floating jig attached with end loop.

salmon and steelhead country you'll find such drift-fishing rigs ready-made at any tackle shop, but elsewhere they might be hard to come by. They're easy enough to make and work well with floating jigs.

To make your own pencil-lead rigs you'll need cross-line (T-shaped) swivels, a few feet of surgical tubing, a small spool of fine wire, wire-cutting pliers, and a pair of scissors.

For each rig, cut a two-inch length of surgical tubing with scissors. Slide the tubing onto the dropper eye of a cross-line swivel and secure it with several wraps of wire. Twist the ends of the wire and bend it back against the wraps. Now fold the upper end of the tubing over the wire wrap to conceal it, and you're ready to put the rig together.

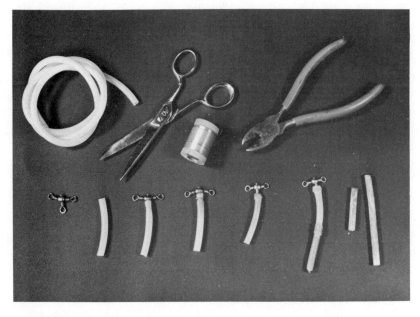

Everything you need to make your own pencil-lead rigs. Bottom row shows assembly steps, left to right.

Tie your fishing line to one of the remaining eyes of the swivel. To the other eye, attach a leader with an end loop.

Push a piece of pencil lead into the open end of the surgical tubing · until it is held securely (normally about a quarter-inch). As with the split-shot rigs above, the length of pencil lead is determined by current and water depth, and again, you'll just have to experiment until you are making good drifts.

This, too, is a breakaway-type rig. When the pencil lead becomes snagged, a steady pull on the line will cause it to pop out of the surgical tubing. Push another lead into the tubing and you're ready for the next drift.

Of course, you'll want to assemble the swivel/surgical-tube portions of these rigs at home and carry a good supply of them when you head for your favorite river. The rest of the rig can be put together on the stream bank.

Deadly Double-Jig Rig

My favorite rig for working a floating jig provides a double-barreled approach because, instead of using a sinker, this rig employs a leadhead jig as the weight.

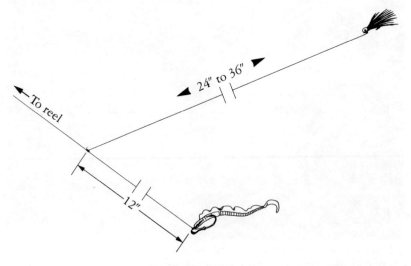

Deadly double-jig rig.

Although the rig can be tied with a three-way swivel or split ring, I prefer to use a simple dropper, tied into my line. In gin-clear waters, however, where lighter lines are called for, I use a split ring tied to the end of my line with light leaders then tied to the split ring.

I like a dropper of about 12 inches tied into my line about 24 to 36 inches from the end. To keep the rig relatively snagproof I use either a weedless jig, or a jig and worm rigged Texas style, attached to the dropper.

To the end of the line extending beyond the dropper, I tie a floating-jig head. When I'm fishing for largemouth bass, I normally rig the floating head with a twist-tail. In salt water I sometimes use the same rig, but I have also found that rigging the floating head with strip bait is highly effective.

My favorite combination for largemouth bass is a six-inch or eight-inch black plastic worm on the worm jig and a four-inch pearl-white twist-tail on the floating head. When the rig is worked slowly over the bottom with short twitches of the rod, the floating jig darts downward, toward the plastic worm, as if a small fish is nipping at some slithering bottom-dwelling creature.

I suspect the floating jig appears the easier target, as this is the one the bass seem to favor. But at times it merely acts as the attractor for the more desirable plastic worm.

Jig-and-Float Rigs

Floats are widely used by bait fishermen to keep baits suspended off bottom, over weedbeds, flooded brush, and the like, but they can be equally useful to the jig fisherman. A float is a great aid to crappie fishermen who want to work jigs slowly and present them to schools of crappie that are suspended only a few feet below the surface, such as they often are in the spring. The rig works equally well for other school fish, such as bluegill and white bass. And it can be employed whenever you need to keep a leadhead jig suspended off bottom or above weedbeds and other cover.

I like to use a small, clear-plastic bubble float and a jig of ⅛ ounce or smaller when I'm fishing during the day. For taking crappie at night by lantern light, I prefer a fluorescent-colored float that is more visible.

When using a float with a jig, you can effectively fish from near surface to maximum depths of about six to eight feet, depending on the length of the rod you're using. It's best to experiment with various depths until you locate fish. Then keep your float set for that depth, and work your jig very slowly with a twitching rod action. When you jerk your rod, the jig will rise. On the hesitation, it will fall again until the float stops its downward motion. Your strikes will most often come as the jig is falling, so be prepared.

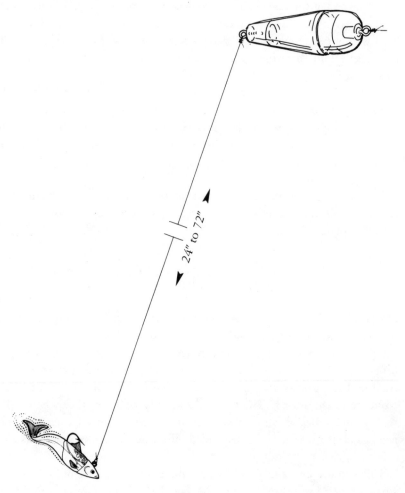

Jig-and-float rig.

In the southern coastal waters, jigs are also used with popping floats by seatrout anglers. The popping float is tied to the fishing line. Then a leader is tied to the float and a jig is tied to the end of the leader. The rig is cast into a likely seatrout haunt and the float is popped and gurgled across the surface with jerks of the rod to attract the fish to the jig. Identical or similar rigs and techniques are used for several other species as well.

I've had popping floats struck often enough that I much prefer to use a popping lure, instead, to which I attach a dropper line and jig. It is every bit as effective as a popping rig, but offers the added advantage of hooking those fish that go for the attractor instead of the jig.

8. ![jig illustration] Jigs Plus

The jig is an outstanding lure in its own right—unmatched by any other single lure on the market today. But there are times when jigs in multiple rigs with other lures can be even more effective.

Jigs and jig heads can be used with nearly all the soft-plastic lures. They can be trailed or led by plugs of various kinds. And they can be used with other jigs to improve the angler's odds of connecting with fish.

Jigs Plus Plastic

Most largemouth-bass fishermen will agree that the plastic worm has no equal among lures designed to attract bass. But the invention of that simple lure not only led to the great bass boom that has been going on since the sixties—gaining legions of followers every year since—it also paved the way for the development of countless other lures that have excelled in the catching of numerous species in fresh water and salt. Nick Creme's plastic worm was important—perhaps the single most important angling development of the century—but the discovery of a formula for making the soft plastic from which lures could be molded was of greatest impact.

Soft plastics can also claim a significant amount of responsibility for putting the leadhead jig at the top of the list of "Most Versatile and Effective Artificial Lures." The jig is a natural companion to most soft-plastic lures and is an integral component of many; some simply do not function without the leadhead.

Jig/Worm Rigs

The forerunner of our modern plastic-worm rigs was the old jig-'n'-eel rig that boated a lot of big bass in years past and continues to be a favorite of many veteran bass anglers. With the introduction of a plastic worm that

174

worked, anglers started switching to the synthetic nightcrawlers, most rigging them the same way as they had the pork-rind eels—with leadhead jigs. Then along came the sliding worm sinker and special worm hooks, and the leadheads were put aside.

Rig after rig was touted by tournament fishermen and angling scribes until the now-famous Texas rig shook out on top as the most universally effective and widely popular of all.

Strange, though, how so many things tend to go full circle. In recent years, some of the newborn bass anglers have found that the Texas rig isn't the perfect do-everything setup some claimed it to be. They began to realize that certain conditions call for a stationary weight on the line, instead of the sliding sinker. Some started jamming the sinkers down to the hook eye and wedging them in place with pieces of tooth picks. The technique, known as "pegging" the sinker, was soon discovered and reported on by the writing fraternity as something revolutionary. A few of the brighter boys realized that a pegged worm sinker is no more in principle and practice than a leadhead jig.

Now special worm jigs are on the market and are fast gaining popularity among the bass-boat set. Some folks are even whispering that maybe the sliding-sinker rigs aren't so great after all.

I must confess to having rather thoughtlessly followed the fad. I don't remember when I first used a plastic worm to catch a bass, but I do know we called the lures "rubber nightcrawlers" then, if that gives you any indication. I vividly recall, however, my discovery of the effectiveness of the plastic worm and my undaunted devotion to it for several reasons.

I was living in Florida in 1963-64, trying sedulously and seriously to become a fishing bum. When I wasn't wandering around the Keys, exploring the glades, or scuffling along the south Atlantic or Gulf coast, fishing for just about anything to be found in those fertile salt waters, I was dropping plastic worms into every convenient body of fresh or brackish water.

I fished the plastic worms on jigs, in the style of the jig-'n'-eel rigs. The jigs were black. The worms were black. The bass were of the black variety, also, and I caught plenty of them—more bass than I had ever caught in my life. And I didn't miss many strikes. It's all so clear in retrospect.

What isn't so clear is how I one day ended up with a huge tackle box full of plastic worms of every color and size imaginable, worm hooks of two styles and eight different sizes, dozens of sliding worm sinkers, and

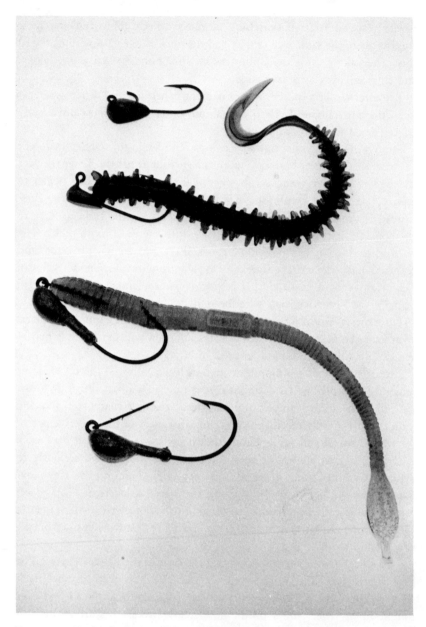

Two worm jig heads designed for weedless rigging. *Top*, the Worth/Aquacone LUR/LOC glider head rigged with a Burke Hook Worm; *bottom*, the Mister Twister "Keeper" head rigged with a Mann's Jelly Worm.

narry a jig. That was my worm box, and it went with me on all my bass-fishing trips.

I had also taken up casting tackle again for the first time in years, because everybody knows spinning tackle is no good for worm fishing.

Of course, I continued using jigs of various sorts for freshwater and saltwater fishing, but not for worming. I caught a fair number of bass on my plastic worms and Texas rigs, but not like the "good old days." What with water pollution, more fishermen, fewer fish, water too muddy, water too clear, cold weather, hot weather . . .

All the angler's laments came readily to mind, except the most obvious one: stupidity. I had given up a simple, effective system for catching bass in lieu of something that was less successful for me and certainly more cumbersome and uncomfortable.

About four years ago, I noticed that I was doing more and more jig fishing for bass and proportionately less plastic-worm fishing. I also noticed that my jig fishing was much simpler and more enjoyable for that simplicity.

Two years ago, I started leaving my casting gear at home. I rigged a spinning outfit for worm fishing and started using jig heads instead of sliding sinkers and worm hooks. I began catching more bass and missing fewer strikes.

Last year, I cleaned out my worm box. I got rid of all the various colors and sizes of worms that had not produced or had caught only a few stray fish. I emptied all the compartments of their sliding sinkers and most of the worm-hook compartments and filled them with the jigs that should have been there all along.

Now I carry only two sizes of worm hooks and use them only when I need a weightless worm. At all other times I rig my worms with some sort of jig or jig head.

I'm not going to be so presumptuous as to suggest you follow suit. If you like worm fishing with the conventional accoutrements, by all means, don't give up a winning combination. But if you haven't tried worm fishing with jigs or jig heads or are having any difficulties with your present tackle and techniques, give the jig/worm rigs a try.

There is much room for debate on which rigging is best for plastic-worm fishing. Certainly, individual preferences are important: the system you prefer is the best system for *you*. Nevertheless, I'm convinced that for some circumstances, the jig/worm rig is the best. In shallow water, for example, the jig/worm rig will outfish all others. And in the lily pads, a sliding sinker is useless; the pads are jig/worm territory.

Several companies now offer keeper-type jig heads for plastic-worm fishing, among them Mister Twister and Worth/Aquacone. If you're set up for casting your own heads, you might want to invest in the worming-jig mold offered by Do-It Corporation.

These heads are designed to be rigged weedless and are every bit as snagproof as the Texas rig. Although they don't allow a free-line pickup as a sliding-sinker rig does, I find they afford far more control. And on those occasions when a slack-line free fall is called for, there's no problem with the weight plummetting to the bottom too far ahead of the worm, as a sliding sinker sometimes will; worm and weight drop together.

To rig one of these heads, simply impale the head of the worm on the keeper barb or wire (depending on the style of jig) and slip the hook point into the body of the worm as you would with a worm hook, concealing the point inside the worm.

One problem with any such weedless rig (jig or worm hook rigged Texas style) is that setting the hook is more difficult, as the point must be driven through the worm and into the fish. More than one trophy bass has been lost because the barb wasn't driven home. This is one reason most plastic-worm fishermen use heavy rods with all the appearance and action of pool cues.

One way to improve the hook-setting abilities of such rigs is to prepare them in a slightly different manner from what you are accustomed to. Most experts recommend pushing the point of the hook into the worm only far enough to hold the worm in place and make the rig weedless. But by pushing it through the worm until it almost pokes through the side opposite the entry hole, the worm will be just as secure (if not more so), every bit as weedless, and far more efficient in hooking fish.

Toward this same end, I have taken to keeping a supply of Burke Hook Worms in my tackle box. Because of their design, these worms allow the hook to be run all the way through the worm's body until the point actually protrudes. The bodies of these worms are covered by plastic bristles that act as weed guards for the hook point. With them, I have greatly reduced misses caused by hooks not firmly set.

Another advantage that the worming jigs offer is greater penetration. Along with the surge in popularity of plastic-worm fishing, came a preference for large hooks. In my opinion, too many anglers began using hooks that were unnecessarily large. The smaller hooks in the worming-jig heads are totally adequate, yet their narrower gauge allows quicker and deeper penetration through the plastic worm and into the fish's jaw. Whereas I once used 3/o hooks with six-inch worms and 5/o hooks with eight-inch worms, I now use jig heads weighing ⅛, ³/₁₆, ¼, ½, and ¾ ounce, equipped respectively with size 1, 1/o, 2/o, 3/o, and 4/o hooks. I do most of my fishing with the three smallest sizes.

I seldom use the ½-ounce and ¾-ounce worming jigs, and then only for deep-water worm fishing. My favorite rig is the ⅛-ounce head with a six-inch worm. When necessary I'll switch to the ³/₁₆-ounce or ¼-ounce head to work deeper waters, dropoffs, ledges, and the like. And in murky waters, or where fish tend to run large, I will sometimes switch to an eight-inch worm. I no longer carry worms larger than eight inches and sometimes find it necessary to pinch back the worms I use to make them even smaller.

Some worm fishermen, who have experienced the characteristic problems of the Texas rig, prefer to rig their worms with weedless hooks instead. With these hooks the worm can be threaded on with the entire hook gap exposed; the barb is then easier to sink into the fish, as it need not be yanked through the worm body first. Also, such rigs tend to prolong worm life, as they don't tear up the worm body as much as the Texas-rigged hooks do.

Although the wire weed guards on weedless hooks do a good job of preventing snags and are easier to set than Texas-rigged hooks, they're not as efficient as weedless jigs and jig heads. Thanks to the development of nylon weed guards (stiff-but-bendable bristles molded into the leadhead) weedless jigs are finding favor among anglers who regularly work the weedbeds, lily pads, sunken brush, and flooded timber. These weed guards afford all the snag resistance of the wire weed guards, yet their hooking ability is much better.

Weedless jigs are available in a variety of dressings and colors or as plain jig heads. Recently, I've been using those dressed with living rubber almost exclusively. I rig them with six-inch worms.

A fully exposed hook is always more effective in hooking fish than a weedless one or one rigged to be weedless. But it is also more prone to snags. You must remember, however, that the jig, by design, is relatively snag-resistant because of its attitude on the retrieve and its upriding hook.

Consequently, in relatively open water (along gravel bars, sandy

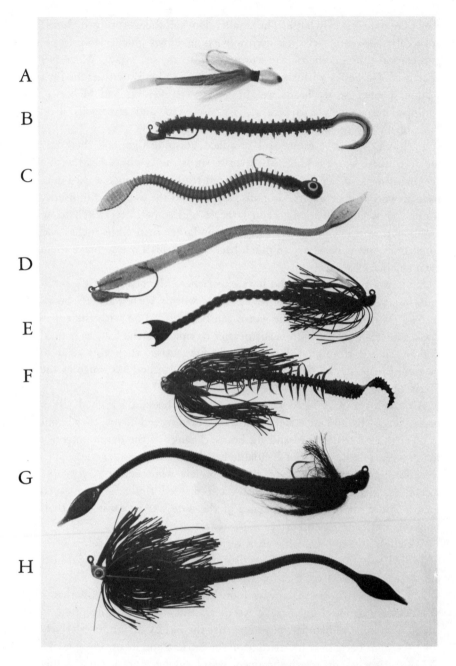

Various jig-and-worm rigs. (A) Bomber Flare Hair Jig; (B) Worth/Aquacone LUR/LOC glider head with Burke Hook Worm; (C) Rebel Ring Worm on Mann's leadhead; (D) Mann's Jelly Worm rigged Texas style on Mister Twister "Keeper" head; (E) Burke Buckshot worm on Cordell Crazy Leg weedless jig; (F) Worth/Aquacone Hawg Hackle worm and Poly Whopper jig rigged Texas style; (G) Mann's Jelly Worm on a synthetic hair jig with nylon weed guard; and (H) Worth/Aquacone Sow Belly jig rigged with Mann's Jelly Worm.

beaches, and the like) a nonweedless jig/worm rig is your best choice and is far superior to other nonweedless worm rigs in resisting even the occasional snag. It's also a good choice for working dropoffs and ledges.

For this rig I use a dressed jig, usually a bucktail, and a short worm. Although I have used six-inch worms, I find the shorter worms allow me to hook more nibblers and short strikers without noticeably detracting from the rig's attractiveness. I prefer the thicker body of a six-inch worm to that of a four-inch worm, so I use a six-incher pinched back to four inches.

Not only are such rigs good in reasonably open fresh water, they can be dynamite on a number of inshore saltwater species. Larger versions are also good for vertical deep-water jigging in fresh and salt water. They can also be used in a number of trolling rigs in conjunction with other lures.

I wouldn't dare tell you with any pretense of authority what color of worms you should use. Although, characteristically, black bass are the same fish wherever they exist and their feeding preferences will be similar, water conditions—depth, clarity, structure, cover, oxygen content, temperature—will vary greatly from region to region, even from one body of water to another. These conditions can and often do affect the way bass live and feed. So local preferences and your own experimentation should guide you in your choice of worm colors.

My standing supply of plastic worms once included a fair variety of colors: black, purple, blue, red, yellow, green, white, chartreuse, natural brown, and amber. And some of these I stocked in various color densities; for example, I carried solid black and translucent black or smoke-colored worms, as well as deep purple and light purple. Although I never did go for the stripes and polka dots, I did carry a variety of Fire-tail, Glo-Tail, and other multi-colored selections.

It's good to experiment with various colors and color combinations to determine which worms work best under different conditions, but a bit of common sense and moderation is essential if you are to retain your sanity. Since worms of different colors must be stored separately, the logistics alone can be problematical if the variety is too great. And since the possible combinations are nearly infinite, so are the attendant hassles. But most important, I think you'll find that a few colors will see to all your needs, no matter what the conditions are. And certainly when the selection is smaller, the decisions come easier and you'll spend more time fishing and less time browsing and shopping in your tackle box for the elusive "perfect color."

I have fished plastic worms in every region of the country except the southwest, and the one color that seems to be universal is black. It's the one and only color I would recommend to anyone, regardless of where he lives and fishes. It's the color I started worm fishing with, and for several seasons it was the only color I used. Even now, when I'm fishing unfamiliar waters I normally start with black and often find no need to change.

When I did most of my fishing in the midwest and south, purple was another standby and one I came to prefer over black in some waters. Since living and fishing in the western states, however, I have acquired a preference for blue as the second most productive worm color. Black is still first, and purple has slid to third place.

Before I cleaned out and reorganized my worm box, I studied my fishing log to determine the most and least productive colors. For some reason I won't attempt to explain, translucent red has been a good color at certain times. I haven't done well with it in roiled waters, in early morning, or during the spring. Nor has it proved to be a good deep-water color for me. But I've caught fish with red worms in the late afternoons on clear, sunny days, in clear water, when other colors couldn't get a bump or a nod. And I've made some dandy catches in shallow water in the fall, after we've had our first autumn storm, but before our seasonal rains have begun in earnest, during Indian summer.

So, I've kept the red worms in my tackle box, but I use them selectively. And, currently, black, blue, purple, and red are the only colors I use. My worm fishing has again become simple and basic. It is now as enjoyable as it once was, and every bit as productive.

Again, I'm not recommending that you carry only four colors or these four colors. My fishing style has changed, and had it not, I would be carrying a few other colors, which I'll discuss later.

A good rule of thumb for selecting worm colors is to use the dark, solid colors in stained or murky waters; use the lighter colors and translucents in clearer waters. Time of day and sky conditions can play an important part in color selection, too, and I'll cover that momentarily when I discuss jigs and twist-tails.

Plastic-worm anatomy, it seems to me, is not as important as other considerations. The counterfeit worms are available in configurations ranging from true copies of nature's counterpart to strange-looking objects that might well have come to earth from another galaxy. Take your pick; I don't think the fish care one whit.

I happen to carry four different styles of worms for my own personal reasons. I use the worms with the natural ribs, collars, contours, and flat tails molded in, namely because that's the type I started with and have used for years. I have bought them in bulk quantities and have molded countless dozens. I also use the beaded-body pinch-off type worms (such as the Burke Buckshot worms) that can be pinched back to any length and still retain the same general appearance, which matters more to me than to the fish.

As I mentioned earlier, I have been using the Burke Hook Worms with worming jig heads. This is the one style that I do believe makes a difference, as it allows me to expose the hook point while still keeping the rig weedless. The Rebel Ringworm can be similarly rigged, as can any other plastic worm with prominent ribs or ridges molded in.

Another I've been using recently—most often with living rubber jigs—is Worth/Aquacone's Hawg Hackle worm. This one has several features I like, including a beaded body, a serrated twist-tail, and holes molded into the body which trap air and release tiny bubbles when the worm is worked. Its soft-plastic legs or hackles make it a pretty fair imitation of a hellgrammite for freshwater fishing. In black, it's nearly a dead ringer for the sea worms that are such great bait in salt water. The Burke Hook Worm is another that resembles a sea worm and is a good saltwater lure.

Incidentally, since I almost always work a worm slowly, often in clear water, where fish have the opportunity to thoroughly examine it before striking, I always attach worming jigs and jig heads to my line with an end loop instead of a lure snap.

Jig/Twist-Tail Rigs

Something that led to my rather drastic change in plastic-worm fishing and the subsequent reorganization of my tackle box was the development of the plastic twist-tail and related lures. When the swirling, swimming tail was introduced some years ago, I was already an avid plastic-worm fisherman. I liked the idea of the curly tail and began at once to use the twist-tail worms. I rigged them as I rigged other plastic worms and fished them the same way. And I caught fish with them, as I had with conventional worms. In other words, I had not used the twist-tails to their full potential or as effectively as I might.

In looking back, I suppose it was the twist-tail that brought about my return to using jigs with all soft plastics. I normally fish a plastic worm slowly, along bottom structure, sometimes in heavy cover, but the twist-tail requires a bit more speed for the seductive tail to swim naturally. I later found, too, that it can be fished at any depth.

When I switched to the shorter four-inch tail and jig head and began working it in a greater variety of ways I started catching more fish. For several seasons I experimented with different colors and sizes and ultimately settled on those which worked best for me. In the process, I developed a system of fishing from which I seldom veer on bass waters.

I said earlier that my style of fishing has changed and had it not, I would undoubtedly carry worms in a greater range of colors. My tactics would likely differ considerably also.

When I was a diehard worm fisherman, my first bait to touch the water in the early morning was a plastic worm. Now I rarely ever use a worm until the sun is high in the sky and I must start looking for bass somewhere other than my usual targets. A notable exception is late winter and early spring when the water is cold and the bass are deep and sluggish. I'll often start with a jig/worm rig then and will work it slowly in the holes and along the dropoffs where the fish congregate. But it's still not an early-morning tactic, as I normally don't bother to get out on the lake before nine or ten o'clock in cold weather.

In late March and early April, as the water begins to warm and the bass become more active, I switch to the system that will see me through till mid-autumn. I start with jig/twist-tails and stay with them as long as the fish continue hitting them. Often, early in the season (April to early June) this means all day, especially on overcast days. Even in middle or late summer, on those rare overcast or drizzly days, the jigs will take fish all day long.

The rig I do most of my bass fishing with consists of a ⅛-ounce or ¼-ounce jig head to which I have attached a four-inch twist-tail. I occasionally drop back to a ¹/₁₆-ounce head if I want something that sinks slower, or a ⁵/₁₆-ounce head for a quicker drop. In early spring I also use two-inch and three-inch tails, as bass often like smaller baits then. Additionally, there are times during mid-summer and early fall when bass show a preference for smaller offerings and I'll use the two- and three-inch tails and lighter heads then.

Again, I'm not going to recommend specific colors to you. Ask around at your local marinas and tackle shops, talk to other fishermen, and experiment on your own—especially the latter. I will tell you, though, which colors I have settled on and why.

A quick survey of my tackle box shows that I currently have compartments filled with three-inch and four-inch twist-tails in black, purple,

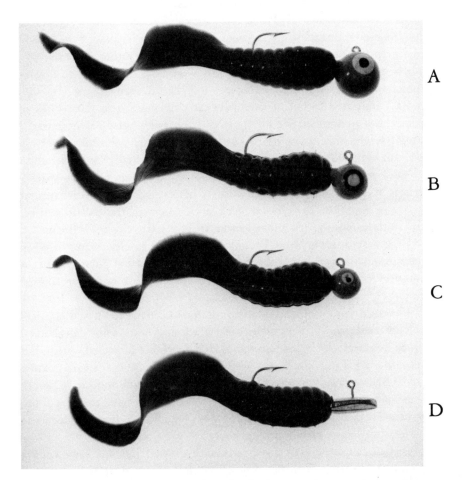

Author's favorite four-inch twist-tail will take bass nearly everywhere, at any depth, by merely matching the jig head to the conditions. (A) tail is rigged on $^5/16$-ounce roundhead for quick drop or deep water; (B) same tail is attached to ¼-ounce roundhead for working most waters; (C) ⅛-ounce roundhead is a good choice when a slower-sinking rig is required; (D) ⅛-ounce slider head is perfect for the slowest drop in shallowest water or for swimming the tail.

blue, red, amber (root beer), chartreuse, yellow, white, and pearl white. The purple, blue, red, amber, and chartreuse are translucent or semitransparent; the others are solid colors.

The two-inch tails that I mainly use for panfish and trout, and occasionally for bass, are stocked in black, yellow, white, and pearl white in solid colors, as well as translucent chartreuse.

As with plastic worms, I have tried a greater variety of colors and color combinations, but these are the ones I've settled on for now. I might add that even these colors will likely change a bit in the future. For example, when my current supply of white tails is gone, I don't plan to replace them. I much prefer the pearl white, and the fish seem to also.

As I indicated earlier, I would be carrying more than four colors of plastic worms were it not for the way I use twist-tails. For example, I would surely stock a few chartreuse worms. But chartreuse is one of my early-morning colors, and early in the morning I normally use twist-tails.

Solid yellow is another good color for early morning. Semitransparent yellow is good, too, but chartreuse is better and the semitransparent yellow is too close in color to stock both. As with the plastic worms, translucent dark red has proved to be strictly a late-day color for me.

I normally use purple and blue in the evening in clear water or when nothing else is working and I'm searching for the right color. Amber is another occasional producer that I might well phase out after another season.

If pressed to recommend the best all-around producer, I'd find no small amount of difficulty picking between black and pearl white, although I probably use black in more situations. It's my choice for roiled waters, but it's also a good pick for clear waters, possibly because it is such a natural color. Black is also the color I use at night. But my wife and I have caught a lot of fish on pearl-white tails, and we'd hate to have to do without either. The pearl-white tails, by the way, are also excellent producers in clear water in the early-morning hours.

Although I have used twist-tails with dressed jigs and have caught plenty of fish with such rigs, I now use plain, painted jig heads most of the time. I either match or contrast the head colors to the twist-tail colors. When I've run out of painted jig heads in the middle of the season, I have used unpainted heads, and it apparently makes no difference.

For most situations, I prefer a roundhead jig for this rig, and one with a barbed collar is best for keeping the tail in place, although any of the collared varieties will help secure the tail. I also like the Aberdeen hooks used in such heads, as they bend enough to pop free of most snags.

For shallow-water twist-tail fishing, I like the slider jig head. When I need a fast-sinking head for deeper waters, I use any of the vertically thinner heads, such as the lima bean, walleye, or arrowhead.

I have also used jigs and twist-tails in salt water ever since I moved to the Oregon coast, but until recently I was in a tiny minority of anglers here. In fact, as recently as four or five years ago, I knew of only one other angler working the Coos Bay area who used soft plastics. He fished plastic worms off the jetties for lingcod and rockfish.

I used to get a lot of skeptical looks from seasoned old salts when I walked aboard a party boat with my medium-weight spinning tackle and jigs. When, at the end of the trip, however, I walked off with a gunny sack full of fish, the looks had changed to amazed belief.

In a small coastal town it doesn't take long for a successful fishing system to catch on. The same tackle shops that once carried only a token selection of plastic worms for the rare bass fisherman and a few bucktail jigs for tourists and eastern transplants now stock a fair number of jigs and are beginning to carry twist-tails. Most of the charter boats still use bait on their bottom-fishing trips, but many of the local anglers going afloat in their own boats are using jigs and twist-tails and are outfishing the charter boats by a long shot.

My selection of jig heads and twist-tails differs somewhat for saltwater fishing. For offshore fishing—casting to kelp beds and deep-water jigging—I use heads running from ¼ ounce to two ounces. I use the same heads in the surf and in the bay, but I also use smaller ones on lighter tackle for some inshore species.

Most of my saltwater jig heads are of four different designs: lima bean or Upperman, arrowhead, bullet, and banana. They're molded with the stronger O'Shaughnessy hooks that are normally cadmium plated and tinned to resist saltwater corrosion.

On the lighter jigs, I use the same-size twist-tails as I do in fresh water. On larger heads, I often use six-inch twist-tails and occasionally even longer ones, but I switch to shorter tails when I have problems with short strikers and broken tails.

I haven't found a need to carry much of a variety of colors for saltwater fishing, particularly offshore. Pearl white and solid yellow have been my best producers and are my favorites. I've also made some good catches on fluorescent orange and chartreuse when the fish weren't taking the white or yellow offerings.

For inshore fishing, I have found twist-tails in these same colors to be productive. And though I've done well with black in the bays and backwaters, I've done rather poorly with it offshore for some reason unknown to me.

When I'm using jig heads with plastic twist-tails, whether in fresh or salt water, I invariably attach them to the line via a lure snap.

For several reasons, the jig/twist-tail rigs are my favorites. Except when specific conditions or target species dictate otherwise, I always start a day of fishing with these rigs. They're easier to use than plastic worms; they're less prone to snags than crankbaits, spinners, and spoons; they can be adapted to just about any water depth; and, during the course of a season, they catch more fish than anything else in my tackle boxes.

Jig/Grub Rigs

Several years ago the soft-plastic grub tails took the country's waterways by storm. They caught the fancy of fishermen and fish alike. They became, at once, favored by freshwater and saltwater anglers, mainly because they proved so effective on the ever-popular black bass in fresh water and weakfish and seatrout in salt water.

Plastic grubs are among the aforementioned lures to which jig heads are integral. Without a leadhead, a plastic grub would be relatively useless. But together, the jig and grub are a deadly combination.

I view the conventional grubs, such as Mann's Sting Ray grubs, as specialized hybrids. They're something between a plastic worm and a plastic twist-tail. They share some of the advantages of each as well as some of the drawbacks. But used properly, they will sometimes take fish when nothing else will.

Their versatility lies in their adaptability to various sizes of jig heads. A two-inch grub on a ⅛-ounce head sinks slowly and can be worked in shallow water, over weedbeds, or above sunken brush and flooded timber. That same tail on a ½-ounce head will drop to the bottom like a Danforth anchor. The larger four-inch tails can be used the same way and are also good lures for vertical jigging in deep water when used on heavy heads.

Although jig/grub rigs are my first choice in some situations, for the most part, they're my switch-to lures. That is, I often switch to them when other lures aren't producing.

For example, when I'm casting jigs and twist-tails to cover in relatively shallow water and the bass are in one of their short-striking moods, grabbing the tails and turning them loose before the hook is in striking range, I'll often switch to a fat grub on the same-size head and will work it identically. More often than not, I'll start connecting.

Likewise, when I'm working jig/worm rigs over bottom structure and am missing too many fish, I'll try shortening the worm. When that fails, I'll switch to a grub and will usually start catching fish.

Such phenomena bother me until I can conjure up reasons. I think one reason bass and other fish short-strike lures is that they're not really interested in feeding but are curious or angry about invaders to their domain. A nip at a tail might be enough to scare off the intruder or satisfy the fish's curiosity. Use something with a shorter tail and that nip might put a hook in the fish's jaw.

In other instances, I think a lure's design and characteristics simply make it easier for the fish to find its target. In the case of the grub, its relatively thick and buoyant body gives it a distinctly different attitude on the fall. Even at rest on the bottom, the buoyancy of the body will tip the lure to a head-down/hook-up attitude that facilitates pickups.

Then there's the matter of feel. Surely, there are times when the thick, soft, pliable body of a grub just feels more edible to a fish than hair, feathers, or metal.

Jig/grub rigs are favorites of mine during the cold weather and low water temperatures of late fall, winter, and early spring. During the warmer months of the year, when my wife and I head out for a day of bass fishing, we each have four rods racked in the boat. Two spinning outfits are rigged with jigs and twist-tails. A third is rigged for jig/worm fishing, and an ultralight is set up with a tiny jig of some sort for panfishing. During the colder months we're outfitted similarly, except that the two rods that were rigged with jigs and twist-tails will, instead, have jigs and grubs attached. The ultralight will still have a tiny jig attached, but the target will be trout that are easier to find and are more active then than the panfish are.

For largemouth-bass fishing in lakes and impoundments, white grubs are my favorite, with black running a close second. I also carry solid yellow and translucent purple grubs, but I use them less frequently.

When I'm fishing streams for smallmouth bass, I like two-inch grubs in either white or black and occasionally solid yellow. With head weight

A

B

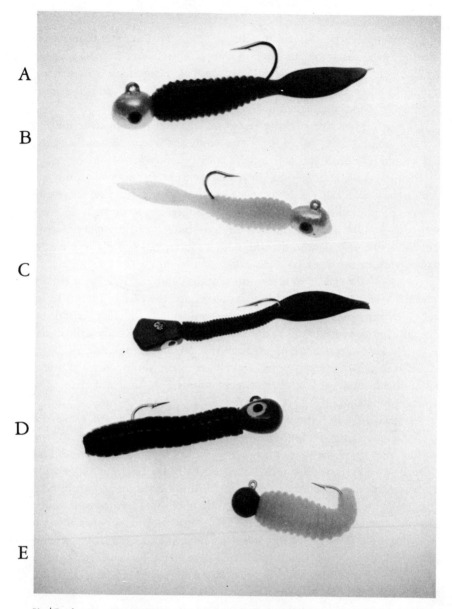

C

D

E

Jig/Grub rigs. (A) and (B) are store-bought grubs. (C) is the tail section of a damaged worm, rigged on a Gapen Ugly Bug head. (D) is the head section pinched off a damaged worm and rigged on a Mann's leadhead. (E) is a commercial grub with tail pinched off, rigged on a roundhead.

to match the current, grubs are excellent lures for drift fishing for a number of larger stream-dwelling species, including channel catfish.

Jig/grub rigs are among the best lures ever designed for taking a number of inshore saltwater species—particularly weakfish on the east coast and its southern cousin, the spotted seatrout. White, yellow, and black are top choices for most species, but as weakfish and seatrout anglers will tell you, any color is okay as long as it's hot pink (which, among manufacturers, might be called fire red, fluorescent red, glo red, etc.). Pink jigs are favorites for taking weaks and specs, but other colors, including translucent green and smoke gray, are also good. Again, while you will probably want to stock a good supply of pink grubs for this kind of fishing, experiment with others in your area.

In multiple-jig rigs and jig/fly rigs used for vertical jigging in salt and fresh water, a jig and grub is a good choice for the bottom-bouncing part of the rig that gets tied to the tag end of the line.

I also use pieces of plastic worms—either salvaged from damaged worms or intentionally broken off—as grubs. The tail sections from six-inch and eight-inch and larger plastic worms, when attached to jig heads, make excellent baits for a number of species in fresh water. The head sections from the same worms, rigged with the nose trailing, are great saltwater lures.

With two-inch plastic worms (usually marketed as panfish worms) you can make deadly grubs that at times will outfish anything else you might normally use for bluegill, perch, and other panfish, as well as trout.

A half-inch piece pinched off the tail of one of these tiny worms and hooked onto a tiny marabou, feather, or hair jig can markedly improve your catch. But the rig my wife and I have found to be most successful is a miniature grub that we make with short pieces of plastic worms that we thread onto jig heads of $1/32$ or $1/64$ ounce. The heads are either painted black or left unpainted.

We used to buy our panfish worms, but often experienced difficulty finding them. We now mold our own, and the only colors we use are black and white, as we've never had a need to experiment with other colors. Also, these colors duplicate natural grubs and insects that panfish and trout relish.

To rig our trout and panfish grubs, we pinch off about a half-inch piece of a two-inch worm and thread it onto the jig hook the way we would with any grub tail. In ponds, lakes, and reservoirs, we cast to schools and likely cover. In streams, we drift the grubs in currents, usually on a cast that quarters upstream.

We vary our retrieves until we find the one that's most attractive to the fish. In still waters we use slow, steady retrieves that simply allow the grub to fall to the feeding fish. Sometimes we retrieve with short flicks of the wrist. When fish are near the surface and working a hatch, we keep rod tips high and retrieve fast enough to keep the grubs from sinking too deep. In streams, we either dead-drift the grubs or impart slight action until we connect.

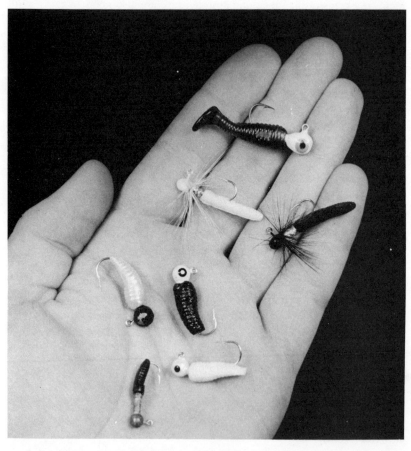

Grubs for trout and panfish. Three displayed on the fingers are commercially available. Those in the palm are some of the author's favorites: the fat-bodied grubs are made from two-inch twist-tails with the tails pinched off, and the skinny one is a half-inch piece of a two-inch worm rigged on a $1/32$-ounce head.

We use a lot of two-inch twist-tails for trout and panfish, especially for crappie. In a hard day of fishing we might end up with two dozen or more of these lures with torn or severed tails. We keep the bodies for rigging grubs similar to those we make with pieces of worm but which are a bit thicker. We have taken a lot of big bluegills with these fat grubs, as well as some dandy trout. We rig these, with their tails trimmed off neatly at the body, on $^1/_{32}$-ounce heads and sometimes use $^1/_{16}$-ounce heads in deeper waters or when we need some extra weight for casting.

Other Jig/Plastic Rigs

There are numerous other soft-plastic lures that you can experiment with—some extremely popular with jig fishermen, others rarely used by them.

The soft-plastic fish with swimming tails (such as Burke's Wig-Wag Minno) are certainly among the most popular and successful of such lures. I use these in fresh water much the same way I use the jig/twist-tail rigs,

Burke Wig-Wag Minno, one of the most popular jigs, features a soft-plastic body with swimming tails.

but because of the head design that causes them to sink faster, I fish them mainly along the edges of weedbeds, dropoffs, creek channels, and the like. They're also excellent trolling lures.

In salt water I use the heavier models for vertical deep-water jigging and the lighter ones for casting to kelp beds, pilings, rip-rap, and other cover. The ⅛-ounce models are great lures for a wide variety of inshore saltwater panfish.

The soft-plastic shrimp tails are rigged and used much the same as plastic grubs. For some species, such as weakfish, seatrout, snook, tarpon, and others that dine regularly on shrimp, these lures rigged on plain jig heads often prove superior to all other lures and baits, including live shrimp.

Since shrimp occur in nature in a variety of colors and most are, to some degree, translucent or semitransparent, I stock shrimp tails in translucent pink, green, chartreuse, amber, and red.

Those that get damaged while fishing can be pinched off to form short tails of about one inch, which, when rigged on small jig heads, are dandy lures for many inshore and upper-bay species, particularly the panfish.

Many other soft-plastic lures exist that seldom get a nod from even the veteran jig fisherman. They include all the molded plastic minnows, eels, frogs, crayfish, hellgrammites, and various insects that are so natural in appearance as to be lifelike. Pfeiffer's Tackle Crafters catalog carries a good line of such lures that are worth trying. Additionally, both M-F

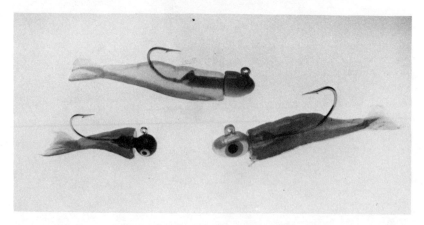

Top and right, commercially available jig/shrimp-tail rigs. *Left,* ⅛-ounch round-head rigged with a piece of damaged shrimp tail for saltwater panfish.

Manufacturing and Limit Manufacturing offer molds for making many of these creatures in your workshop.

Often, these soft plastics are rigged conventionally with down-riding hooks and are used with split-shot or other weights for casting and trolling. A jig head, however, is far superior for rigging them, as the up-riding hook makes them relatively impervious to snags, and the stability of the jig keeps them from twirling when retrieved or trolled, thus preventing severe line twist.

A plain, roundhead-style jig head is ideal for rigging most of these lures naturally. When I want to jig or swim a plastic frog or minnow through shallow water, though, I prefer a ⅛-ounce slider head. For working frogs in lily pads, a weedless head is my choice. And a deadly combination in just about any type of fresh water is a weedless jig dressed with living rubber with a plastic crawfish impaled through the tail on the jig's hook.

Soft-plastic minnows (from Pfeiffer's Tackle Crafters) rigged on various jigs and jig heads.

Other soft-plastic lures from Pfeiffer's: stonecat and frog rigged on round jig-heads, and crawfish rigged on brown-and-orange bucktail jig.

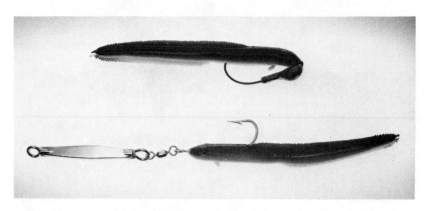

Top, plastic eel, rigged Texas style on Mister Twister "Keeper" head. *Bottom,* plastic eel rigged on diamond jig.

Jig Heads and Skirts

One of the quickest and easiest ways to dress a plain jig head is with a skirt. Suitable skirts, made of rubber, living rubber, vinyl, or soft plastic are available from a number of manufacturers and mail-order suppliers, such as Burke, Limit Manufacturing, Mister Twister, Netcraft, and Worth/Aquacone, to name but five.

Jigs rigged with rubber and vinyl skirts from Limit Manufacturing and Netcraft. Skirts on right have been reversed and rigged backwards to produce fuller body.

Worth/Aquacone Jig'un Skirt.

Burke two-piece Squirm Skirt is a molded soft-plastic skirt, ideal for use with jigs and worms or twist-tails. Worth/Aquacone Worm-in skirt slips onto jig collar for a tight fit and can be trailed by a plastic worm or twist-tail.

The skirts simply slip over the hooks and onto the collars of the jig heads. Some lock in place; others are held on by friction or the elasticity of the material.

Skirted jigs are often effective when used without further adornments, but the addition of a plastic worm, twist-tail, or grub can add even more appeal.

One advantage of skirted jigs over those tied traditionally is that the angler can carry an assortment of skirts of various materials, in different sizes and colors, and can switch them quickly. Also, damaged skirts are easily replaced.

Jig/Plug Trolling Rigs

Jigs are now being used with great success in conjunction with a number of swimming and diving lures for trolling rigs. One of the most popular of such rigs consists of a 1700 Series Bomber Water Dog, trailed by a Bomber Flare Hair Jig.

This has become a favorite rig for taking freshwater striped bass in deep water during the summer months. It will get down to 40 or 50 feet where the lunkers lurk.

The 600 Series Bomber is another good lure for similar rigging. It can be trolled as deep as 30 to 35 feet.

Depending on the depth of water, you can choose swimming lures to meet your needs, from those that will dive to no more than six feet to others that easily work in water of 12 to 15 feet and deep divers that sound to 25 feet or more.

There are several ways to rig these lures with jigs. One way is to tie one end of a monofilament leader to the jig and the other end to one tine of the forward treble hook. Leaders should be about 18 inches long or longer.

Large lures can usually have small jigs attached, via leaders, to the aft end without impairing the lure's action. You can either tie the leader to the trailing treble hook, or you can remove the rear hook entirely and attach the leader to the screw eye. For best action, use a snap to attach the leader to the lure's eye.

The possible lure/jig combinations are innumerable. Just about any good swimming-type lure can be used, but remember that a heavy jig will not usually work well with a small plug. And be sure to pick a jig-head design that is suitable for trolling, such as the roundhead, bullet, arrowhead, or dart.

These rigs are not only effective on freshwater stripers, but on their saltwater brethren as well. They will also take a host of other gamefish in fresh or salt water.

The Winneconne rig is another way to use jigs with swimming lures. Normally in the Winneconne rig, a lure trails a three-way swivel on a monofilament leader of 18 to 36 inches. The trolling weight (usually a dipsey sinker) is tied to a 12-inch dropper that is suspended from the three-way swivel. The remaining swivel eye is tied to the tag end of the fishing line.

The idea is to use enough weight and the right trolling speed to allow the sinker to bounce on bottom as the lure trails. Why not substitute a leadhead jig of comparable weight for the dipsey sinker and double your

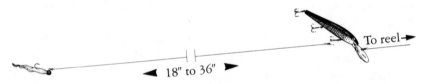

This jig/plug trolling rig consists of a Cordell Red Fin Deep Diver, followed by a Burke Wig-Wag jig.

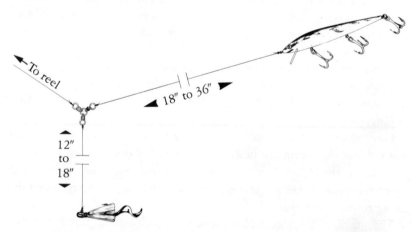

Jig/plug Winneconne rig for trolling.

chances for a hookup? Jigs dressed with any of the conventional tying materials or with plastic twist-tails work fine. I find roundhead jigs the best design, as they drop readily to the bottom and their rounded edges don't wedge in rocks as easily as others might.

If you cast your own jigs and thus only pay pennies for them, you might want to tie them to dropper lines that test lighter than the rest of the rig. When snagged they can be broken off, leaving the rest of the rig (especially the expensive swimming lure) intact.

My favorite lures for Winneconne rigs are Rebels, Rapalas, and other buoyant lures that have good swimming actions but do not dive deeply. Their buoyancy keeps them swimming well above the jig line, preventing possible entanglement.

Popper/Dropper Rigs

For casting to surface feeders, schooling fish, and other shallow-water targets, it's hard to beat a surface lure trailed by a jig on a dropper line.

As with the trolling rigs, above, jigs should be tied to monofilament

A few of the lures suitable for jig/plug trolling rigs.

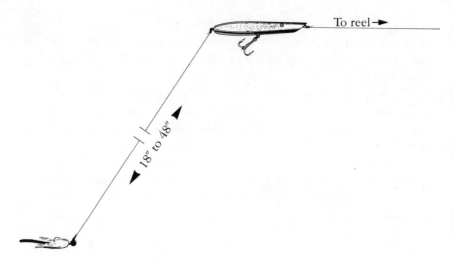

To reel →

18" to 48"

This saltwater popper/dropper rig consists of Cordell Pencil Popper trailed by Gapen's Hairy Worm Jig.

←To reel

18" to 48"

An excellent popper/dropper rig for bass and panfish consists of an Arbogast Hula Popper trailed by Gapen's cockroach jig.

leaders of 18 inches or more, depending on water depth and personal preference. They can then be tied to the trailing hook of the surface plug; or the rear hook can be removed from multihooked poppers and the leader attached via a snap to the screw eye.

Although just about any type of surface lure will work, the poppers, gurglers, and others that cause surface commotion are best. The lure-size:jig-weight ratio is not as important with these rigs as with the

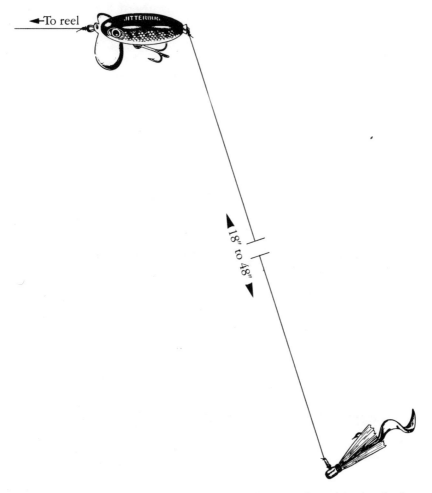

Arbogast Jitterbug trailed by jig and twist-tail is a good combination for bass or pike.

trolling rigs, but good sense dictates that you avoid jigs so large as to render the surface lures ineffective.

When you're after a single target species, such as white bass, northern pike, striped bass, snook, tarpon, and seatrout, pick plugs and jigs of sizes appropriate for that species.

In waters where you might encounter larger and smaller species, this rig will offer you chances at each if you assemble the rig with double duty in mind. For example, in my part of the country our coastal rivers during certain times in the spring will harbor both striped bass and shad. A favorite rig of mine, then, consists of a large popping lure trailed by a shad dart on a two-foot leader. Often, in the evening, schools of shad come to the surface and create quite a commotion. When this rig is cast in their midst, the noise of the popper is usually lost in the turmoil and the jig attracts strikes from the shad.

Stripers on or near the surface normally smash the popper, and the trailing jig doesn't seem to bother them a bit. In fact, when the smaller schoolie stripers are working the surface, they'll as often as not hit the jig instead of the popper.

The rig works equally as well on other species combinations, such as largemouth bass and bluegill. The same kind of rigs are great for "pop-

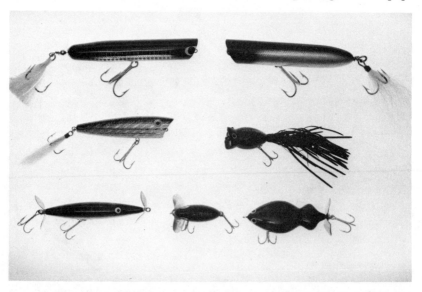

A few of the surface lures that can be used in popper/dropper rigs.

ping" in coastal waters for seatrout and are better, in my estimation, than the traditional popping-float rigs.

Jig/Fly Rigs

Jig/fly rigs can be adapted to vertical jigging for a number of gamefish and panfish in fresh or salt water. You can closely match fly size with jig size in any one rig to attract a single species or fish of like size, or you can set up one rig for taking both large and small fish.

The rigs are simple to make and all are similar, except for the lures that get tied to them. You need only tie two or more droppers into your line, spaced about 12 inches or so apart, leaving 18 to 24 inches of line hanging from the bottommost dropper.

An excellent deep-water rig for salt water consists of large streamer flies tied to the droppers and a heavy leadhead jig tied to the tag end of the line with an end loop. If you're after bottom fish that dwell in waters deeper than 50 feet, you might prefer substituting a heavier diamond jig for the leadhead.

For most freshwater gamefish, you can use a similar rig, or you might prefer to set one up for gamefish and panfish. To accomplish this, tie small wet flies or nymphs to the droppers and a ¼-ounce or larger leadhead jig to the tag end of the line. Leadheads with plastic grubs or twist-tails are excellent for such rigs.

On light tackle in relatively shallow water, you can make a panfish rig by using wet flies or nymphs on the droppers and a ⅛-ounce or $^{1}/_{16}$-ounce jig at the end of the line.

A productive variation of these rigs calls for substituting soft plastics for the flies. In the case of the larger rigs, tie sliced-shank bait-holder hooks to the droppers. For most freshwater gamefish and smaller saltwater species, hook sizes from 1/0 to 4/0 will suffice. To these, attach two-inch plastic grubs, four-inch twist-tails, or a combination of both. For larger saltwater fishes, use 5/0 or larger hooks to which are attached four-inch grubs, or twist-tails of six inches or larger.

For crappie, tie No. 4 sliced-shank hooks to the droppers and rig them with two-inch twist tails. For smaller-mouthed panfish, such as bluegills, drop down to No. 8 or No. 10 hooks, each rigged with a half-inch piece of plastic panfish worms.

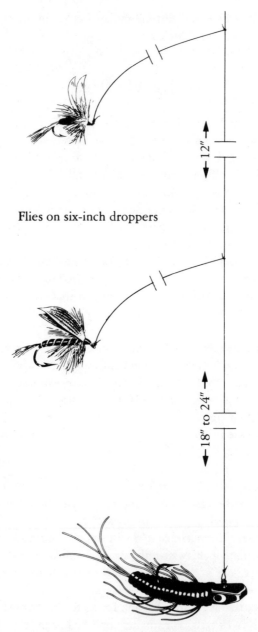

Flies on six-inch droppers

A jig/fly rig that is ideal for bass and panfish consists of Gapen's Ugly Bug jig with flies tied above on six-inch droppers.

All of these rigs are worked in similar fashion, with a few notable variations. Let the rig sink to the bottom on a taut line that will signal any pickups on the fall. Once you feel the jig touch bottom, reel in a foot or so of line and bounce it along the bottom by jigging your rod. You can often locate suspended fish by continuing the jigging action as you slowly retrieve the rig. Keep track of the depth by counting turns of your reel handle so you can quickly get back to the same depth after you catch your first fish.

These rigs and techniques are suitable for use from an anchored or drifting boat, or from docks, piers, and bridges.

Diamond-Jig/Tube-Lure Rigs

A popular rig on the east coast for large cod and pollack is similar to the rigs described above, but this one calls for tying a tube lure or two into the line with about two feet of line left beneath. To the end of the line a large diamond jig is tied. Depending on the depth being fished and local currents, anglers use diamond jigs ranging in weight from about eight to 12 ounces or more, lines of 40-pound test or heavier, and heavy-duty boat rods with conventional reels.

Jig/Trailer-Hook Rigs

When fish are short-striking your jigs or are only nipping at the dressings, there are several ways to rig your jigs for catching these troublesome fish.

Burke Fishing Lures is currently marketing a plastic tail specifically designed for rigging jigs with trailer hooks. Called the Split-Tail Eel, it can be purchased with or without the special large-eyed trailer hooks.

To rig the trailer eel, first slip the point of the jig hook through the eye of the trailer hook. Now run the point of the jig hook through the head of the eel. Then run the point of the trailer hook into the Split-Tail eel near the crotch and the rig is ready to use.

Eagle Claw brand trailer hooks are available in a variety of sizes and finishes from tackle shops or directly from Wright & McGill. These hooks can be used bare or rigged with soft-plastic tails.

For bare rigging, you'll need to use a short piece of surgical tubing to keep the trailer hook from sliding off the jig hook. To rig it, cut a short piece of tubing to cover the hook eye. Slip it over the eye, then run the point of the jig hook through the tubing and the eye of the trailer hook, and move the trailer hook down the bend of the jig hook; now it's ready to use. Eagle Claw trailer hooks come with the necessary surgical tubing.

If you prefer to rig the trailer hook with a plastic worm, grub, or twist-tail, thread the plastic lure onto the hook as you might attach it to a jig. Slide the lure up the hook until the eye is buried in the plastic. Now run the point of the jig hook through the plastic and the eye of the trailer hook, and slide the trailer hook down to the middle of the bend of the jig hook. This rig not only takes the short strikers, but it's an excellent way to rig bucktail and marabou jigs with soft-plastic tails.

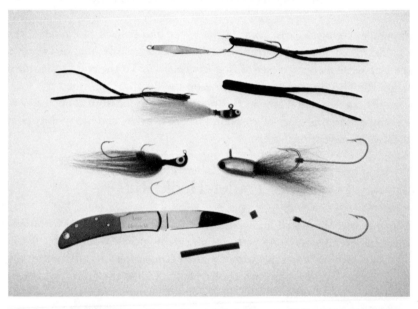

Jig/trailer-hook rigs. *Top,* diamond and bucktail jigs rigged with Burke Split-Tail Eels and trailer hooks; *bottom,* jigs rigged with Eagle Claw trailer hooks that come with required surgical tubing.

9. Jig-'n'-Pig Rigs

In 1921, Alan Jones and Urban Schreiner, a pair of Wisconsin bass fishermen, were looking for a suitable substitute for the live frogs they had been using to catch bass. After some experimenting, they settled on "phony phrogs" carved from fatty hog hide. The bass loved the pork chunks, and Jones and Schreiner soon found themselves in the business of producing the baits for other fishermen. Dubbing their new business "Uncle Josh," the company has since grown to become the world's leading producer of pork-rind baits.

Pork rinds are made from narrow strips of tough, fatty hide found along either side of the pig's spine. During the manufacturing process, the material is split and carved into various shapes and thicknesses, requiring a good bit of handwork. The resulting baits are soft and pliable, yet are among the toughest and most tenacious materials ever put on a hook. They combine the durability and long life of an artificial with the texture and taste of a natural bait: a winning combination.

It wasn't long after pork rinds won widespread popularity that other companies began making and marketing the baits. Pork rinds enjoyed widespread acceptance among anglers and were used extensively for more than a quarter-century. But with the invention of the plastic worm and the subsequent development of other soft plastics, the popularity of pork rinds waned for a number of years. While the plastics stole the limelight, pork-rind producers were forced to improve their products and offer greater selection, or get out of the business. Most got out, but Uncle Josh met the challenge and now offers nearly three dozen different styles and sizes of pork-rind baits, some available in as many as eleven different colors.

A generation of anglers has grown up knowing and using only soft plastics, spinnerbaits, spoons, plugs, and other popular lures. Now they're beginning to discover pork rind and its natural partner, the jig. Their results are forcing some oldtimers to rediscover the deadly duo. To be sure, though, some of the more silent types have been using the jig-'n'-pig rigs all along, catching plenty of fish, but not broadcasting their successes.

Pork Problems Solved

Pork-rind baits had a number of things going for them from the beginning. Besides the characteristics already mentioned and their proven fish-catching abilities, they were (and still are) relatively cheap. Moreover, they can be used over and over again, which further decreases the cost of fishing with them.

But the soft plastics are also comparatively cheap, and fishermen found them every bit as productive as pork rinds in many situations, if not as durable. Additionally, the plastics were easier to store and not nearly as troublesome to use.

One problem in the old days was the brine the pork rinds were packed in. Although the salty liquid kept the baits from spoiling, it led to other problems. Not only would spills rust nearby hardware, but the salt that dried around the jar rims prevented a good seal. And since salt draws moisture, fighting corrosion was always an ongoing and tedious battle that pork-rind fishermen faced. Now, though, the rinds are packed in a salt-free preservative, and the corrosion problem has been solved.

To stay sufficiently soft, though, the rinds must be kept wet at all times. If they're allowed to dry out they become tough and stiff and virtually useless. Even a short run from one fishing spot to another on a warm day can cause a rind left exposed to dry out. So, during any extended periods between casts, the pork rind should be returned to its jar. But since the rinds can be tough to get off the hook, this can be a nuisance.

If you're taking a lunch break or are moving slowly from one spot to another, you can simply trail your jig-'n'-pig rig in the water to keep it soft. Another way I have solved the problem is to remove the entire rig from my lure snap and put the whole thing in the jar of preservative. In a new jar of rinds there won't be enough room to do this, so keep a couple of jars of the preservative after you've used all the baits, and carry them in your boat or tackle box for this purpose.

Some anglers like a pork bait that's even softer than those fresh out of the jar. To soften them, they add two drops of glycerine to each jar. Do this only to the rinds you'll be using in any given season, though, as the glycerine will reduce the useful life of the baits to about a year or so.

You will also find the rinds mighty tough to cut. Sometimes the hook holes aren't quite large enough, especially if you want to use a small rind on a large jig, and must be made bigger to fit over the hook's barb. You might also have need from time to time to trim pork rinds—perhaps to shorten one that's too long, or to cut back a worn or damaged head and make a new hook hole. Although a sharp and finely pointed pocketknife will suffice, I have found a pocket X-Acto knife with a razor-sharp pointed blade to be the best instrument for trimming tough rinds. When the blade dulls on this knife, it is easily replaced.

Favorite Jig-'n'-Pig Rigs

A dozen different Uncle Josh pork-rind baits are described in Chapter 3, all of which can be used with jigs and jig heads. For details on the rest of

You can alter the action and reduce the buoyancy of a pork frog or pork chunk by trimming away some of the body meat. An X-Acto knife will handle this tough job with ease.

the line, write Uncle Josh for a copy of the company's latest catalog. When you do, be sure to ask for a copy of the booklet, "How to Fish Pork Rind in Fresh Water."

As with other jig rigs, you should talk to anglers in your area and seek the advice of tackle-shop and marina proprietors about the most productive jig-and-pork-rind combinations to use in the waters you fish. I also recommend that you try a number of different sizes, styles, and colors of rinds and combine them with various types of jigs until you can settle on your own personal favorites. Meanwhile, I would like to tell you about the rigs I use, some of which are fast becoming nationwide favorites.

For starters, let me generalize by saying that virtually all the pork-rind baits currently available are suitable for use with jigs. Moreover, it's my considered opinion that just about any type of jig will produce more fish when a pork rind is added to it than it will if fished bare. That is not to say I always use pork rinds on my jigs or that I never use plain jigs without tipping their hooks. You already know better than that. You know that I

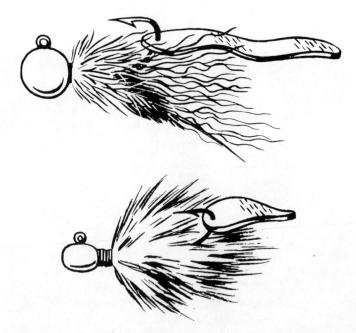

Two jig-'n'-pig combinations that are good for trout and panfish. *Top,* Uncle Josh No. 1 Fly Strip on a marabou jig; *bottom,* small jig tipped with an Uncle Josh Fly Flick.

use soft plastics extensively, and of course, I use unadorned jigs for a variety of purposes. I also use bait of various sorts in conjunction with jigs. In short, I fit my jigs and rigs to the particular situations I face. But, to put it hypothetically, if I were to be restricted to using only jigs with or without pork rind (no plastics, no bait, etc.) I would certainly do about 90 percent of my fishing with pork added to my jigs.

The smallest pork-rind baits are good choices for use with small marabou, Dynel, and bucktail jigs for panfish and trout. The Fly Strip and the Little Vee are excellent for tipping crappie jigs. Fly Flicks are good for tipping $1/32$-ounce and $1/64$-ounce jigs for trout and bluegill. White is the only color of these particular rinds that I use.

For bass and pike in fresh water, as well as for a number of inshore marine species, I use the larger strips, skirts, and split tails, but I've come to favor the Ripple Rind above all others when I simply want a pork rind for tipping a jig and adding fish appeal to it. When I'm after toothy critters, such as northern pike in fresh water and barracuda in salt water (two of my favorites), I invariably pick a Ripple Rind over a plastic twist-tail, as it will not succumb to the destructive dentures of these species as soft plastics will.

That's the discussion on my general uses of pork rinds with jigs, though I'll go into more specifics later on. Right now, I would like to get to the rigs I use most often and most purposefully. One is an old rig I used as a youngster and revived a few years back when others weren't serving me well. The other is a born-again bass buster that I've only recently grown fond of and am still learning how to use to its ultimate efficiency.

It was in the fall of 1963 that I discovered the plastic worm and immediately became a devotee of counterfeit crawlers of the black persuasion. I had just returned from a fifteen-month stint in the Aleutian Islands (compliments of the Army Security Agency) where I had fished for trout, salmon, and a variety of saltwater species whenever my olive-drab superiors were unable to keep me otherwise occupied, or when they simply couldn't find me.

I loaded the trunk of my '57 Ford with every bit of fishing tackle I owned and whatever more I could afford to buy, pointed it south, and headed for Florida, hankering to do battle with the legendary Florida largemouth, and amusing myself with dreams of snook (another of my all-time favorites), tarpon, bonefish, seatrout, permit, and jacks wild.

On my first day of bass fishing in Florida, I caught and released thirty scrappy fish—all taken on black plastic worms—and found two huge old mossybacks that I would stalk and coax for another month before moving one of them to attack. Although my plastic worms were of no interest to the ten-pound-plus lunkers I discovered, they took all the fish of one to four pounds I could handle, and tempted plenty others that I missed for one reason or another.

It was not only that black was the most widely available and popular of plastic-worm colors then that led me to use it to the exclusion of all others; I had been introduced to the lure's forerunner some years earlier and had subsequently caught a fair number of fish with it. I'm talking about the black pork-rind eel.

Although I was only twelve years old in 1955, I had been fishing for six years, had been reading everything about angling I could lay my hands on for the past four years, and was already a devoted and studious follower of the great guru of modern angling, A.J. McClane. It was in December of that year that McClane introduced me and countless thousands of other anglers to the black pork-rind eel in his article, "That New Black Magic."

Even at that early age I was able to separate the scribblers from the scribes, and I found McClane to be always a step or two ahead of everyone else with his reporting on various new lures, tackle, and techiques. I would not have been at all surprised to learn that McClane, once each month, just prior to deadline, ascended a mountain and later returned to his desk and typewriter with notes for that month's column chiseled into tablets of stone.

It was nothing out of the ordinary, then, when I hung on every word of his report on Black Magic, the trade name for the long, thick strips of black pork rind. But it was months before I could lay hands on a jar of the stuff, and it took a good while longer before I found the best way (for me) to fish it.

I tried fishing it first sans weight. I had better luck with it, though, when I added split-shot to my line. But it wasn't until I started using it with jigs that I gained true control of the bait and began finding regular takers.

Perhaps it was because fish I normally caught were a good bit smaller than those McClane was able to tempt, but I had trouble with short-strikers. When I started cutting the big rinds back, however, from their normal eight or nine inches to about six inches, I missed fewer fish.

Of course, the rig I was fishing came to be called the jig 'n' eel, and would take a lot of big bass in this country before the plastic worm took over. I later foolishly joined the legions of bass anglers who put the pork aside and took up the plastics. We weren't stupid for using the soft plastics, only for using them to the total exclusion of pork rinds. A few of the sharper gents had learned that there were times when nothing but the big, black pork eels would take fish, and they kept right on using the jig 'n' eel to fill stringers.

I haven't seen a jar of Black Magic eels for a good number of years now, and I wouldn't be at all surprised to learn that this particular brand is no longer available since the plastic-worm boom put most of the pork-rind makers out of business. But Uncle Josh does offer Black Widow Eels in four-, six-, and nine-inch lengths and a half-dozen different colors.

In fresh water, I fish the six-inch eel almost exclusively. I sometimes use the same size for inshore saltwater fishing, but as often will rig the nine-inch eel on a black jig (a dynamite combination for snook in the mangrove tangles). The only color I use and have ever used is black, but I suspect that white eels rigged on bucktail jigs might prove powerful

One of the author's favorite pork-rind rigs is a six-inch Black Widow Eel impaled on a weedless Fishair jig.

medicine in offshore salt water, and I intend to give them a workout next season.

The jigs I've been using on these rigs for the past several years are black banana jigs with molded-in nylon weed guards and are dressed in black Dynel Fishair. Lately, I've also begun using black living-rubber jigs that are identical in all respects, except that they're dressed with bulky bodies of living rubber instead of Dynel.

One innovation that certainly led to the recent rind renaissance was the development of the nylon-fiber weed guard. Molded right into the head of the jig, it is strong enough to fend off most snags, yet is flexible enough to allow a sure and certain hookup on the strike. Several manufacturers have combined this feature with the highly effective bodies of living rubber to turn out jigs that are becoming standard for use with pork frogs. The Arkie is one such jig, as are Cordell's Crazy Leg jig and Mister Twister's Living Rubber jig.

For several years, anglers in various parts of the country (most notably in Arkansas, Kentucky, Louisiana, Oklahoma, Tennessee, and Texas) have been using the living-rubber jigs and pork frogs to make phenomenal catches of large bass. They're able to toss these weedless rigs right into the sauerkraut and stickups and come out with mossybacked old bass that snoot their broad noses at other offerings.

Jiggin' and piggin', as anglers call the technique, is rapidly gaining in popularity in all bass waters in the U.S., certainly due in no small part to Bo Dowden's winning of the tenth annual Bass Masters Classic. The Louisiana bass fisherman took his Arkie jigs and pork frogs to the St. Lawrence Seaway for the 1980 tournament and caught a three-day limit of fifteen bass that totalled 54 pounds, 10 ounces—beating Roland Martin's second-place catch by more than 10 pounds. A rig that can do that isn't likely to remain only regionally popular for very long.

According to Uncle Josh's Jim Vander Mause, the best-selling pork frogs used to be the green-spotted ones, but now these have taken a back seat to black, brown, and orange, and in some parts of the country there are shortages of these colors during the fishing season.

Year-Round Jig-'n'-Pig Fishing

As I see it, anglers, in general, have made four important mistakes regarding pork rinds, from about the mid-1960s on. First, many switched

The jig-'n'-pig rig that has
virtually stormed the country
is an Uncle Josh Pork Frog
rigged on a weedless
living-rubber jig.

A weedless living-rubber jig rigged with an Uncle Josh Pork Frog, when fished properly, imitates the bass's favorite food—the crawfish.

entirely from pork rinds to soft plastics when the latter began dominating tackle-shop offerings and the contents of the nation's outdoor magazines. Secondly, those who were smart enough to keep using pork rinds as well as the soft plastics tended to think of the former as good during cold weather only. Third, too many concentrated their use of pork rind on freshwater fishing while ignoring its many saltwater applications. Fourth, the average fisherman got into a pork-rind rut—that is, he restricted his methods to one or two he had learned about from others or read about, and failed to experiment with other techniques.

My own switch to plastic worms for all my bass fishing, although radical at first, tempered after two seasons, and I started using other lures and baits again. Of course, I continued using plastic worms and, later, other soft plastics. But, gradually, I approached my fishing more moderately, with more thought. And eventually I got back to fishing pork rinds.

I never did give up the rinds totally for all species. Even when I wasn't using them for bass fishing, I used pork-rind strips with spoons, spinners, and jigs for a good bit of saltwater fishing as well as for some freshwater species, namely, northern pike. But it took me a number of years to get back to the jig-'n'-eel fishing with the black pork-rind eels; when I did, I used the combination exclusively during the colder months when the bass seemed to prefer pork over plastic.

Although I have and still do catch cold-weather bass on plastic worms, I think the jig 'n' eel is a better producer under certain conditions. When bass become lethargic because of lower temperatures that slow their metabolic rate, they don't feed with vigor. They continue to eat, but they require less food then. And they're picky. They aren't as likely to chase a fast-moving or even moderately moving lure then. They tend to mouth their meals more and will usually reject anything that is even remotely unappealing to them.

My first indication that the bass have become moody and picky is when the fishing slows considerably, often after a strong cold front—perhaps only a few days or a week after the same waters were giving up frequent strikes and good catches. Usually simultaneously, I will notice that I'm getting little pecks at my plastic worms that seldom or never result in hookups. Many anglers mistake these gentle bumps or tics in the line for nibbling bluegills, or they fail to notice them at all. Occasionally, they

On February 7, 1981, Texas angler John Alexander established a new state record when he hauled up a 15½-pound largemouth with an Arkie jig and Uncle Josh black Pork Frog. He took two more bass the same day that exceeded 11 pounds apiece. The previous Texas record largemouth of 14 pounds 3½ ounces had been taken only one month earlier—by John Alexander, with an Arkie jig and Uncle Josh Split-Tail Eel. *(Photo courtesy Uncle Josh Bait Co.)*

will be bluegills, but most often they are bass that have nipped at the offerings and rejected them. This is my signal to switch to a jig 'n' eel.

I work this rig much the same as a jig and plastic worm, but not as actively. I creep it over the bottom, hesitating frequently. Occasionally, I hop it up off the bottom a few inches, but then let it settle and stay put for at least a full minute. Then, with my rod tip near the surface of the water, I twitch it only a couple of inches and watch my line closely for any sign of a pickup.

Bass are usually hard to come by in such situations, even when they are densely schooled. But if I manage to locate them, this technique will usually get me a few fish. And when I do get a pickup, it almost always comes after the jig 'n' eel has rested on bottom for a while and then has been twitched just a few inches. With my mind's eye under water, watching the entire process, I see the slowly working rig attract a bass, or perhaps several. The fish move closer for a better look, hovering near the rig, waiting to see what it will do next. Were it to dart off quickly, any distance at all, the fish would likely move back to where they were holding when it all began. But when the slithery black eel moves, it only scoots a few inches across the bottom, stirring up a bit of silt to lightly cloud the water around it; then it stops again. The most aggressive, or perhaps the hungriest or most curious, of the onlookers swishes his caudal fin almost imperceptibly, moving him toward the eel. He glides up to it, a turn of his pectoral fins raising his tail and tipping his nose to the eel. He opens his mouth and flaps his gill covers simultaneously, sucking the eel into his mouth. The eel's natural feel and taste appeal to him, and he again works his mouth and gills to suck it in the rest of the way, at the same time turning to cruise back to his holding area. The barb of the jig hook, however, alters his course.

This is hard fishing that takes plenty of patience and concentration. It is typical of cold-weather bass angling. It also gets this tough at times during the warmer months.

In the heat of a mid-summer day, bass will often avoid the areas where they can be taken early in the morning, in the evening, and at night. They search out and find areas elsewhere in the lake or impoundment where they are content to hold, breaking their pattern now and then to move and feed ravenously but briefly, and they return again to their holding area. Often, they'll be suspended over deep water, and such fish are difficult, if not impossible, to tempt with the jig-'n'-eel rig. But if the depth at which the fish are found can be matched up with bottom structure and cover, the jig 'n' eel will take fish.

A sudden weather front, usually signalled by a falling barometer, will also cause bass and other fish to change their patterns. This can also make for some tough fishing—so tough, in fact, that many anglers don't even bother to try, reasoning that the front has caused the fish to stop hitting. The conditions might cause the fish to move from their usual haunts and might make them behave differently, but they can still be caught. In fact, I have found such times to be highly productive when I've been able to find the fish.

During weather fronts in the warmer months (June through September) I like to prospect with small jigs and twist-tails on an ultralight spinning rod, switching off regularly to a spinning outfit rigged with a jig 'n' eel and another rigged with a jig and pork frog.

I prefer small offerings then, or I should say, the bass do—hence, the ⅛-ounce or ¹/₁₆-ounce jigs with two-inch twist-tails. I also switch from my normal six-inch Black Widow Eel to one of four inches and rig it on a ¼-ounce weedless jig. I also put aside my usual No. 11 Bait Frog and use, instead, the No. 101 Spinning Frog.

I begin my search for fish amidst the pockets and avenues in lily-pad beds where I often find them feeding actively. If such areas don't give up fish after a reasonable amount of prospecting, I then move off to the sloping gravel bars, underwater humps and reefs, dense brush, flooded timber, and root tangles. More often than not, one of these spots will turn over some fish.

So I have learned that pork rinds are not winter-only baits. They can, indeed, be used year-round. But there is no denying, as cold-weather offerings, they can't be beat.

As mentioned earlier, I have used pork in salt water for years, but not as extensively as I might. And certainly, I have a good bit of experimenting to do before I can report on the full line of pork-rind baits with authority.

A pork-rind strip or Ripple Rind is my first choice for dressing bucktail jigs when I'm fishing for such toothy critters as barracuda. And I like smaller strips on light jigs for flounder and other bay and backwater species. To be sure, the tough rinds are a top choice for dressing bucktail and diamond jigs for bluefish. And they're favorites among many striper fishermen.

Two rinds I should have used by now for deep-water vertical jigging offshore are the Uncle Josh Offshore Big Boy and the largest Black Widow Eel. So here, you would do well to follow my advice instead of my

Pork is better than plastic for the toothy critters. This fine northern pike fell for a black jig rigged with an Uncle Josh Spring Lizard. Angler is Michigan fishing instructor and guide Bob Musselman. *(Photo courtesy Uncle Josh Bait Co.)*

example. Chances are, by the time you read this I will have already put these big rinds to work on some of my favorite bottom-dwelling species. By the way, I'll use white eels for the offshore angling, as I suspect that will prove the most productive color there.

As for the fourth mistake I cited—falling into the pork-rind rut—I've done much in the past two years to work my way out of it, and you should do likewise. I've learned other ways to fish these baits, and I will continue experimenting and adding more techniques to my repertoire.

I suppose the most radical changes I have made are associated with my use of the old pork frog—a bait that's been catching fish for more than a half-century. And I'm certainly not alone in my change of tactics with this rind. Earlier, I said that the development of the fiber weed guard for jigs had much to do with the resurgence of interest in the pork frog and other pork-rind baits. Also linked with this renewed popularity are the living-rubber dressings being used on these jigs.

But every bit as important as the materials are the methods. These rigs are catching fish in shallow water, deep water, and middle depths. They are taking active feeders, suspended bass, and bottom-hugging wintering bass. They're catching fish in all waters, from the deep south to Canada, and from coast to coast. And they're not only making large aggregate catches, but they're bringing up the lunkers.

Any rig that's going to accomplish all this surely cannot be restricted to one or two methods. And it can't be considered only a seasonal lure. With an acute awareness of prevailing conditions and a knowledge of which rigs to use when, the angler will soon learn that jig-'n'-pig rigs can catch fish in practically any type of water, any time of year.

10. ![jig illustration] Jig-and-Bait Rigs

I don't rise before dawn has even dreamed of cracking, drive countless miles each year, wade slippery-bottomed streams, float endless miles of river, hike over dunes of talcum-powdery sand, wrestle the helm of a boat in evil winds and worse waters, and spend untold dollars and hours maintaining all my gear just to catch a few small fish. I do it to catch a *lot* of *big* fish.

I like to catch fish. I like to catch a lot of fish. I like to catch big fish. Most of all, I like to catch a lot of big fish. I don't always succeed, but I always try. On every outing, I try to catch as many fish as possible; on every cast I'm after the biggest fish I can find, with no apologies offered.

When it comes to fishing, I am in no way a purist. Within the realm of good sportsmanship and sound conservation practices, I'll use any damned method or tackle that will catch fish. And the techniques and gear that produce the most fish and the biggest fish with greatest consistency are the ones I favor. So I readily admit, here and now, in front of everyone, with no compunctions whatsoever, that *I use bait.* Sometimes bait is best. And to my way of thinking, if you're not using what's best, you're not really interested in catching fish.

Some people have it in their heads, though, that bait is always best, and for that reason is something less than the sporting thing to use. Of course, both notions are faulty. First, bait is not always best. Secondly, even if it were, there's nothing unethical or gauche about its use.

Basic Jig-and-Bait Rigs

There's a rather large variety of natural and prepared baits that can be used successfully with jigs and jig heads, and there are three basic ways to employ jig-and-bait rigs. For the sake of discussion, I'll call the first

Walleye anglers often tip their jigs with worms or minnows to sweeten the offering. Here, expert angler and tackle manufacturer Dan Gapen hoists a stringer of proof. (*Photo courtesy Gapen's World of Fishin', Inc.*)

"jig-primary rig"; the second, "jig-bait rig"; and the third, "jig-secondary rig."

In the jig-primary rig, the jig is "tipped" with bait. Worms, minnows, and other baitfish are most often used for such purposes; they can be used whole or cut into pieces. In such a rig, the bait is secondary or subordinate to the jig. The jig is the primary attractor; the bait is only added to "sweeten" the offering. Freshwater fishermen, particularly walleye anglers, are the main users of such rigs, but the method works well on a number of species in fresh or salt water.

In the jig-bait rig, both the jig and the bait are equal partners. Jig and bait are carefully chosen and matched to perform a task as a unit, with one component complementing the other. Bucktail jigs dressed with strip baits are among the most popular of such marriages. They're most often used for inshore and offshore saltwater angling, but are also highly effective on many freshwater gamefish and panfish.

In the jig-secondary rig, which as well might be called a bait-primary rig, the bait is the main element, and the jig functions merely as the vehicle for presenting it. Although in such a rig the jig is relegated to the ranks of terminal tackle, it is nonetheless important, if somewhat less glamorous. Most often, plain jig heads are best for such rigs, although for some specialized purposes, dressed jigs are better.

The jig-secondary rig is probably the least used in fresh or salt water, but can prove to be the most effective under certain circumstances and for some species. It warrants the consideration of every serious angler and certainly should be subjected to more experimentation than it gets.

Largely, I suppose attitude plays an important part in the use of jig-secondary rigs. In employing the baits that are normally used for any given species or that are regionally popular, you must learn to "think jigs." Consider the sort of terminal rigging you are currently using, and ask yourself whether or not you might substitute a lead jig head for the hook and sinker. If it is possible to do so, might the rig be improved by such substitution? If you think it will be, then, by all means, experiment with it.

I have used a number of these rigs for trout, grayling, whitefish, bluegill, various bullheads, and channel catfish. In the salt chuck, I've taken flounder, sole, surf perch, cod, cabezone, greenling, croaker, pompano, several varieties of jacks, snapper, and a host of bay and backwater residents I didn't bother to keep track of.

Advantages of Jig-and-Bait Rigs

Bait has several important qualities, missing totally or partially from artificial baits, that appeal to the quarry's keenest senses—smell, taste, and feel. Bait smells, tastes, and feels natural and edible.

Live baits, as well as some dead baits and cut baits, are also visually appealing. Indeed, a wriggling worm or swimming minnow has an attractive action that cannot be duplicated.

It follows, then, that baits will normally work better when weather or water conditions reduce the effectiveness of artificial lures or cause fish to change their feeding habits. Of course, some baits for certain species will *always* outperform artificial lures.

Consequently, jig-and-bait rigs are most successful and are often your best choice when weather extremes drastically change fishing conditions. They're also the rigs to use anytime your quarry simply shows a preference for natural baits.

In turbid waters, for example, where fish feed less by sight than by other senses, a jig-and-bait rig provides something for the fish to home in on by smell. When water temperatures are low and fish feed with less frequency and vigor, the taste and texture afforded by the bait portion of your rig can lead to more frequent hookups. And when fish are feeding selectively, you can often simulate their natural foods best with a jig-and-bait rig.

Favorite Freshwater Jig-and-Bait Rigs

Freshwater anglers often tip their jigs with small minnows, redworms, or pieces of nightcrawler to add appeal to their lures in the early spring. In lakes where water temperatures are still low at that time of the year and the fish are not yet feeding vigorously, a tipped jig is a good choice for walleye, white bass, yellow perch, and even largemouth bass and bluegill.

Rivers and creeks in many parts of the country are high and roily in the spring, either from winter runoff or seasonal rains. Then, jigs dressed with redworms, whole nightcrawlers, minnows, and strip baits will draw more strikes than anything else. Even diehard bait fishermen, who normally outfish anglers using artificials under such conditions, would do well to switch to jig-and-bait rigs, because with such tackle the angler can cover much more water with greater efficiency than with traditional still-fishing gear.

Small jigs tipped with one or two cured salmon eggs are always good bets for trout, grayling, spring chinook, and summer steelhead. During the fall and winter salmon and steelhead migrations, try drifting jig-and-egg rigs on the streams that harbor these anadromous species. Use plain jig heads or jigs only sparsely dressed with fluorescent-orange bucktail, marabou, or wool yarn and with heads painted fluorescent orange or bright red. Use the dressed jigs with spawn sacks or cured egg clusters. Use commercially cured single salmon eggs with the plain jig heads, and completely fill the jig hook with them, from jig head to hook point.

Grubs and meal worms are excellent baits to use with plain jig heads any time of year. Fat white grubs that are usually found by digging in the roots of grass, weeds, and other vegetation or by crumbling apart rotting wood make dandy trout baits. Meal worms, available at most bait shops, are good for trout, whitefish, and panfish.

Use small, roundhead jigs with heads painted black or brown or left unpainted. Rig the grubs or meal worms by inserting the hook point at the head and running the hook lengthwise through the body so that the tail curls naturally around the bend of the hook.

In streams, these rigs are best fished by dead-drifting them in a current, or by casting into a riffle and letting the rig drift into a nearby pool or

Small jig heads baited with meal worms consistently take the big bluegills, especially during weather extremes, when the big fish can be tough to tempt.

eddy. In lakes and ponds, use the rig for vertical jigging, or you can suspend it from a float and work it slowly.

The favorite food of stream-dwelling smallmouth bass is the hellgrammite. Use a plain jig head painted black and hook the hellgrammite from the underside, either up through or just behind the collar. Since the hellgrammite uses its tail to cling to rocks, you can avoid snags by snipping off the end of the tail with a pair of scissors or nail clippers. Work the jig-and-hellgrammite rig slowly over the bottom of pools, or drift it through riffles into pools, around boulders, and beneath undercut banks.

Minnows are excellent bait for most freshwater gamefish and many panfish, and one of the main advantages of using them with jigs is that you need not keep them alive. For most fish, however, they should be fresh. If you seine your own minnows, you can lay in a good supply and freeze them for later use. You will also find frozen minnows at many bait shops at prices far below those charged for live minnows. Moreover, you can use the dead-minnow rigs in states where fishing with live minnows is prohibited.

The tail-end half of a small minnow is good for tipping small marabou jigs used for crappie fishing. Use tails cut from larger minnows to tip jigs for walleye, white bass, and black bass. Tails, fillets, and belly-meat strips cut from large chub minnows are good for dressing large bucktail jigs for big bass, pike, and muskie.

To use whole dead minnows, match them with appropriately sized jigs and jig heads, and fit the rigs to the species you're after. Use jigs of ⅛ ounce or smaller for minnows up to two inches for crappie and yellow perch. For white bass, smallmouth bass, and sauger, use minnows of two to three inches and jigs of ⅛ to ⅜ ounces, depending on water depth and current. For largemouth bass, walleye, and pike, as well as channel, blue, and flathead catfish, minnows from two to six inches or more can be used—depending on the species and normal running sizes—with jigs of ¼ to ¾ ounce, or even larger in deep water and heavy currents.

If you use bucktail, marabou, or other dressed jigs, hook the minnows through the lips. With plain jig heads, you can either hook them through the lips or you can run the hook into the mouth and out the dorsal side, behind the head, so that the hook shank is concealed inside the minnow.

Another favorite food of most freshwater fishes is the crawfish. As with minnows, these too can be caught ahead of time and frozen for later use.

Package them for particular species of fish according to size. Small crawfish of about two inches or so are good baits for trout, smallmouth bass, rock bass, and bullheads. The medium-size craws are best for largemouth bass and channel catfish. Your best bet with the largest crawfish is to pinch off the tails and freeze them for catfish and panfish bait.

I've fished crawfish in a lot of different ways, but I consider the jig the best way to rig these baits. I simply run the jig hook up through the underside of the crawfish's tail and work the bait backwards, as it moves in nature. With the smaller craws I like to use an orange and brown bucktail. With larger ones I use a weedless living-rubber jig.

One bait that many freshwater anglers overlook is saltwater shrimp. Shrimp exude a strong, fishy odor that naturally attracts bullhead, catfish, and many varieties of panfish, particularly bluegill. And the best way to fish with shrimp in fresh water is with a jig.

The tails are the only part of the shrimp I use as bait in fresh water, but I often use the rest of the shrimp as chum, after cutting it into pieces.

Saltwater shrimp is an excellent freshwater bait for bullheads and panfish and is a top choice in early spring for trout and grayling. A small shrimp tail will yield four or more small baits that should be used with tiny jig heads on ultralight tackle. Head and shell remains can be cut up and used as chum.

For channel catfish, I sometimes use a whole unpeeled shrimp tail rigged on a marabou or bucktail jig. I work this rig slowly over the bottom, with quick, short twitches of the rod, and long pauses between the twitches.

For bullheads and bluegills, I use plain jig heads—usually $1/16$ or $1/8$ ounce. I peel the shrimp tails and use only enough meat to conceal the hook. Most tails will yield at least two baits, and larger ones can be cut into three or more pieces. The baited heads are then jigged vertically from an anchored or drifting boat.

Bullheads and catfish are often overlooked by jig fishermen, and that's too bad because these are great fish in many ways, and contrary to popular belief, they are not reserved for trotliners and still-fishermen. Bullheads are tasty and prolific; in a good spot you can jig up a boatload. The so-called large catfishes (white, channel, blue, and flathead) are efficient predators and sporty gamefish, perfect targets for the jig-and-bait fisherman.

Most bullheads, as well as white, channel, and blue catfish, will come

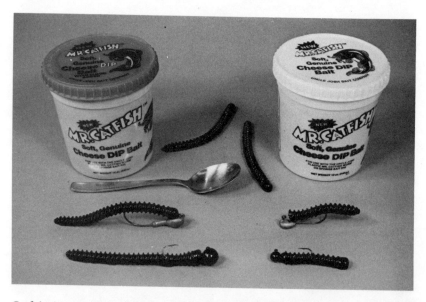

Catfish rigs can be used whole or pinched in half. They can be rigged Texas style on worm heads, or with hooks exposed on other types of jig heads. Rigs are then dipped into soft scent bait, which is spread between the ridges of the plastic body.

readily to cheese-based or blood-based scent baits and other fragrant concoctions. There are now commercially available soft scent baits, such as those offered by Uncle Josh Bait Co., that are ideal for use with molded soft-plastic catfish rigs.

You can buy these plastic rigs or make them with molds available from M-F Manufacturing Co. Although many anglers use these rigs with treble hooks, jig heads are a far better choice as they don't get snagged as readily.

Rig the soft plastic on a plain jig head as you would a grub or twist-tail. For small jigs, you can pinch back the plastic body to fit. When you have the rig ready, dip it into the prepared bait and use a stick or spoon to spread the scent bait into the ridges of the soft plastic.

In ponds, lakes, and reservoirs, work the rigs slowly over the bottom, or vertically jig them with very little action. In streams, look for deep, quiet pools. In either still or running water, at night, you can work the shallows where catfish come to feed.

Jig-and-worm rigs are also good for bullhead and catfish. Sometimes a single nightcrawler on a plain jig head is enough to tempt bullhead and channel catfish, but one of the best rigs for big flathead, blue, and channel catfish is a gob of nightcrawlers impaled on a plain jig head and worked along the bottom, jigged vertically, or drifted in a current.

Strip baits cut from beef or pork liver and from cheap cuts of beef, then rigged on bucktail or marabou jigs are great for channel catfish, but will also take other freshwater fish, such as trout, bass, and panfish.

Frogs are popular baits for a variety of freshwater gamefish. They will take bass, pike, the large catfishes, and big brown trout; and jigs are perfect for working live frogs. Use either dressed jigs or plain jig heads, and match the weight of the jig to the size of the frog and type of water you plan to fish. Hook the frog through the lips and cast it to lily pads, weedbeds, and shoreline cover. Retrieve it with quick, short rod twitches to impart a natural action. You can skim the jig-and-frog rig across the water just beneath the surface by using a light jig and holding your rod high on the retrieve. You can also swim it through the middle depths, or let it drop to the bottom and hop it back on the retrieve.

On streams, you can work the jig-and-frog rig in a variety of ways, allowing the current to sweep it into likely spots. You should give the rig some rod action, though, instead of dead-drifting as you might with other rigs.

Favorite Saltwater Jig-and-Bait Rigs

As in fresh water, many of the traditional saltwater baits can be used in jig-and-bait rigs. In fact, bait of some sort is probably used more by saltwater jig fishermen than by freshwater anglers.

Although whole baitfish can be used with jigs in salt water, much the same as minnows are used in fresh water, the preference seems to be for strip baits. The strips can be cut from the sides of most popular bait species—such as herring, anchovy, menhaden, mullet, sculpin, balao, and others; they also can be cut from the bellies of saltwater panfish and gamefish.

Sometimes fillets are cut from baitfish and used as they are to dress jigs. Some anglers prefer to do some additional trimming to alter or improve the action. Strips can be cut into long, narrow ribbons; they can be tapered; they can be slit to form a forked tail; and they can be cut to any desirable length. Bellymeat strips can be similarly carved and can even have the fins left in place.

Skins should be left on strip baits for two reasons. First, the color of the skin and sparkle of scales are often attractive to the target species. Also, the skin makes the strip bait a tough and durable addition to the jig.

If you use strip baits cut from oily or bloody fish, you can lightly score the skin with several shallow slashes to cause the bait to release fish-attracting oil or blood in the water.

For most inshore species, bucktail jigs are the top choice of many anglers for use with strip baits. Large bucktails are also used in offshore waters, but for deep-water jigging, diamond jigs with strip baits are the top producers.

Killifish are popular baitfish along the east and gulf coasts and can be worked effectively with small bucktail or marabou jigs or with plain jig heads. To use them live, hook them through the lips. Fresh dead killifish can be rigged by running the hook into the mouth and out the dorsal side behind the head, but most are used live.

Since the various members of the killifish family (including mummichogs and sheepshead minnows) are hardy fish that don't die easily, they are best rigged with small, plain (roundhead) jig heads. They can be cast to likely cover and structure in bays and backwaters where they will take most popular inshore species. They are tops for working over the flats for flounder. They can also be jigged vertically from boats, bridges, docks and piers, or can be drifted in tidal currents.

Live or dead shrimp can also be used with jigs for most inshore species. With live shrimp, use plain jig heads that are heavy enough to get the shrimp down but not so heavy as to anchor it to the bottom. Run the hook up through the underside of the tail. Cast it gently and work it with short twitches of the rod and brief pauses between twitches.

A big bucktail, dressed with an eight-inch sculpin fillet tempted this big lingcod.

Dead shrimp should be fresh or fresh-frozen. Although whole dead shrimp can be used as live ones are, I prefer live shrimp for such purposes. With dead shrimp I use only the tails. For vertical jigging or working quiet backwaters for the smaller inshore species, I often use plain jig heads dressed with peeled shrimp tails.

Bloodworms and other sea worms are popular saltwater baits that are excellent for use with jigs. Bucktail and marabou jigs can be tipped with pieces of worms or dressed with whole worms. Plain jig heads can also be used for rigging whole worms or several worms at once.

One bait overlooked by most saltwater fishermen is the nightcrawler. A surprising variety of inshore marine species will readily take night-crawlers but are seldom offered the opportunity. In some areas, night-crawlers are much easier to come by than bloodworms and other saltwater baits and will often produce as many or more fish than the traditional baits. Try tipping your jigs with small pieces or rigging them with whole nightcrawlers.

Tough and effective strip baits can be made from squid. You can use the small tentacles or can cut strips from the arms and body to use on leadhead and diamond jigs. Although some anglers use squid to take

Some effective jig-and-bait rigs for saltwater fishing. *Top,* a whole herring rigged on a bucktail jig; *center,* a Bomber nylon jig rigged with trailer hook and strip bait; *bottom left,* nylon jig tipped with bellymeat strip; *bottom right,* diamond jig rigged with a baitfish tail.

Jig-and-bait rigs account for a lot of saltwater fish in U.S. coastal waters. Here, angler hauls a black rockfish aboard a party boat.

inshore species, most fish this bait offshore by trolling, casting to kelp beds, or vertical jigging in deep water.

Clam necks make excellent bait in many waters for two reasons. First, the neck is the toughest part of the clam; the body, though a good bait, is fragile and difficult to keep on the hook. Also, the neck is the only part of the clam that most fish ever eat. A variety of inshore species move onto the flats on the high tide searching for food. That's also when clams raise their siphons (necks) to feed, and the fish simply move in and bite the necks off.

For best results, use Erie or standup jig heads, either painted a dull, dark color or left unpainted. Rig them with whole clam necks and fish them on the flats by casting and letting them rest on bottom. Every few minutes, move the rig several feet, until you've brought the rig all the way in. Make your next cast to a different spot, and continue working the rig this way until you find fish.

Clam necks can also be cut into strips and used as any other strip bait to dress jigs for inshore and offshore fishing.

Other Jig-and-Bait Rigs

No matter whether you're fishing fresh or salt water, an excellent way to rig for short-strikers is to use a leadhead jig with a trailer hook and baitfish strip. Slip the eye of the trailer hook onto the jig hook. Then run the jig hook through the leading end of the strip bait. Now put the point of the trailer hook through the middle or tail of the strip bait, and you're ready to fish the rig.

The floating-jig rigs, discussed in Chapter 7, are also good for jig-and-bait rigs. They can be used in almost any body of fresh water as well as inshore saltwater. And most of the baits discussed in this chapter are suitable for use with the floating-jig heads.

The double-jig rig is a good one to use when you're searching for the right bait. You can rig a plain leadhead with one type of bait and the floating head with another. When one bait starts producing more fish than the other, rig both jig heads with it.

Certainly, there are other rigs you can use and many popular baits I haven't mentioned. Experiment, and remember that most baits that catch fish in your part of the country can be used with even greater success on a jig-and-bait rig. When it comes to bait fishing, think jigs.

Part Four

Jig Fishing: Tackle and Tactics

Now that you have a sound understanding of jig function and design and know which jigs work best in various situations, how to make your own jigs, and how to rig them effectively, you should have sufficient knowledge to put your jigs to work catching fish. But before you head off to your favorite lake, stream, bay, or backwater area, you might wish to consider the tackle that's best for jig fishing. A discussion of some favorite jig-fishing tactics for use on popular freshwater and saltwater species should provide the polish to make you a top-notch jig fisherman.

In the remaining chapters, then, we'll cap off our study of jigs and jig fishing with some of the fine points of the sport—namely, picking the right tackle and matching that tackle with proven tactics for taking gamefish and panfish.

Here, I primarily want to talk about the tackle I use and why, but I also want to emphasize the importance of each individual choosing gear he's most comfortable with, provided that it is good equipment that will hold up to the rigors of the sport. And I want to pass on some of the tips and tricks that have proved successful for me and for other jig fishermen.

I won't pretend to have the last word on jig tackle or to know all there is to know about jig-fishing tactics. If I couldn't learn from others and look forward to picking up a tip or two on just about every fishing trip, angling wouldn't be nearly as much fun as it is for me.

239

11. Jig-Fishing
Tackle and Totes

Although there are no hard and fast rules pertaining to the selection of tackle for jig fishing, a few pointers should help you match your jigs to the right rods, reels, and lines and to fit the tackle to particular fishing conditions. While some serious jig fishermen have developed rather specialized tackle for their kind of fishing, most of the gear used by the average angler can be adapted to fishing with jigs in a variety of situations. So, chances are, you already own tackle that is adequate.

If you're just starting out, however, or are considering the exploration of new fishing horizons, some careful study of the array of tackle available to you might be in order.

No matter what your angling status is, you would do well to examine your tackle and to reassess it in terms of what you expect it to do for you, how you want it to perform. Make sure it is delicate enough to handle the tiny, nymph-size jigs for trout and panfish, or that it has sufficient backbone for sinking a jig hook into the bony jaw of a lunker largemouth or big northern pike, or that it will stand up to the rigors of deep-water jigging for reef species.

Tantamount to angling efficiency is a convenient, orderly, and systemized means of storing and carrying all your jigs and related tackle. If you fish one type of water exclusively and normally pursue only a few species, you will probably get along quite well with a single tackle box. If, on the other hand, you're an all-around angler who fishes for a large variety of fishes in different types of water, you will undoubtedly need several tackle-toting systems to meet your needs.

Freshwater Jigging Tackle

The only freshwater tackle not well suited to jig fishing is fly-fishing gear and, perhaps, simple cane poles. To be sure, though, the lightest leadhead

241

jigs, $^1/_{64}$ to $^1/_{80}$ ounce, can be worked quite easily with a fly rod, much the same way weighted nymphs are used. And some fishermen, particularly crappie anglers, do use jigs with cane poles. But because such tackle is restrictive by nature, I would not recommend it to the well-rounded jig fisherman.

My choice for fishing the greatest variety of water types and using the broadest range of jigs is spinning tackle. With the proper spinning rod, reel, and line I can cast and work tiny jigs for trout and panfish, or the middle-weight jigs for black bass and walleye, or heavier jigs for bigger fish and greater depths.

I use open-face spinning reels, each of which has been carefully matched with a particular rod for balance, control, comfort, and hook-setting ability relative to the type of fishing for which it is normally used. I keep my reels clean and well lubricated so they won't fail me when I need to put the pressure on them.

Bing McClellan with 4¾-pound smallmouth bass taken from Grand Traverse Bay on ⅛-ounce pearl Wig-Wag Minno and light spinning tackle. (*Photo courtesy Burke Fishing Lures.*)

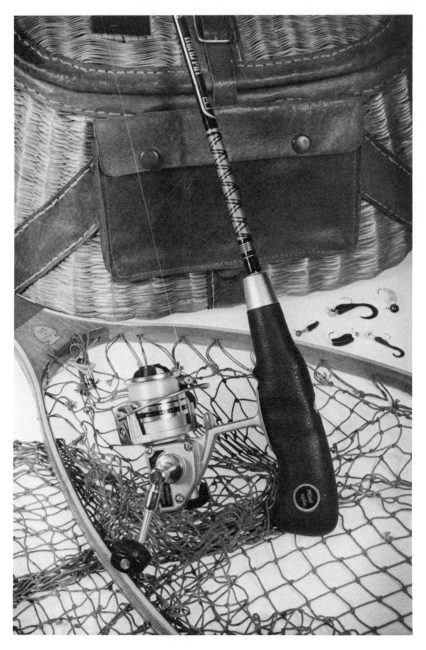

Author's choice for lightest jig fishing is the Daiwa Mini Spin outfit.

Although I've tried more than a dozen different brands of spinning reels over the years, I use Mitchell reels almost exclusively. I've been using Mitchell reels for more than twenty years, and they have always served me well. They balance nicely with my rods, function smoothly and comfortably, and, most important, are equipped with excellent drags.

My workhorse reel for freshwater fishing is the Mitchell 300A (formerly, Model 300). I have three of these on active duty right now, and my wife has three Model 301A reels (the southpaw version). For heavier duty, I use a Mitchell 406, and for light work, a Mitchell 308.

For our lightest jig fishing, my wife and I use Daiwa Mini Spin outfits, each consisting of an ultralight reel, filled with four-pound-test line, mounted on a 4½-foot ultralight-action rod. With these outfits we use jigs of ⅛ ounce and smaller, usually for trout and panfish.

My Mitchell 308 is filled with six-pound-test line and is matched with a 5½-foot, light-action, fast-taper rod that I use for trout and panfish, but also for largemouth bass when they prefer smaller offerings. But this is

Author's favorite Mitchell 300A reel and medium-action rod *(bottom)* is a suitable combination for most freshwater and light saltwater jig fishing. Mitchell 406 reel and salmon/steelhead rod *(top)* see to heavier tasks in fresh and salt water.

primarily my smallmouth outfit, and is ideally suited to the task of subduing these scrappy fish. For its size, this rod has a fairly hefty butt section, sufficient for driving hooks home and for handling a fair-size fish, even in a current.

One of my Mitchell 300A reels is mounted on a seven-foot, medium-action spinning rod. This is the outfit I normally use for my jig-and-worm fishing, but it also doubles as a deep-water jigging rod and is the one I use with jig-'n'-eel rigs.

My other two standard freshwater rods, also equipped with the 300A reels, are nearly identical medium-action, fast-taper sticks that perform the bulk of my jig-fishing tasks. With them, I use all sorts of jigs, normally ranging in size from ⅛ to ⅝ ounce. With these, as well as with the jig-and-worm outfit, I most often use 15-pound-test line, but sometimes drop back to 12-pound or 10-pound line when conditions warrant.

The heaviest gear I use in fresh water is the Mitchell 406 reel on an eight-foot salmon/steelhead rod. Mainly, this is a big-water, big-fish outfit with which I use either 15- or 20-pound-test line. I use it for casting, drifting, and trolling.

My preference for spinning tackle is largely a personal one, as it should be. I happen to be more comfortable and more proficient with a spinning rod and reel than I am with casting tackle. And, contrary to popular misconception, spinning tackle, in the right hands, is every bit as accurate and able as casting gear.

Of course, if you happen to be an expert with a casting outfit and a bumbling clutz with spinning tackle, or if you just happen to prefer casting gear, by all means use it. The only drawback I can think of that can be generally applied to casting tackle is that it isn't suitable for fishing the tiny jigs. For that, you need a fixed-spool reel, if you want to cast any distance at all.

Spincasting tackle would seem a good compromise between spinning and casting tackle, but again, the only recommendation I will make is that you pick what you are most comfortable with. I personally haven't cared for any of the spincasting tackle I've owned over the years, mainly because the reels have fouled more frequently than either spinning or casting tackle has, and none I've owned has had a reliable drag system.

One characteristic problem associated with spinning tackle and jig fishing that you should know about, though, is that the jigging, stop-and-go retrieve can cause line snarls if you don't pay attention to how your

If you use casting or spincasting tackle, palm the reel and run the line through thumb and forefinger to load spool with even tension and avoid reeling in slack line.

line is loading on the spool. In such a retrieve, if you're not careful, you can reel slack line onto the spool, followed by tight line, more slack line, and so on. When line is loaded unevenly this way, a subsequent cast can come off the spool several coils at a time, causing a bird's nest of a tangle that will rival any casting-reel backlash.

The only sure way to solve this problem is to avoid reeling in slack line. Keep your line taut, even when you're retrieving with a pumping rod action. Do this by twitching your rod upward to bounce the jig off the bottom, then reeling down to a lower rod position, keeping constant tension on the line at all times.

Check your spool frequently to make sure the line is loading evenly. If loose coils are evident, pull line off the reel until you reach the point where the line is evenly loaded. Then rewind the spool while running the line betwen your thumb and forefinger to maintain tension on it. You must be careful not to let all this loose line get tangled when you pull it off the reel. If you're in a boat, you can simply pay the line out behind the boat until the potential snarl is gone. If you're on shore, you can walk the line off your reel to keep it stretched out and free of snarls.

Although uneven loading is as much a problem with spincasting tackle and can even lead to snarls with baitcasting tackle, it's easier to prevent tangles with this gear. When using a jigging retrieve with spincasting or casting tackle, palm the reel and keep the tension on the line by running it between the thumb and forefinger of your palming hand.

Saltwater Jigging Tackle

For the same reasons I use spinning tackle in fresh water, it's my favorite in salt water as well. But I also use other tackle in the salt chuck.

My smallmouth-bass outfit (the Mitchell 308 and 5½-foot light-action rod) also doubles as my saltwater ultralight outfit. For my kind of fishing, the Daiwa Mini Spin outfit is just a bit too light for saltwater jig fishing, although I would certainly put it to that use if I owned no other ultralight tackle. But I would spool the reel with six-pound-test line instead of the four-pound line I use in fresh water.

The standard freshwater outfits, what I call bass-weight gear, are ideal for many kinds of saltwater jig fishing. All of my Mitchell 300A reels and medium-action rods have seen saltwater action. In fact, I have taken far more saltwater fish with such tackle than with any other, because it adapts so readily to the kind of fishing I do most.

If I had to be restricted to one rod and reel for all of my fishing in fresh and salt water or had to recommend one all-purpose outfit for jig fishing, my first choice would be the Mitchell 300A or comparable reel and a seven-foot, medium-action, fast-taper spinning rod. With several extra interchangeable spools of line in various weights, the jig fisherman can use such an outfit for casting jigs as small as $^{1}/16$ ounce (or even smaller with the assistance of a casting bubble) or as large as one ounce or more. Although a rod of this sort isn't perfect for handling the light and heavy extremes, it is adequate. Moreover, it is ideally suited to fishing with jigs in the ¼-ounce-to-⅝-ounce range, which are the most popular sizes for freshwater and inshore saltwater fishing.

Not only have I taken all the popular freshwater gamefish and panfish with an identical outfit, but I have caught all sorts of marine gamefish and panfish with the same tackle in lagoons, bays, estuaries, and backwaters of the Atlantic, Gulf of Mexico, Pacific, and Bering Sea.

Since I'm not forced to use only one rod and reel, though, I use this middle-weight tackle whenever it's the best choice. When I need something bigger for handling heavier jigs and larger fish, or for making longer

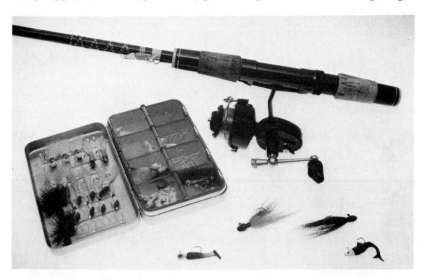

Author's "smallmouth-bass outfit"—a Mitchell 308 reel and light-action rod—doubles as his saltwater ultralight outfit.

casts or working stronger currents or deeper water, I pick one of the three other outfits that I use predominantly or exclusively in salt water.

My eight-foot salmon/steelhead rod is a medium-action, fast-taper stick that sees more saltwater than freshwater action. With the Mitchell 406 reel, it will handle leadheads and small diamond jigs from ⅜ ounce to 2½ ounces, with lures of one to two ounces being perfect for its action.

I spend a fair amount of time walking the shores of bays, fishing the inlets, channels, and flats, casting to pilings, bridge abutments, rip-rap, and the like. This is the outfit I prefer when I need to put some distance into my casts and work large leadheads in strong tidal flows or in the tidewater reaches of our coastal rivers, especially when there are striped bass about. It's also my first choice for what we call rockfishing, which is actually a form of surf fishing done along the rocky shores of the Pacific Northwest. It's a good outfit for fishing from jetties, and I frequently use it offshore for casting leadhead jigs to floating kelp beds and working jigs over shallow-water reefs and ledges.

For reaching out beyond the combers, I use a surf-fishing combination comprised of a Mitchell 302 reel filled with 20-pound-test line and a

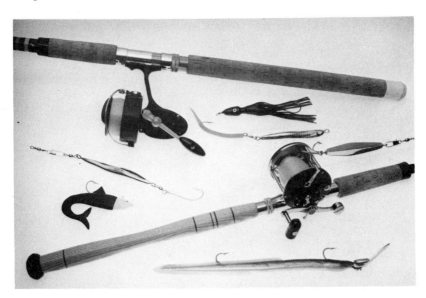

For heaviest surfcasting, trolling, and deep-water jigging duties, author prefers a Mitchell 302 reel and 10-foot rod *(top)* and the Heddon 409 reel on a 6½-foot heavy-action boat rod *(bottom)*.

10-foot, medium-action, fast-taper, saltwater spinning rod. This is also a good choice for fishing from big jetties where huge boulders extend beneath the surface of the water for some distance beyond the breakwater. In such places the heavy jigs and squids needed for long casts and strong currents must be worked up and over the boulders on the retrieve, and the long rod helps immensely here. When a fish is hooked in such water, it should be hauled up in a hurry and brought over the rocks with the authority only such a heavy-duty outfit can afford.

When I'm heading offshore for a day of deep-water vertical jigging, I switch from spinning to conventional tackle, mainly because I find it easier to use. My reel is a Heddon 409, heavy-duty trolling reel, filled with 40-pound-test line. This is matched with a 6½-foot heavy-action boat rod.

When I'm freespooling a big leadhead or heavy diamond jig into the depths, I feel that I have much better control with a revolving-spool reel than I would with a fixed-spool reel. And if the lure gets hit on the way down, as often happens, I think it's quicker and easier to engage the revolving spool and set the hook than it is to throw the bail and set the hook with a spinning reel.

Another advantage that conventional tackle offers the offshore angler is better rod control and surer footing in rough water. The swells in even fairly calm water can have the angler dancing around the deck when he's got a fish on, trying at once to fight his adversary and stay on board while doing so. Many a time, I've had to brace myself against a gunwale or side railing to steady myself while struggling with a fish. The upright position of a conventional reel is certainly preferable to that of a spinning reel then.

The only time I ever need anything larger than the rods and reels I have discussed is when I occasionally spend the bucks for a charter trip. Then, I let the skipper furnish the big gear, as I don't use such equipment often enough to warrant buying my own.

Reel Drags

It should go without saying that you ought to keep your tackle clean and in good repair if you want it to serve you well for years to come. But reel drags (the clutch systems that allow line to be paid out automatically when needed) bear special mention, because they are so widely misunderstood and misused.

There are times when fish are lost due to angler error: the fisherman reels line in when he should be letting the fish run, he lifts his rod tip when he should lower it, he tries to set the hook too soon or too hard, he fails to set the hook firmly or to set it several times, he zigs when he should zag. These are common mistakes we all have made from time to time. And there are rocks and ledges that can abrade a line, or brush and branches that can tangle a line, or weeds and other natural obstacles that can get in the way of landing fish. To be sure, there are occasions when fish simply outmaneuver anglers or wear them down to a point where the fishermen begin making mistakes. This is all part of the sport.

But I would venture a guess, based on my observations of many hundreds of anglers, that more fish are lost due to faulty or improperly set drags than for any other single reason.

The first thing that the experienced angler does before touching any lure or bait to the water is check his drag and make any needed adjustments. And he continues to check it periodically all the while he's fishing. He oils the drag mechanism before he starts fishing, several times while he's fishing, and at the end of the day. And when any reel's drag doesn't pay line out smoothly on demand, the skilled angler works on the mechanism until it functions properly or sends his reel off to the repair shop.

I've seen fishermen do some mighty strange things with reel drags, simply because they had no idea of what the gizmos were supposed to do. One day last spring, I watched an angler fishing for seaperch from a dock at the local boat basin. After baiting his hook, he unscrewed the drag-adjusting knob on his spinning reel until the spool turned freely. Then he stripped the line off the spool by hand and fed it through the rod guides until his rig hit bottom. Then he screwed the drag knob back down tight. Every time he reeled in, he would repeat the process all over again. Not once did he flip the bail to let the line off the reel as he should have. What's most important, here, is that had a fish of any size taken his bait, it would have snapped the line in short order when the tightened drag failed to let the fish run. Or at best, he would have had to do a lot of fumbling around with the adjusting knob to get the drag to work properly—the time to do that is *before* you have a fish on.

That's an extreme example of drag misuse and misunderstanding, but even the more common misconceptions about reel drags have the same end results: lost fish. So pay special attention to your drag system, and make sure it is functioning properly and is set correctly at all times.

Although with experience you'll gain the ability to check your drag as you're fishing by simply pulling line off the reel with your hand, this is not the way for the novice to set or check his drag, nor is it the right way for any veteran angler to make initial settings before he starts fishing.

Generally, most drags are set too tight. One reason for this is what I just mentioned—setting the drag directly off the reel by pulling on the line. Another reason is the incomplete advice often given: "Set the drag just below the breaking point of the line."

First, when you merely adjust the drag by pulling line off the reel and setting the adjustment knob to release line just before it would break, you are failing to take rod tension into consideration. We don't fight fish directly off the reel. We use a rod that is flexed and acts as a shock absorber. The rod also functions to increase the effective strength of the line, and for that reason, among others, we are able to land fish that are much heavier than the pound-test rating of the line.

So the right way to initially set a drag is to thread the line through the rod guides and have someone hold the end of the line at a distance from you of about 20 feet. With the line held taut, raise the rod to the eleven o'clock position and continue raising the rod and adjusting the drag until it will slip between the eleven o'clock and twelve o'clock position. Then return the rod to a nine o'clock position and raise it again against a taut line to double check. If it slips before eleven o'clock, it should be tightened. If it does not slip by the time you reach the twelve o'clock position, loosen it. Now return the rod to the eleven o'clock position and have your partner pull the line sharply, as a fighting fish would. The drag should now slip at the eleven o'clock position.

If you now pull line directly off the reel, you'll notice that the drag is set much more lightly than when it was adjusted without the rod.

I would much rather have a drag adjusted on the light side than one that's too tight. If my drag is too tight, a fish might well snap my line before I can get to the adjusting knob. And if I manage to hold a good fish, I could easily lose it while I'm attempting to reset the drag. If a fish is running against a drag set a bit too light, however, I need only touch a fingertip to the reel spool to slow him down.

Tips on Picking the Right Jigging Rod

Although there are some custom rod-makers currently building specialized jigging rods that are mainly used by saltwater fishermen, I know of no manufacturer that is offering jig rods. Perhaps as jig fishing continues to grow in popularity we'll find some companies building rods that are perfectly suited to this type of fishing. Meanwhile, a few pointers should help you pick a rod that will do an admirable job for you.

Rod actions relate to the size and type of rod and to the sizes of lines that are used with or recommended for any particular rod. For example, my wife and I own a number of spinning rods labeled "medium action, fast taper," but those ratings are relative to line size and rod purpose. One such rod is a seven-foot, standard freshwater rod that is rated for 8- to 15-pound-test line. Another is an eight-foot salmon/steelhead rod, rated for 10- to 20-pound-test line. Another is a 10-foot surf spinning rod, rated for 12- to 30-pound-test line. Butt sections of these rods are proportionally larger, and the larger the rod the heavier the lures and fish it will handle. But each is still a medium-action, fast-taper rod.

I prefer a fast taper on all my jigging rods, except those I use for jig-and-worm fishing and deep-water jigging. The medium-action shafts give me sufficient backbone for setting hooks and getting fish up and out of heavy cover and dense vegetation. The fast tapers give me tips that easily flip even the light jigs to likely targets. These tips are quite sensitive, yet fully responsive. It is important that rod tips recover quickly in jig fishing, and this quality becomes increasingly important in deeper waters. For that reason, soft-action rods are virtually useless to the jig fisherman.

Action is imparted to the jig by rod movement, and if the rod is too soft, it will absorb all or most of the action, relaying little or none to the jig. Moreover, the barbs of jig hooks must be driven home with authority, and the deeper you're fishing, the harder you must set the hook to offset line stretch and the lengthening of reaction time. A soft-action rod simply won't get the job done right, and too many fish will be lost.

So, if you're shopping for a good jig-fishing rod, whether it be a spinning rod, spincasting, or casting rod, make sure that it has a hefty butt section and a shaft stiff enough to impart action to your jigs and to set hooks properly. For most fishing, you should find fast tapers a good choice, but you would do well to stick with a standard taper for jig-and-worm fishing and deep jigging. For such purposes in fresh water and inshore salt water, the so-called worm rods do nicely. For offshore work in deep water, a stiff boat rod is the ticket.

Lines for Jig Fishing

Lines are getting easier to buy all the time, mainly because they keep getting better. We have some mighty fine monofilament lines on the market now, and I really can't think of many ways they can be improved, short of some unlikely breakthroughs that would make lines glow brightly, day or night, above the surface and become invisible under water, or perhaps something that would make them abrasionproof, tangleproof, and twistproof.

Getting back to reality, today's monofilament lines are a far cry from those of yesteryear. They are manufactured with better abrasion resistance and less elasticity, and are balanced with the limpness needed to keep them from taking a set and enough stiffness to spring freely from the spool of a spinning reel.

In fact, the monos have made such great strides that I see very few braided lines being used these days on casting reels and even on trolling and deep-jigging reels. Except for the Cortland Polyspin braided multi-filament line I use on my casting reels and the dacron backing and fly lines I use on my fly reels, I use monofilament lines exclusively.

As for line color, I would first recommend that you use lines that are least likely to show up in the waters you fish. There are blue, green, amber, and clear lines to match any shade of water you might encounter. Mostly, I use amber-colored or clear lines to fit the waters I fish most.

As far as I'm concerned, the jury is still out on fluorescent-pigmented lines. Despite the claims of manufacturers that these are lines that fishermen can see and fish can't, I haven't seen sufficient proof that they are indeed difficult or impossible to detect under water, particularly in clear water. I suspect the contrary: that they are much more visible under water than the nonfluorescent lines. In fact, one very artfully produced and dramatically photographed television commercial shows a popular brand of fluorescent line strung through all manner of underwater obstacles. As the video camera follows the line over barnacle-encrusted pilings, through brush, over rocks and other snags it ultimately comes to the tag end where a big bass is trying his best to break loose. It's an effective bit of film footage that speaks highly of the line's ability to hold a fish, even when tangled and raked across all manner of abrasive objects. But the bright yellow line that the camera records so clearly and that I can see so plainly in the film certainly must be obvious to the fish, right?

Nevertheless, I have taken to using fluorescent line in recent years for jig-and-worm and jig-'n'-eel fishing and for other jig fishing when the fish are gently slurping the lures instead of smashing them vigorously. When I'm worm fishing, I'm a determined line-watcher, and here I think the fluorescent lines are a distinct advantage. Even if they do put off the shy fish, as I suspect they might, they indicate pickups so much better than nonfluorescent lines that, I think in the long run, they account for more hookups. The only proof I have to support my theory are the larger catches I've made since switching to fluorescent lines for worm fishing. It may not be sufficient evidence for you, but I'll continue using the lines I can see for this kind of fishing.

The only other recommendation I will make as regards lines is that you buy only premium-quality lines from the top manufacturers. Stay away from the no-name and bargain-basement varieties, as they will end up costing you more in grief and lost fishing time. You can't go wrong with the premium lines made by such manufacturers as Garcia, Berkley, DuPont, Cortland, Ande, and Maxima, to name but a few. My favorite mono lines and the ones I use almost exclusively are Garcia Royal Bonnyl II, DuPont Stren, and Berkley Trilene.

Many fishermen tend to leave old line on their reels far too long. Aging and prolonged exposure to sunlight will gradually weaken monofilament lines, so you should change your line regularly. For some anglers, this might amount to annual line changes; for others, several changes per season might be in order.

I change my lines as I see fit. All my reels get new line each winter during my tackle-tinkering time prior to fishing season. Then I change lines on any reel when the level has been significantly reduced from cutting back frayed portions. This might mean several more changes during the year (depending upon how often I'm able to get out and where I'm fishing) or it could mean several changes during one weekend trip.

For the jig fisherman, more breakoffs probably result from frayed line than from any other single cause. We're usually sending our jigs into snag-strewn waters where barnacle-covered pilings, sharp rocks, ledges, bridge abutments, and the like wreak havoc on fishing line. For this reason, it's wise to frequently check the last few feet of your line for fraying, and at the first sign of a weak spot, cut back your line and retie your jig. And always check your line carefully after each large fish you catch or lose, and after every snag you work out.

Some anglers run the line between their fingers to check for fraying, but tough and possibly calloused fingertips are not sensitive enough to detect slight fraying. Consequently, many experienced anglers run their line between their lips to search for fraying, as lips are much more sensitive. If you're bothered by such an idea, as I am when I'm fishing waters that are less than pristine, try checking for fraying by running your line over the sensitive skin at the second joint of your little finger on the hand opposite the one you favor. It works.

Jig Totes

Jigs and related tackle can be stored in just about any kind of tackle box, but there are a few features you should look for if you're planning to buy a new box. Also, some boxes are better suited to the requirements of the jig fisherman than others. And if you're a busy angler who fishes a variety of water types for several different species, you will likely have a need for more than one tackle box.

Make sure any tackle box you buy is reasonably waterproof. Those with hinged lids should be equipped with rain lips that shed water. Handle fasteners should be properly sealed to prevent leaks.

Though not a necessity, a recessed handle is a convenience. It allows other gear or another tackle box to be stacked atop the box in transit or at home. Handle recesses also trap water when it's raining: another reason to make doubly sure that handle fasteners don't leak.

Even if you don't currently use soft plastics, it's a good idea to buy a tackle box with so-called wormproof trays or drawers in the likely event that you will one day need this feature. Soft plastics will react with most paints and with plastics that are not specially formulated to resist this reaction.

If you do most of your fishing with jigs and you cover a lot of varied territory as a jig fisherman, you'll want a tackle box with plenty of compartments to keep everything tidy and organized. You'll find that for

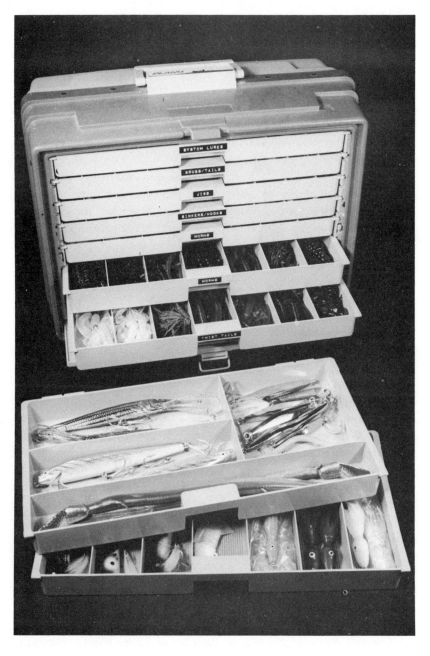

Plano 777R drawer box with interchangeable drawers is an excellent jig-carrying-and-storage system.

most purposes, boxes with an abundance of small compartments are better than boxes of similar size with large compartments. Jigs are more compact than most other lures and can be stored in smaller spaces.

In the purchase of any tackle box, I suggest you carefully consider possible future requirements. Chances are, your angling needs will continue to change from year to year, and you'll regularly acquire more tackle. For that reason, it's a good idea to buy a bigger tackle box than you currently need. You'll not outgrow it as soon, and it will serve you longer than a smaller box will.

I have continually tried to keep my tackle neat and organized, mainly because an orderly box saves fishing time and makes it easy to keep track of inventory for restocking purposes. For years, I searched for the perfect tackle box that would see to all my needs, and in the process used about every type of box available. What I've come to realize is that there's no such thing as the perfect, all-purpose tackle box.

I fish the year around, and my angling takes me to ponds, lakes, reservoirs, impoundments, small creeks, sprawling rivers, estuaries, bays, open ocean beaches, rocky coastline areas, and onto the high seas. Consequently, no single box or type of box will see to all my needs. I have, however, developed a decided preference for three types of tackle totes that combine to do everything I expect of a tackle-carrying and tackle-storage system.

I have come to prefer the drawer-type tackle box for housing most of my gear. I think the drawer boxes are easier to organize and I find them much more convenient in a boat than other types of boxes are. Furthermore, their interchangeable drawers allow me to exchange tackle quickly to fit the needs of any particular type of fishing I'm planning.

I'm in the process of changing over entirely to a drawer-box system to store and carry the bulk of my tackle. I started with a Plano Model 777R box and subsequently purchased extra drawers for it. I have sorted and organized most of my tackle to fit in these drawers and have labeled the drawer fronts as to contents. Some of the drawers hold tackle that I normally carry on most fishing trips. Others hold lures that I use only in fresh water, while still others hold saltwater lures, terminal tackle, and other gear.

I'm building a simple cabinet to hold all the extra drawers of tackle and to allow ready access to all my gear. Prior to any fishing trip I'm planning, a quick scan of the labels on the drawers in the tackle box will tell me if I have all the tackle I need, or whether I must exchange any of the drawers.

Although I spend more fishing hours in a boat than out of one, in any given season my shore-angling outings will be greater in number than my boat trips. For the simple fact that I can get away quickly to take advantage of a spare hour or two, I frequently grab a rod and head for the bay or for a nearby pond, lake, stream, or slough. I also go on foot to fish the surf, the jetties, the upper reaches of our coastal rivers, and the mountain streams.

For this kind of fishing I don't lug along the giant tackle box and twenty pounds or more of jigs and other lures that accompany me on a boat trip. When I'm on foot, I need something lighter and more portable, but nonetheless convenient and organized.

When I'm wading a trout or smallmouth-bass stream, I like to wear a fishing vest. For years, I've kept my flies in Perrine aluminum fly boxes that are distributed nationally by Orbex, Inc. Recently, I filled four such boxes with various bucktail and marabou jigs I use for trout, panfish, and smallmouth bass and now carry these in my fishing vest when I plan to be jigging instead of fly fishing. Orbex offers a large assortment of well-made

Perrine aluminum fly boxes are great for small jigs. *Top left* box has foam strips; *top right,* coil clips; *bottom left,* polly clips; *bottom right,* both point clips and individual compartments.

Flambeau's Adventurer Velure boxes are wormproof and come in a variety of styles and sizes.

boxes that feature several different styles of lure holders to keep jigs organized and tanglefree. You can pick boxes equipped with coil clips, point clips, polly clips, foam strips, or individual compartments.

For quick outings, when I don't anticipate a need for all the tackle I normally carry in my fishing vest, I usually just grab an ultralight rod and reel, stuff a fly box or two full of jigs into my parka pocket, and in minutes I'm off for an evening of fishing.

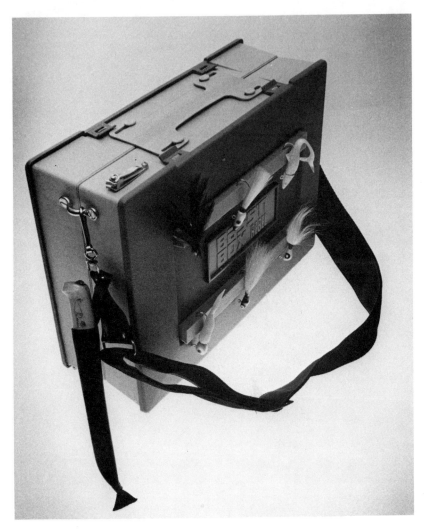

Luggage-style tackle box author converted for carrying over the shoulder.

For carrying small jig heads and soft-plastic tails when I'm traveling light, I like the wormproof Adventurer Velure boxes made by Flambeau Products Corporation. I have several small boxes with removable compartments that are ideal for jig heads and tails as well as a pocket-size worm box with individual compartments.

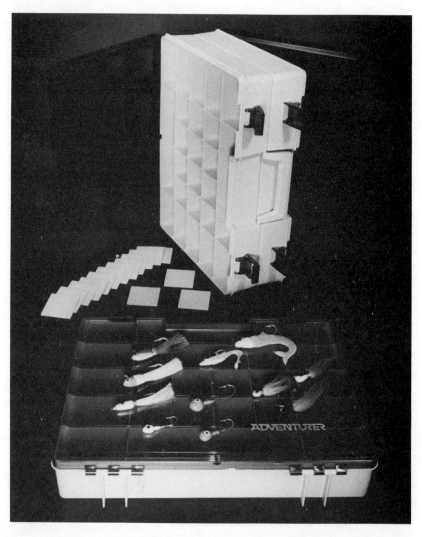

Flambeau Adventurer luggage-style boxes (single- or double-sided) are convenient, easily organized, and can also be converted for carrying over the shoulder.

For striper fishing on the bay and sloughs, for surf fishing, working the jetties, and fishing along the rocky coast, I carry heavier tackle and then need a more substantial tote. Over the years, I have tried a number of pouches, bags, creels, and boxes for carrying a large assortment of gear and found nothing that met my requirements for capacity, organization, and portability. Some totes were better than others, but every one fell short of my expectations in at least one area.

Last year, though, I solved my problem with a few simple modifications of a luggage-style tackle box that I've had for several years and never particularly cared for. The box, made by Rebel and called the Bass'n (sic) Box, is wormproof, roomy, and easily organized with removable partitions. But it was not as portable as I wanted it to be. I needed something I could carry by means of a shoulder strap. By installing two small eye straps on the box with machine bolts and nuts, I was able to snap on a wide-web camera strap, thus converting the box to a shoulder tote.

Similar luggage-style boxes (both double- and single-sided) are available from Plano Molding Co. and Flambeau Products. You'll find the adjustable camera straps at any photo-supply shop and most discount department stores. Look for a two-inch-wide strap that will distribute weight better than a narrower one will. Get one with foam backing to keep it from sliding off your shoulder, and make sure it is equipped with quick-release snaps.

You can further refine yours, as I did mine, by attaching a pair of nail clippers to the top of the box where they'll always be handy for cutting fishing line. I also put two strips of self-adhesive foam insulating tape on the outside lid of the box for hanging lures to dry. A small bait knife in a sheath can be hung from the carrying strap.

12. Freshwater Jig-Fishing Tactics

The United States—indeed, North America—is blessed with an overwhelming abundance of fresh water. There are cascading mountain streams and broad, slow-moving rivers. There are thousands of glacier-made lakes, millions of farm and ranch ponds, and thousands of reservoirs ranging in size from a few acres to several thousand acres. Many of these waters harbor at least one species of gamefish, but most hold several varieties and panfish as well. Some are home to a great array of fishes. And nearly all can be successfully fished with jigs.

Stream Fishing with Jigs

There are countless miles of moving water in the United States—streams of all sizes, from tiny mountain and meadow brooks that an angler can step across in spots to creeks, small rivers, and sprawling waterways that traverse the boundaries of several states. Although each has its own character, all share one common trait: movement. Streams are constantly on the move, and consequently are forever changing, sometimes subtly, sometimes drastically. Current is what makes each different from the other and what makes them all similar.

Current affects the fish that reside in these waters and it determines the tactics we use to catch them. Currents can attract and congregate dense schools of fish, or they can scatter the fish in all directions. Currents can create havens, carry food, and spur seasonal migrations. Currents can also scour stream beds, deposit silt, ruin spawning grounds, carry sewage, disperse industrial and agricultural wastes, and generally wreak havoc, killing fish for many miles along the stream's course.

Current is at once the angler's assistant and adversary. Knowing what currents do and how they normally affect the streams we fish is the basis for understanding stream fishing. To fish a stream successfully, you must know the currents and how to deal with them.

An angler can learn much from a small stream like this in only a season or two of fishing. The knowledge gained can then be applied to other streams and bigger waters.

Brooks, Creeks, and Small Rivers

No type of water appeals to me more than small streams. I do more lake and bay fishing than anything else now, but that's only because I live so near the lakes and bays.

Small streams have much in their favor. An angler can become intimate with a small stream and can come to know it well in only a season or two. And much of what he learns from one can be applied on other streams, even the larger ones.

I don't think there's any place better for learning how to fish than a small stream. I'm not talking about the tiny meadow brooks, although they can be great, too. And I'm not talking about creeks that are drastically affected by the seasons—that run high and roily and are laden with silt during spring runoff, then dry up into a series of potholes in the summer. I'm talking about the countless creeks and small rivers throughout the country that carry enough water to flow year around, but are easily waded. Such a stream will have occasional pools too deep to wade or cross, frequent riffles, perhaps moderate rapids in spots, and many ledges, boulders, cutbanks, gravel bars, fallen trees, and fish—plenty of fish.

These streams are abundant in many parts of the U.S. They are often highly productive, and most are underfished; some are virtually unfished for many miles of their courses. Depending on altitude and latitude, they can either be cold-water, cool-water, or warm-water streams. In turn, such a stream might harbor trout of one or several species, whitefish, or grayling, or it might be home to such species as pickerel, sauger, or smallmouth bass, or perhaps largemouth or spotted bass, crappie, white bass, and channel catfish. Sculpins, darters, shiners, or other forage species will be abundant in some stretches, and the waters will be rich with various insect larvae, nymphs, and crustacea. Some will experience seasonal migrations of prey or predator species, or both.

In central and northern latitudes and higher altitudes, the winter fishery will be spotty to nonexistent. In the south, fishing might be good all year long. Characteristically, early spring snowmelt or rains will make the streams high and muddy, but as the season progresses and waters begin to drop and clear, fishing will pick up. Mid-spring through summer will be the best times to fish in most parts of the country, with the low, clear waters of early autumn normally the most difficult to fish. Late summer and early fall hatches can trigger great feeding sprees on some of these streams, as can the first autumnal rains that freshen and color the waters and induce the resident fishes to take on their winter fat. Periods following mid-summer storms can provide the best fishing of all for some species.

On these streams, the light-tackle jig fisherman is in his element. With a fly box or two full of jigs and an ultralight spinning outfit, he can cover every likely spot and any depth during the entire fishing season.

Although some of these streams meander through urban and suburban areas, most are country creeks that wend their way through rural America. They're crossed and sometimes paralleled by county roads and state high-ways. Those that get any fishing pressure at all will usually be overfished at and near the access areas, parks, and parking spots, so these are places to avoid. Oddly enough, though, good fishing and untouched waters are often just around the first bend or no more than a few hundred yards from the high-use areas, so the best approach is to wade and walk the banks.

Your first trip or two to any such stream should be considered exploratory, and it should be preceded by the study of a good road map. Plan the length of stream you'll cover by the amount of time you have: two hours per stream mile should be a good starting gauge.

Of course, you will want to work your way upstream from your starting point. On many streams there will be relatively frequent access areas and bridge crossings, allowing you to start at one and finish at another upstream. Where the stream runs cross-country in a sparsely populated area with few roads, you might have to plan to fish your way upstream and hike back down the same way.

With a partner you can plan a full day of fishing in which you might cover as much as four or five miles of stream. By taking two vehicles and stationing one at the upstream access and parking the other at your put-in point, you won't have to face a long hike back to your vehicle at the day's end. Or you can do as my brother Phil has done and find a compatible fishing partner who's also a marathon runner. At the end of one of their trips, Phil relaxes on the bank of the stream while his partner Tom Rybus strips out of his waders, dons his running shoes, and runs back to get the vehicle.

In a season you should be able to learn different stretches of stream and be able to match them to the amount of time you have to spend. For example, you'll probably have one or several short stretches of a mile or two that are perfect for an evening of fishing, others that take all day to work adequately, and still others that are best for weekend trips and overnight camping. On your early trips, though, remember that stream miles and road miles often differ greatly. While roads are normally built in a relatively straight path, streams wind and turn and meander over the land. So two road-access points only a mile apart could have two miles or more of stream bed between them.

In cold-water streams and on others during the colder months, you'll need waders of some sort. Some streams might be deep enough to require chest waders, while on others you can get by with hip boots. During the warmer months on the cool-water and warm-water streams, though, you can wade wet, which is my favorite way to go. Don't ever try it barefoot, though, as there's always the possibility of suffering a serious cut or other injury some distance from where you parked. Wear sneakers to protect your feet and provide sure footing, and wear long pants instead of shorts or swimming trunks to ward off insect bites and sunburn.

The jigs you'll find most useful for small-stream fishing are those which

Wading is an excellent way to reach the most productive waters of a small stream. (*Photo by Pat Oberrecht.*)

imitate forage fishes, hellgrammites, crawfish, and various insects and larvae. Those of ⅛ ounce and smaller will probably serve you best, although you might need a few of ¼ ounce to work stronger currents and deeper waters. Carry a good variety of bucktail and marabou jigs as well as plain heads that can be used with small grubs, twist-tails, and pieces of plastic worms. The ⅛-ounce Wig-Wag Minno is a favorite of mine for small-stream fishing, particularly for smallmouth bass.

It won't take many trips to learn the most productive spots on your stream and the best jigs for working those areas. During your exploratory trips, the first thing to remember is to go slowly and study any stretch of stream from a distance before approaching it. Find out what types of forage fish are present, and turn over rocks from time to time to see what scurries from beneath them. And be sure to check the stomach contents of any fish you keep for the frying pan to determine what makes up their natural diets.

Stream curves are often productive spots. Sometimes they gouge out undercut banks along the outside edge of the curve, and these are often havens for fish. Be especially watchful for tree-lined banks where the stream has eroded earth away from the root structure of the trees. If there is a riffle upstream of the undercut bank or a good current running toward the bank, as there usually is on the outside of a curve, cast your jig upstream and let the current wash it into the pool beneath the bank. Such areas are often large enough to warrant several casts. Make sure that your jig is heavy enough to bounce bottom, but not so heavy as to plow the stream bed.

Always be alert for midstream boulders. Where there is a good current, fish will hold in the slower water created by the boulder. Most anglers know to fish the deep pool below the boulder, but many fail to fish above it where another pool is created as the current divides to travel around each side of the boulder.

Although fish will move into fast-moving water for brief periods to feed, they don't hold in such water. They prefer the gentler currents along the edges of stronger, food-bearing currents. Most anglers know this and normally avoid the fast water. But, there is fast water and there is fast water. Where a stream narrows and is funneled into a chute of fast water, whether or not these narrows will contain fish is largely a matter of bottom structure. If the bottom is smooth rock, clay, or hardpan, the narrows will probably contain neither gamefish nor forage species. If the

Waterfalls are often barriers to upstream migration, and the pools beneath them will seasonally abound in forage and game species. Such pools also are midsummer havens for resident gamefish that often gather in dense schools in the oxygen-rich waters.

bottom is gravel and small stones, there will probably be some forage species present as well as other food, and gamefish will enter these waters from time to time. Then it's probably worth trying a cast or two through the chute. If there are large rocks and boulders in the chute, chances are it will hold fish since the water won't really be moving as fast as it appears. Surface velocity will be much greater than the deeper currents that are broken up by the rocky bottom.

In broader stretches of fast water, the same criteria may be used for evaluating the probable presence of fish. If the water is only shallow riffles, it will not normally produce fish but might be worth trying early in the morning, in the evening, and at night. If the water is knee-deep or deeper and the bottom is rocky, work it over thoroughly. Midstream boulders will be the best holding areas and should be worked as described earlier. Submerged boulders will appear as bulges in the surface current, usually with the water breaking on the downstream side. Approach such a boulder from the side, with the first cast quartering upstream. Allow the jig to drift down to the front of the boulder and around one side. To work the pool beneath the submerged boulder, cast upstream and let your jig drift on a taut line with your rod held high. As the jig washes over the top of the boulder, quickly lower your rod, thus slackening your line and allowing the jig to drop into the pocket of calm water beneath the boulder.

Fallen trees and log jams are other good targets. Downed timber will often divert currents, creating eddies and backwashes and causing pools to be dug out of the stream bed beneath the tree. Floating trees, branches, and other debris often accumulate at stream bends and will channel the stream into deep pools.

Rock ledges along stream banks often provide broken structure that not only slows the current but also offers protection and shade to fish. Work these areas carefully at all depths, as there might be breaks along the ledges from just beneath the surface through the mid-depths to the bottom, any one of which might hold fish.

Rock ledges across a stream create tumbling water that churns out bottom sand and gravel, usually creating a deep pool. Such pools are almost always good bets, but are particularly productive during warmer months when the depths are cool and shaded, and the tumbling water is well oxygenated. Cast your jig above the ledge and let the water tumble it into the pool. Lower your rod to slacken the line just as the jig falls over the ledge; it will sink to the depths rapidly then. If the pool is a large one, work it thoroughly and carefully.

Stay alert for springs and the evidence of spring holes. Often clay or rock ledges running parallel to the stream will spout springs that feed cold waters into the stream. Look for trickling water along such ledges. Where there are no ledges, unusually dense vegetation generally means there's a spring nearby. Submerged spring holes foster the growth of lush water vegetation. Although such areas will usually hold fish year-round, they are gathering spots for gamefish during the warmer months. Never pass one by, and always work it over thoroughly. If the water is exceptionally clear, as is often the case in late summer, keep your profile low and work the pool from a distance with long casts.

Portions of small streams will physically change from year to year, especially those areas where the bottom is loose gravel or sand. New pools will be created where there were none before. And some pools will be turned into shallow riffles. In spots, currents will eventually erode new channels. Banks will cave in. Landslides will create natural dams, and beavers will build ponds. But, by and large, most of the stream and its overall character will go unchanged from year to year. The stable pools, boulders, waterfalls, rapids, and springs will be there for you to enjoy on every trip. And many of these spots will produce fish year after year.

By working such a stream for a season or two, wading its waters, observing and feeling the effects of currents, and learning to distinguish among the various types of current and cover, you'll not only gain a good bit of stream savvy that can be applied elsewhere, but you'll catch fish while you're getting smart. And the smarter you get, the more fish you'll catch.

With the possible exception of the southwestern United States and a few arid and semiarid areas elsewhere, small streams are within easy reach of most anglers. Surprisingly, though, they get much less pressure than they can tolerate, which is certainly not the case with many waters we're accustomed to fishing these days.

It is actually possible to live in a densely populated and highly industrialized area that's within a few miles of several small streams that are seldom fished. And when you do encounter another person on one of these streams, he'll probably turn out to be a serious angler with a love for solitude and an appreciation of what small-stream fishing has to offer. He will likely be a chap worth meeting and talking to.

Big Rivers

Although big rivers share common traits with the smaller rivers, creeks, and brooks, it's difficult to characterize them generally, because they differ broadly from one another. Moreover, the hand of man has altered most of them in some way. In the days of the pioneers, the big rivers were much more like the smaller streams, only greater in size, depth, and water volume. But most have now been dammed at least once, broadened, narrowed, channelized, levied, diverted, and in other ways changed by man and machine.

To be sure, some of our great rivers have been raped and pillaged and in other ways all but destroyed by man in the name of progress. But all the changes we've wrought aren't entirely bad, and some have even had beneficial side effects. On the whole, the rivers were a lot better off before our ancestors started tampering with them, but that is all "water over the dam." There's not much we can do about the structural changes made to our major rivers and many of their larger tributaries, except to take advantage of any positive effects.

It's difficult to come up with a good definition of a big river. Of course, the Mississippi is our largest, stretching some 2,348 miles from Minnesota's Lake Itasca to the Gulf of Mexico. Annually discharging 133 cubic miles of water into the Gulf, the Mississippi drains an area of nearly 1¼ million square miles, or 40 percent of the total area of the contiguous states. That's a big river. But so are the Mississippi's major tributaries (the 2,315-mile-long Missouri and the 981-mile-long Ohio rivers) and some of the tributaries of these rivers as well as tributaries of tributaries. In the United States there are more than 140 rivers that are 100 miles long or longer. Of these, more than half are greater than 300 miles in length. Additionally, there are plenty of streams shorter than 100 miles that qualify as big rivers. In short, there's at least one big river within reach of every United States angler.

While these rivers differ greatly from one another in many respects, they do share some similarities. Most are small streams at their headwaters, some no larger than tiny creeks and brooks. As they traverse their courses and are fed by their tributaries, they gain volume and usually increase in width or depth, or both, while decreasing in gradient and current velocity. Some rise in northern latitudes and flow southerly, or originate at high or moderately high altitudes and flow into lowlands, and consequently hold cold-water fishes in their upper reaches and warm-water species downstream. Some are silt-laden; others are clear; most are influenced by seasonal fluctuations.

An angler could spend a lifetime learning only a relatively small part of a big river, but in most cases that's all he would need to know. A productive stretch of river will give up fish year after year. Moreover, fish populations in most rivers are in a constant state of change, due mainly to seasonal temperature fluctuations and spawning migrations of both predator and prey species.

Unlike the smaller rivers, creeks, and brooks, big rivers aren't easy to get to know, but the patient angler who is willing to work at it has the chance of being rewarded with great catches and large fish. And one of the best ways to probe the pockets and pools of big rivers is with jigs.

Some stretches of big rivers are wadable; others are not. Wading can help you reach productive waters, but you must be particularly careful when wading any large river, especially in roiled waters. Check your footing on every step and go slowly. Get into the habit of carrying a wading staff.

Of course, bank anglers take plenty of fish from rivers, but there's no better way to get to fish than by boat, and few pleasures exceed those associated with river float trips. The type of boat to use for floating rivers depends largely on the kind of water the angler is likely to encounter. To be sure, just about every kind of craft imaginable has been used to fish the rivers; but on most of our large rivers, canoes and jonboats seem to be the most popular. I have used both for a number of years and have found that my preference for one over another depends mainly on the type of water I'll be running. Both types of craft have shallow drafts—a necessity for floating all but the deepest rivers—but I have found canoes a bit more maneuverable and better suited to running moderately fast water. The jonboat, on the other hand, is a more stable and comfortable fishing platform in the slower waters its suited to.

Of course, there are waters where neither type of craft is adequate. In the fast, whitewater rivers of the west, the McKenzie drift boat or a whitewater inflatable boat is a much better choice. For running heavy water under power, jet sleds are the answer. But the waters where such craft are necessary are best traveled by experienced boatsmen. Personally, I prefer to hire a guide on these waters and put navigation in more capable hands than mine.

As with walking and wading a small stream, floating a river will get you off the proverbial beaten path and into some underfished if not unfished waters. But, again, you'll have to carefully plan any float trip on unfamiliar waters. As with wading, it helps to have a partner and to take two vehicles so you can station one at your take-out point and drive the other back to your launch area. Remember, too, that road miles and river miles are often different, sometimes drastically so.

I recall that several years ago, when I was living in Alaska, two fishermen were reported overdue one evening when they failed to return home as expected, having set out that afternoon for a casual five-mile float down a local river. The weather had turned nasty, and it was feared that the anglers might have met with tragedy.

The next day the two showed up, hungry and tired, but none the worse for wear. It seems they had slowly fished the first three or four miles of river and then, as evening approached, had gotten down to some serious

Many anglers find canoes ideal for float trips on North American rivers. But don't make the mistake of covering too much water; better to beach or anchor your canoe frequently to fish the promising pools, such as this one on Canada's Missinaidi River. (*Photo by Roger Losier, courtesy Blue Hole Canoe Co.*)

paddling to reach their take-out point. When they had traveled well over the five miles and were facing inclement weather, they decided to over-night on the river bank and head out again the following day. It took them most of the next morning to reach their other vehicle.

This was the first time either angler had floated the river. While they launched their boat only five road miles upstream of their take-out point and second vehicle, they had to cover considerably more territory along the winding course of the river. When they later took time to check a map of the river, they discovered that they had floated 21 miles, point to point.

The moral, of course, is to plan your float trips carefully and study maps *before you set out*. Even then, many anglers bite off too big a chunk of river the first time out. For a day-long float on a productive stretch of river, plan to cover no more than five miles. You'll find some stretches of only a couple of miles that take all day to work adequately.

Most anglers, even seasoned riverboaters, cover much more water on float trips, but to my way of thinking, floating long stretches amounts, at best, to hit-and-miss fishing. It takes time to work promising pools and pockets; if there's any speed at all to the water, a boat will move through and past such areas much too quickly. The way to do it right is to proceed slowly and, if necessary, anchor the boat or beach it and work an area by wading or casting from shore.

My way of floating a river is to cover one relatively short stretch by drifting or paddling quickly through unattractive water and slowing down or stopping for any that looks like a potential fish-holding spot. When I'm underway in the unproductive waters, I don't bother casting; rather, I focus my attention on boat-handling chores and keep watch ahead for any signs that indicate fishy waters. Whenever it's possible to do so, I beach the boat above any spot I want to try; then I walk the bank downstream and wade up on the spot to work it efficiently from a down-stream position.

If you decide to try a floating/wading trip, don't fall into the habit of wearing waders or hip boots while afloat or underway as so many foolish anglers do. There's no greater potential hazard than falling overboard or capsizing while wearing waders that will quickly fill with water and take you down. It doesn't take much time to slip into or out of waders whenever necessary.

Actually, you'll only need waders if you make float trips during the colder months or on cold-water streams. On cool-water or warm-water streams, from late spring through early autumn, you can wade wet. Wear sneakers for sure footing and protection and long pants to protect you from insect bites and sunburn. You'll find that your clothes will dry quickly between wading sessions on a warm day, and the wading itself can be quite refreshing.

On big rivers, be alert for all the likely fish-holding areas you might find on the smaller streams: midstream boulders, undercut banks, log jams, fallen trees, dropoffs at the edges of sand or gravel bars, springs, and spring holes.

When you're on unfamiliar water, it pays to approach all curves in the river with caution. For two reasons you should beach your boat and check out every sharp (blind) curve on foot. First, if you can't see around the bend, you have no way of knowing what kind of water you're approaching. If there are hazards ahead, the time to find out is not when you're midway around the bend in a fast-moving boat. Secondly, good fish-holding waters are often near the bends in a stream, and you certainly don't want to blunder blindly onto them.

Feeder streams are always good bets, too, and when you come onto one, you would do well to beach the boat and fish it thoroughly. The mouth of the tributary will often hold fish. If the feeder stream rushes into the slower waters of the main stream, gamefish will usually hold near the edges of the converging currents, waiting for food to be washed down from the tributary, particularly after a storm has muddied the feeder stream.

The tributary itself might be worth fishing, especially in the summer months if the temperature of the feeder stream is lower than that of the main stream. In the spring and fall, spawning migrations mean concentrations of gamefish that often are easy pickings. But forage fish migrations are equally important, as the game species will lie in ambush for the migrating forage fish and will feed in a frenzy, particularly at the mouth of the feeder stream.

On most big rivers, you'll find that casting to cover will be the most productive way to fish jigs. Drifting jigs in a current will also take fish. In deep stretches, vertical jigging with heavy jigs is often the only way for an angler to reach the fish.

As you will encounter greatly varied water conditions on most big rivers, you should go equipped with a suitable array of tackle to fit the situations. That's one reason a boat is so handy for big-river fishing: you can tote along several rods and reels and plenty of jigs.

You'll want jigs that imitate forage fish: bucktail and marabou jigs, jig heads and twist-tails, and swimming-tail jigs such as the Burke Wig-Wag Minno and Mann's Jelly Shad. These are good choices for prospecting, but they're ideal in any spot where gamefish are feeding on or chasing minnows. Watch for schools of gamefish or individuals working on schools of baitfish. Cast your jig to the edge of the baitfish school upstream of the feeding fish in such a way as to intercept the predator's path.

In early morning and late evening, gamefish often move into shallow water no more than two or three feet deep to feed. Feeding fish will drive forage fish to the surface where the smaller fish will jump and dart, attempting to escape. When you come onto such a situation, you would do best to keep your jig moving and off the bottom. Snap a casting bubble onto your line, a foot or two above the jig (depending on the depth of the water) and cast well upstream of the jumping baitfish. Allow the rig to drift down the current to the feeding fish, and watch your casting bubble closely for any quick change of direction or halting. As your jig will be drifting above bottom, any change in the movement of the casting bubble will probably be a strike; set the hook at once. When such feeding activity is apparent in slower-moving waters, a popper/dropper rig can be most productive.

Jig heads and plastic grub tails are also great river lures. The large jig/grub rigs are excellent for working deep, slow-moving pools for bass and large catfishes, mainly channel and blue. They're also tops for working the mouths of feeder streams after a storm, where they will take a variety of predator species.

The small grub rigs ($^1/_{16}$-ounce or smaller jig head with a half-inch piece of plastic worm attached) work well in any waters where trout or panfish are holding. They're particularly effective wherever schooling fish are feeding on nymphs or insects. In clear, relatively shallow water, try drifting a small grub rig a foot or two behind a casting bubble.

Don't overlook jig-'n'-pig rigs for river fishing. Among the best producers are black pork-rind eels, pork-rind leeches, and pork frogs. Short eels and leeches are great for drift fishing. Pick a jig head that will get the rind to the bottom but will still allow it to drift with the current. Pork frogs can be worked the same way, but I prefer to use these on a Dynel or living-rubber jig along the edges of gravel bars and rocky ledges, with a retrieve that portrays the rig as a skittering crawfish. Black, orange, and brown are good colors for such purposes.

Tailwaters

There are few streams in this country that haven't had at least one small dam built across them; many have been dammed in several spots, and some have been nearly dammed to death. Some dams have killed off migratory fish runs; others have destroyed spawning habitat; still others have eliminated certain species in some rivers.

Dams are among those structural changes I mentioned earlier that we can do nothing about—except to take advantage of any positive side effects. What many dams have done for the angler is to create extraordinary fisheries in the tailraces. Additionally, much research has gone into the management of tailraces for sport fishing, and many such waters have been stocked with fish that were unable to survive in those same rivers before the dams were built.

Some formerly warm-water rivers now provide trophy trout fishing in the cold discharge waters beneath dams. On other streams, where fishing was spotty at best during the cold of winter and the heat of summer, excellent angling is available all year in the productive tailwaters of dams.

Man has been damming streams for a lot of years and for a variety of reasons. Early dams were most often built to use the power of the stream's current to turn water wheels at grist mills. Similarly, modern hydroelectric dams use stream currents to turn giant hydroturbines and create electricity. Dams are also built for purposes of navigation, irrigation, recreation, flood control, and to create reservoirs for municipal water supplies.

Most large hydroelectric dams impound many miles of stream, creating deep-water reservoirs that stratify during the summer months. Since most of these dams discharge water from the cold depths of the reservoirs, the tailraces beneath the dams and the river for some miles downstream will be cold, even during summer months in southerly latitudes. Fisheries biologists have found that the best way to manage these cold tailwaters is to stock them heavily with trout fingerlings, mainly rainbow and brown. Since the trout are thermally restricted to those waters downstream of the dam that are cold enough to support them and have no way to reach spawning grounds, the tailwaters must be restocked periodically.

This is not unlike the put-and-take fishery that exists in so many of our streams these days. Even our cold-water streams that once supported good populations of wild fish now must be stocked and replenished with hatchery fish to satisfy the demands of increasing numbers of anglers. Where tailwaters fisheries differ mostly is in the phenomenal growth rate of trout. Fingerlings, there, grow as much as an inch a month so that a fish in its second year will normally be 15 to 18 inches long, with 20-inchers not uncommon.

It doesn't take many years after the completion of a dam and the stocking of the tailwaters for trophy trout of five to eight pounds or larger to be taken with some regularity. And jigs are the ideal lures for these big trout.

Unlike the typical trout stream, where insect hatches are frequent and fly fishing is a favored method of angling, the broad, often deep, and usually turbulent tailwaters are not conducive to the kinds of hatches that occur on most trout streams. Moreover, tailwaters are often brimming with schools of forage fish. So the big trout are mainly minnow eaters, and the jigs that resemble forage fishes are best: leadheads dressed with bucktail, marabou, feathers, and synthetic materials, and soft-plastic twisttails impaled on jig heads, as well as small diamond jigs.

The tailwaters beneath many dams throughout the country harbor a variety of fish species and often provide year-round angling. Here, the author's brother Phil perches atop a wing dike while probing the tailwaters beneath a hydroelectric dam on Idaho's Snake River.

More than 200 large dams in the U.S.—built for flood control, navigation, or power production—do not discharge cold water. Consequently,
the tailwaters there are warm during the summer months and warm-water
species predominate. In many of these tailwaters, seasonal migrations of
gamefish have produced year-round angling and the opportunities to take
a greater variety and abundance of gamefish than in any other type of
freshwater habitat.

The Ohio River and a number of its tributaries provide a good case in
point. The Ohio River, once ravaged by industrial and municipal pollution, has been cleaned up considerably in recent years and once again
harbors good populations of gamefish and forage species. The tailwaters
beneath the dams on the Ohio provide some outstanding fishing, but so
do the numerous creeks and rivers that feed the Ohio and the tailwaters
beneath tributary dams. Kentucky Dam on the Tennessee River, for
example, provides exceptional angling all year long.

In late fall and early winter, sauger migrate up the Tennessee from the
Ohio by the tens of thousands and hold in the tailwaters beneath Kentucky Dam. Small white or yellow bucktails are dynamite lures for the
sauger, and often a jig tipped with a piece of nightcrawler or minnow will
outperform all other lures and baits.

About the time the sauger run begins to taper off, white bass pour into the Tennessee and huge schools fill the tailwaters beneath Kentucky
Dam. The same jigs used on the sauger will take plenty of white bass,
as will small jig heads dressed with two-inch or three-inch soft-plastic
twist-tails.

Crappie follow the white bass, and a switch to tiny marabou jigs and
⅛-ounce and smaller heads dressed with two-inch twist-tails is in order.
A top producer of crappie, white bass, and sauger is the ⅛-ounce Wig-
Wag Minno in pearl white.

Late spring, summer, and early fall on most of these warm tailwaters is
characterized by consistent action from black bass, channel catfish, and
blue catfish and varying success with the aforementioned species. Some
tailwaters produce largemouth or spotted bass, while others provide some
of the best smallmouth-bass fishing to be had anywhere. And no lure can
match the jig for consistently taking full stringers of these species.

The fish too often overlooked by the angler who uses artificial lures is
the catfish, most notably the channel, blue, and flathead. These are
efficient predators, quite willing and able to take jigs with regularity.
In the warm-water tailraces, these fish grow to huge sizes, gorging

themselves on the abundant forage fishes as well as on the pieces of fish and other animals that get caught in hydroturbines where they are slashed to ribbons.

Flathead catfish prefer live food and for that reason jigs that imitate forage fish are top producers. Also, jig heads and nightcrawlers worked vertically in deep holes will take flathead.

Channel and blue catfishes are more opportunistic in their feeding habits and will take live fish as well as the bits and pieces of fish spewed forth by the churning hydroturbines. Jigs dressed with strip baits are excellent lures for these fish.

The tailwaters beneath large dams, particularly the hydroelectric dams, can be treacherous, so the angler unfamiliar with them would do well to seek local advice and perhaps hire a guide the first time out. For the wading or boating fisherman and, to some extent, even for the bank-bound angler, these waters can be dangerous. It's imperative to know the discharge schedules and to be well out of the way when the turbines are fired up. Generally, the early morning hours and weekends are the safest times, as turbines will either be shut down then or discharge will be minimal.

The low discharge periods are normally the best times to fish anyway, because the high and turbulent waters that are associated with heavy discharge tend to scatter the fish and will often put them down. The large catfishes are notable exceptions in most tailwaters, however, as they have become accustomed to feeding on the scraps churned out by the turbines and will be quite active when the turbines are running.

Even the small dams found on so many of our streams that do not markedly alter water temperatures in the tailraces will still attract fish. Even the lowest ones impede upstream migration and will at least delay migrating fish, causing them to school up beneath the dams where they are relatively easy targets for the angler. Furthermore, the waters rushing over these dams are very highly oxygenated and often carry food in the surface film that becomes abundant in the tailraces and pools beneath the dams.

In short, the jig fisherman who seeks out tailwaters in his part of the country is almost sure to find an abundance of fish, probably year-round angling opportunities, and trophy-size fish—in other words, just dam-good fishing.

Still-Water Fishing with Jigs

Among the millions of bodies of fresh water in the United States are those made by nature and those built by man. They range in size from tiny beaver ponds, farm ponds, and glacial potholes to sprawling impoundments and ultimately to our inland freshwater seas, the Great Lakes. Their depths run from only a few feet to more than a third of a mile. Most harbor gamefish of some sort, and many are highly productive waters that are home to several varieties of our most popular sport species as well as panfish and forage species.

These waters are classified in many different ways. They can be coldwater, cool-water, or warm-water ponds, lakes, or reservoirs. Biologically, they might be fertile or relatively infertile. Geologically, they can be considered old, middle-aged, or new lakes; but keep in mind that a new lake in geological terms can be several thousand years young.

No matter the type, origin, temperature, or age, if the water holds gamefish, you can catch them with jigs.

Ponds and Small Lakes

Take a midday flight across the country in clear weather, as I have done a number of times, and the abundance of sprawling impoundments and large lakes will surely fascinate you and excite your angling instincts. But even more impressive to me are all the sparkling farm and ranch ponds and tiny lakes that seem ubiquitous in most regions of the United States.

Since 1936, no fewer than three million ponds have been built on farms and ranches in America. Combined, they amount to more than three million surface acres of fresh water, capable of supporting about 150 million pounds of fish, or even more if the ponds are managed for optimum yield.

Although there are perhaps ten million or more anglers who fish farm ponds with some regularity, most ponds are underfished; indeed, some go entirely unfished. Not only could most ponds stand more fishing pressure than they get, but they need it to keep the fish populations healthy and thriving.

Add to these, all the small natural lakes of less than ten acres (about 700 in my own state of Oregon, alone) as well as small municipal reservoirs, park ponds, beaver ponds, and the like, and a picture of abundant and relatively untapped waters should begin to unfold before you.

Cold-water ponds are usually stocked with trout, and although the trout will thrive and often grow to good sizes in these waters, they won't normally spawn. So these ponds must be restocked periodically. Many small natural lakes, however, do have good spawning habitat and trout populations there will be self-sustaining.

Warm-water ponds are normally stocked with largemouth bass and panfish, and in most ponds these species will successfully reproduce. Although many combinations of bass and panfish have been tried with varying degrees of success, the best combination is bass and bluegill. Other panfish species tend to overpopulate too rapidly, causing severe competition for food and eventual stunting. Even bluegills will eventually overpopulate in the confines of a small pond if they are not thinned out regularly and substantially.

A number of warm-water ponds have been stocked with catfish. When managed properly, such waters can provide excellent growth rates and superb angling. Channel catfish are the preferred species, but they will not spawn in a small pond and must be restocked to sustain a favorable yield. Bullheads are prolific and hardy fish that will quickly overpopulate and take over a pond. Moreover, in northern latitudes in shallow ponds that freeze from top to bottom, bullheads are able to survive by burrowing into the mud and hibernating. Consequently, they are not a good choice for stocking small ponds.

Most ponds and many small municipal reservoirs are shallow bodies of water, seldom exceeding ten to twelve feet in depth. The deepest spots in any such body of water will be immediately above the dam and along the creek channel, if a creek was dammed to form the pond. Usually the upper reaches will be extremely shallow, sometimes a foot or less in depth, and often marshy.

Usually, these waters will have some weed growth and in some the vegetation will be dense, particularly during summer months. Weedbeds, lily pads, and shoreline reeds and rushes are the only available cover in some ponds and small lakes. This vegetation not only affords protection to fish fry, but it usually harbors abundant food in the form of water insects, insect larvae, crustacea, and amphibians. The fry, themselves, are forage for predator species. In warm weather, the vegetation also provides shade and perhaps the coolest waters in the pond.

For taking bluegills from small ponds, you can't beat $1/16$-ounce or smaller jigs dressed with white or black plastic grubs.

Since ponds and most small lakes and reservoirs are normally shallower than larger lakes and impoundments in most parts of the country, excluding high mountain areas, these are the first waters to begin warming in the spring. Often, they will provide good fishing weeks before larger waters start showing normal spring activity.

In all but the southernmost ponds, all or most of the weed growth in the ponds will have died off during the cold winter months and new vegetation will begin emerging as the first rays of the spring sun penetrate pond waters. Fish then will be dispersed in the ponds and competition for available food will be keen.

In the cold-water trout ponds and lakes, use ultralight tackle and small crappie jigs as well as leadheads with two-inch twist-tails. Another good choice is a $1/16$-ounce or smaller jig head with a half-inch piece of plastic worm impaled on the hook.

In warm-water ponds, the same jigs used for trout are good bluegill producers. For pond bass in the early spring, I like to work the shallows with a jig head and three-inch twist-tail. If that doesn't produce results or if the fish move off the shallows in midday, I normally switch to a worming jig head and a six-inch plastic worm that I work very slowly over the bottom.

Later in the season, when vegetation is abundant, I look for open areas near weedbeds and work my jigs there. I also look for shoreline willows and overhanging tree branches that offer shade. Submerged tree stumps, flooded brush and timber, and fallen trees are other holding areas that will produce fish during the summer months.

Most ponds and small lakes can be fished from shore with no problem. Many have mud bottoms that make wading difficult, and some have steep banks or dense shoreline vegetation that make fishing them difficult. A canoe or small rowboat is handy for fishing such ponds, but my favorite way, and perhaps the best way, to fish these waters is with a float tube.

My brother Phil introduced me to float-tube fishing several years ago, and I was sold on it my first time out. Phil hails from Boise, Idaho—an area that boasts the largest belly-boat navy in the world. On a late-spring fishing trip to my part of the country, he brought along an extra float tube, swim fins, and the Seal-Dry waders he recommends for float-tubing.

The morning after his arrival on the coast, strong winds and heavy seas kept us from crossing the bar and heading out for a day of offshore fishing aboard a friend's boat. As we were planning to jig-fish from my boat on one of the coastal lakes that afternoon and evening, Phil suggested we try the float tubes on one of the tiny municipal reservoirs nearby.

Our mild winter and warm spring had fostered excessive weed growth in the reservoir, and I was worried about navigating in the dense foliage. Wading would certainly have been impossible in such waters, and even a canoe would have been hard to handle in spots. But with the float tubes we were able to go anywhere we pleased. We sought out open pockets of water between vast and dense weedbeds. We cast to the edges of lily pads and tossed our lures amidst the flooded timber, submerged brush, tree stumps, and the like. And in a single morning, from one small reservoir, we caught trout, bluegill, perch and largemouth bass—one of which went three pounds.

I'm sold on the belly boats now, and if you have ponds or small reservoirs that are difficult to fish from shore, you would do well to consider the purchase of a float tube. With your favorite rod and reel and a small box or two of jigs, you can slowly, silently, and almost effortlessly float your way to all the best fishing spots.

Quarries and Pits

Another type of fresh water that is often overlooked by anglers is the lake that results from open-pit mining. So-called gravel pits and stone quarries are usually deep and clear, and most hold fish. Strip-mine pits are usually too high in acid content to support fish life, but most are reclaimed now (after they've been mined out) and are treated to neutralize the waters, then stocked with fish.

Borrow pits that are relatively abundant in many parts of the country, near or alongside interstate highways, are usually fairly shallow. Highway crews use backhoes and tractor-dozers to dig fill material from roadside areas during highway construction, leaving these pondlike pits behind. Most have been stocked with fish and are available to public angling if on state lands, or fishing by permission if privately owned. In character they're much like ponds and should be fished the same way.

The larger quarries and pits, however, are in a class by themselves as bodies of fresh water go. Their sides are usually steep, and water vegetation is sparse, at least in the younger pits. Even when mining companies have reclaimed the pits and have sloped the banks for easy access, the bottoms drop off sharply only a few feet from shore. Then they descend in a series of broad ledges (at one time these were haul or access roads, or railroad beds) all the way to the bottom, which might be at a depth of 100 feet or more.

Pits dug with big draglines will usually be from 45 to 75 feet deep. If dredges were then used to mine the aggregate, the pits will probably run to depths of about 125 feet.

Since the relatively infertile waters of quarries and pits contain few oxygen-consuming organisms, there is often sufficient oxygen in deep water to support fish life. For that reason, many of these deep pits can be stocked with trout and walleye, even in parts of the country where most ponds and lakes hold only warm-water species. Most, however, are stocked with black bass and panfish.

Because of clear waters and steep sides, pits can be difficult to fish. But with some experimentation and a knowledge of the makeup of any given pit, the jig fisherman can take fish regularly; often the fish he pulls from pits will be big and healthy scrappers, well worth the effort.

I grew up in southern Ohio and started fishing gravel pits as a youngster. Later, when I lived in Florida, my favorite bass spot was an old quarry that had more bass per acre than any body of water I had ever fished or have since. When I returned to Ohio to work and attend college, my first job was with a large aggregate company that had five pits where I fished, gigged frogs, and hunted ducks and geese.

Over the years, I've learned a thing or two about pit fishing. Perhaps most important is the necessity for the angler to maintain a low profile and to go quietly and cautiously when fishing a pit. These clear waters are tough to fish, and fish are usually quite spooky. Early morning and late evening are good times to work the shoreline where gamefish will cruise to feed on forage fish, frogs, and insects; but night fishing is best.

During the day, fish will head for the comfort and protection of deep water, and then you must prospect for them along the submerged ledges. There's no better way I know of to find these fish than by bouncing jigs down the faces of the ledges until the fish are found.

There's no better lure for working the shoreline waters of a pit or quarry than the jig-and-pork-frog combination. As these waters are usually fairly open and free of snags, normally you need not use a weedless jig, except for one very effective technique. If you work from a boat, use a weedless jig and pork frog and cast the combination right up on the edge of the shoreline. Coax it gently into the water, and swim it toward deeper water with a twitching rod action.

Be sure to take advantage of any likely shoreline cover or structure. Gravelly points that protrude from shore into the clear waters and drop

Pit bass are lean, mean, and usually hungry. This one nailed a black Wig-Wag Minno on the fall.

off sharply on each side are good spots to try. Any shoreline vegetation that extends into the water should be equally productive early or late in the day.

For working the deep water during the middle of the day, I like to use a worming jig head and a six-inch plastic worm. Black or translucent purple are good colors to try.

Other productive jigs and jig combinations include jig heads and three-inch or four-inch twist-tails worked along shore and occasionally allowed to sink into deeper water. Jigs that imitate forage fish (bucktails, mar-abous, and Wig-Wag Minnos) are also good along shore and worked along ledges as well. For deep-water jigging in the pits and quarries, the jig-'n'-eel is a consistent producer, especially in the late fall and early winter.

I want to be clear, to the point, and adamant about this: *do not wade the pits.* Even the gently sloping banks of many reclaimed pits and quarries drop off sharply into deep water, and wading such areas is dangerous. Either work from shore or from a boat. Wherever there's a good spot for launching, I prefer to use a boat since I can make a stealthier approach when afloat. And certainly, if there is shoreline where a boat can be launched, you could opt for a float tube instead, which is a dandy craft for carefully and quietly working the clear waters of pits and quarries.

Large Lakes and Reservoirs

In the United States there are more than 70,000 natural lakes larger than 10 surface acres in size. Most contain fish and are used by perhaps as many as 40 million anglers.

These lakes have been formed naturally in a variety of ways. Most were created by glacial action some 10,000 years ago. Others were born from landslides that filled river gorges and canyons, creating natural dams. Volcanoes, earthquakes, and erosion have also been responsible for the formation of numerous natural lakes. When rivers and creeks have carved out new channels, oxbow lakes have often been left where the old channels were. Other lakes, particularly in Florida, have been formed by sink holes, when the earth merely fell away after years of erosion by underground rivers. Some lakes are fed by snowmelt and rainfall—others by rivers, creeks, and springs.

Our large reservoirs are, of course, man-made. In the building of a

Bing McClellan with a 5.2-pound smallmouth bass, taken on ⅛-ounce pearl Wig-Wag Minno from Michigan's Cedar Lake. (*Photo courtesy Burke Fishing Lures.*)

reservoir, usually a river or large creek (sometimes more than one) is dammed and water is impounded behind the dam. Earthen, rock-fill, or concrete dams are used and vary greatly in size and design, depending upon the size of the stream being impounded and the size and purpose of the reservoir planned.

In 1900 there were approximately 100 large reservoirs in the U.S. Since that time more than 1,200 have been made, and others are currently in various stages of completion. These reservoirs comprise well over 12 million surface acres of water and it is estimated that approximately 25 percent of all freshwater angling takes place on reservoirs.

More than fifty species of fish are known to exist in large reservoirs throughout America; but in the warm-water reservoirs, the most often stocked and readily found species include crappie, bluegill, yellow perch, white bass, largemouth bass, and channel catfish. Some also contain blue catfish, flathead catfish, and striped bass. The cold-water reservoirs are most often stocked with rainbow trout or brown trout; but lake trout, cutthroat trout, brook trout, kokanee salmon, and whitefish can be found in some. Other popular reservoir species include smallmouth bass, spotted bass, walleye, sauger, northern pike, and muskellunge.

In addition to the gamefish and panfish present, most large lakes and reservoirs hold several species of forage fishes, such as smelt, minnows of several varieties, or shad. In recent years, threadfin shad have been introduced into many impoundments. These prolific but manageable forage fish keep the population of the larger and less desirable gizzard shad in check while providing abundant food for other species. Threadfin shad are susceptible to winterkill, but are prolific breeders that will spawn continuously, all summer long. Consequently, they die off regularly, preventing overpopulation, are restocked in the spring, and provide a veritable banquet for gamefish during the warm months when feeding activity is greatest.

Naturally, one of the best lures to use in waters where threadfin are present are the shad-type jigs with soft-plastic bodies and swimming tails. These jigs can be cast to cover and worked over structure, but one of the most productive tactics is to seek out roving schools of shad, especially those that have been driven into shallow water or to the surface of deep waters by feeding gamefish, such as white bass, largemouth bass, or stripers. Watch for surface activity and flocks of diving and feeding gulls. A pair of binoculars is handy for spotting and verifying such activity.

Once such a school has been located, get to it as fast as possible, as the feeding can stop as quickly as it started, although it may go on for a half-hour or more, if you're lucky. As you near the school, slow your approach and carefully get within casting range. Make your casts to the edge of the baitfish school, and work your jig back with a darting and falling action that simulates a wounded shad.

If you're fortunate enough to find several large schools of baitfish being worked over by gamefish, it's likely that several schools of gamefish are beneath them. If you catch only small fish, try one of the other schools, as fish of a size tend to run together. Naturally, once you find the school of big fish, try to stay with them as they move.

On a windy day, you can often find the schools of baitfish on the leeward or downwind side of a lake or reservoir. Start searching and fishing there, as the predator species will surely be nearby.

Normally, the aggressive northern pike is sought by jig anglers using large jigs and jig rigs and tackle to match. But this 14-pound brute was tempted with a ⅛-ounce pearl Wig-Wag Minno with spinner arm attached. Bing McClellan—fishing alone in a canoe near Old Mission Point on Lake Michigan—managed to subdue the big pike without a landing net using ultralight tackle and four-pound test line. (*Photo courtesy Burke Fishing Lures.*)

I have mentioned the jig-head/twist-tail combination often enough for you to surmise that it is not only my favorite type of jig but my favorite lure of any kind. The reason is that it is so versatile and can be fished at virtually any depth, when the right head is matched with the right tail.

On the big lakes and reservoirs, my wife and I catch about 90 percent of our fish with jig heads and twist-tails. And invariably when we return to the dock with a good string of fish to show for our efforts, other anglers will ask us what we used to make our catch. When we say jigs and they eye the rigs tied to our lines, the reaction is always the same: "Oh, had to go deep for 'em, eh?"

This is probably the greatest misconception about jigs and jig fishing. The fisherman who hasn't grasped the versatility of the jig thinks that we do all our fishing by bouncing bottom, and nothing could be further from the truth. Certainly, when we need to go deep, the jig does a dandy job of getting there and catching fish. But it will also catch fish in weedy

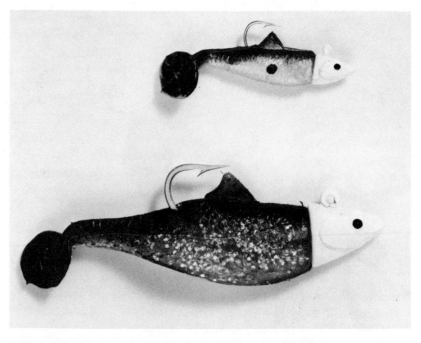

Shad-type jigs, such as Burke's Shifty Shad, are especially effective in reservoirs where threadfin shad are present.

shallows and along shoreline cover. And that's why we rely so much on the jig head and twist-tail.

The soft-plastic tails are buoyant, and they can be used to control the descent of the jig. A four-inch tail rigged on a ⅛-ounce head will sink slowly and can be worked beautifully in only a couple of feet of water. It's ideal for working over flooded brush and weedbeds in the early spring when the water level is up on a natural lake. When the retrieve is fast and the rod is kept high, it will swim just beneath the surface; slow the retrieve and lower the rod, and it will swim to the depths along the edges of weedbeds, dropoffs, ledges, and the like. Rig the same tail on a ¼-ounce head, and it will sink faster and is perfect for working gravel bars and creek mouths. Switch to a ⅜-ounce head, and you have a lure that drops quickly to the bottom in moderately deep water. Need a shallow-water skimmer? Switch to a slider head.

You can also increase or decrease the rate of descent by switching tails. A larger tail will sink slowly; a smaller tail will drop quickly. No lure is more versatile and more adaptable to a wider range of conditions.

In Chapter 9, I discussed the resurgence of jig-'n'-pig rigs that is virtually sweeping the nation. I talked about the effectiveness and efficiency of the weedless living-rubber jigs used with pork frogs, and at the end of that chapter I said that the methods employed with these rigs are every bit as important as the materials comprising them.

For years, pork frogs were used, as you might surmise, to imitate live frogs. They were cast toward shore from a boat, often near lily pads, weedbeds, and other cover, and were retrieved on or near the surface. Some pork-frog anglers "dry-lined" them on the retrieve—that is, they used them without additional weight, cast them as usual, then held their rods high so the line did not touch the water. They cranked them in with the enticing action of a skittering, skimming, frantic frog.

To be sure, these methods worked and still do. They catch fish, particularly fish bent on eating frogs. But in creating the illusion of a frog, the action imparted to the pork-rind bait is every bit as important as the appearance of the bait. Likewise, a different method could be used to create an entirely different illusion, which is what has been happening recently with the pork frogs and living-rubber jigs.

By substituting a brown, orange, or black pork frog for the traditional green-spotted number, and impaling it on a weedless living-rubber jig, the rig can be passed off as the bass's favorite food of all: the crawfish.

Then, if you further the illusion by crawfishing the rig over bottom structure, you're apt to arrive at the perfect combination of materials and method to fool a lot of hungry bass.

That's precisely what a number of jig fishermen have done. Hence, the growing popularity of jig-'n'-pig rigs and seasonal shortages of pork frogs in crawfish colors.

Although these rigs will work in the lily pads, weedbeds, and flooded brush and timber, and are even used to take suspended bass, my favorite spots are creek mouths, creek channels, gravel bars, and rocky dropoffs and ledges. I especially like to cast to visible cover in such areas. After the cast, I let the rig sink to the bottom on a taut line. When it has rested on bottom for a full minute, I twitch my rod to scoot the rig across bottom for a few inches, but no more than a foot. It is usually after one of these scoots, when the rig stops again, that a bass will smash it. Often, it will be nailed on the first scoot.

After the pickup, I usually hesitate only a second or less before setting the hook, to give the fish time to suck the rig into his mouth. Although some anglers do this with a bit of slack in their lines, I like to keep the line taut. Try it both ways and pick the one that works best for you.

The combination of bulky living-rubber dressings and the natural buoyancy of the thick hog-hide frogs causes these rigs to sink slowly, which allows the angler much more control than he would have over a faster-sinking lure. If you need something that sinks faster—for fishing deeper waters, for example—you can use a jig dressed more sparsely. For even less buoyancy, you can trim some of the meat away from the pork frog with a sharp knife. Experiment until you find the combinations that work best for you in the types of water you normally fish.

Here is a good spot to discuss the Aquacone lures I was introduced to recently. Inventor Bob Courtright was good enough to let me have several prototypes of his new lures to try out. The Sow Belly Jig, at first glance, isn't terribly out of the ordinary. It has a molded-in fiber weed guard and is dressed with a bulky body of living rubber. Any experienced jig fisherman would take one look at it and surmise that this jig would be a top-notch fish producer when rigged with a pork frog, pork eel, or plastic twist-tail. But so are most such jigs.

The Sow Belly Jig, however, differs from the others in several ways. First, the hook is finished dull black, for those who fear that hook visibility will put off picky eaters. More important to me is the nifty little wire gizmo attached along the hook shank that has been put there to hold soft plastics (twist-tails, grubs, plastic worms, etc.) in place and to keep them from sliding down around the bend. Most impressive of all, though, is the machine-tied dressing of living rubber. Turn it any which way you please, and I defy you to find any evidence of wrapping material. Moreover, in addition to a generous body dressing of fine living-rubber strands, immediately behind the head is a hackle-style dressing of more living rubber that simulates legs or pectoral fins, depending on how the jig is used.

The clincher is the new, injection-molded, soft-plastic crawfish that Courtright has developed for use with the Sow Belly Jig. I've never seen such accurately detailed crawfish-type lures. They look alive and feel like every soft craw I've ever baited a hook with. They just have to catch bass.

The Gorilla Killa is a real departure in jig design—something I've come to expect from Bob Courtright, who is a research biologist by education, a lure inventor by trade, and a diehard fisherman by passion and avocation. The Gorilla Killa is a leadhead jig sheathed in a pliable plastic body with a molded dorsal hump that completely guards the hook point from snags, yet readily collapses on the strike. Emanating from each side of the jig, just behind the eyes, are living-rubber pectoral fins. Trailing the hook is buoyant plastic "berry" and a bulky skirt of living

Worth/Aquacone Sow Belly jig and soft-plastic crawfish. Molded-in wire holds plastic worms or twist-tails securely on the hook shank.

rubber. The lure is available in eight body colors, and unlike other jigs and jig-type lures each has a light-colored underbelly as is found in nearly all natural prey. Moreover, the tough plastic body will not chip or peel as painted jigs do.

The Gorilla Killa has a striking resemblance to the sculpins that so many saltwater gamefish (most notably, striped bass, lingcod, and various rockfish) like to dine on. When I commented on this, Bob smiled and said, "We call our saltwater version the Rock Hopper Jig."

In working one of these new jigs, the best technique is to cast and let it settle to the bottom. After a pause, twitch your rod to scoot the jig across the bottom—the living-rubber dressing opens like a blooming flower. Then, when you scoot the jig forward, the dressing collapses again in a very seductive manner.

Certainly, there are many other types of jigs and methods of fishing them that I haven't discussed. But I've covered my favorites and the kinds of fresh water where you can put them to the test. In the final chapter, I'll discuss some of my favorite saltwater haunts, the species that inhabit them, and the tactics that will help you catch these great marine fishes.

Worth/Aquacone Gorilla Killa is about the most weedless jig ever designed.

13. ⚓ Saltwater Jig-Fishing Tactics

Modern jigs and jig fishing had their origins in salt water, where leadhead jigs and diamond jigs have been taking fish for more than fifty years. With the growth and widespread popularity of spinning tackle in this country and the subsequent development of smaller, lighter jigs, freshwater anglers soon discovered the effectiveness of these lures and began using them to take all types of freshwater game-fish and panfish. Ironically, although the jig was first a saltwater lure, most of the new jigs that show up on the market these days are designed primarily for freshwater fishing. But, as things tend to go full circle, alert saltwater anglers often see in the freshwater jigs and jig-fishing methods possibilities for saltwater application.

A good case in point is the development of the plastic worm, which was first and foremost a largemouth-bass lure. It and other soft-plastic lures have found their way into many a saltwater tackle box and have taken a wide variety of marine species, both inshore and offshore.

Much of what you have learned about freshwater jigs and jig fishing, then, can be applied to saltwater angling, particularly for inshore species. So I would encourage you to draw on your knowledge of jigs and jig fishing in general when you set out to fish the salt chuck.

If you're an experienced saltwater angler, I needn't acquaint you with the vagaries of the sport. And, most likely, what I have to say about jigs and jig-fishing tactics for saltwater won't be news to you. But if you're mainly a freshwater angler who occasionally makes trips to the coast, or if you're considering your first trip and your first try for saltwater species, perhaps a few tips I have to share will help you take more fish.

Inshore Salt Water

In our discussion of freshwater jig-fishing tactics, we divided our attention and focused first on moving-water (creek and river) angling, then on still-water (pond, lake, and reservoir) methods. Although any body of salt water is a world of its own, some useful comparisons can be drawn between it and various types of fresh water. Moreover, saltwater fishes share many common traits with their freshwater cousins.

Our upper bay areas, salt marshes, and brackish backwaters are not entirely unlike a number of our freshwater lakes and reservoirs and can be fished in similar fashion. In other areas, inshore salt water is much like our freshwater rivers where tidal flows can be compared to stream currents and worked accordingly.

As with the freshwater fishes, marine species can be generally divided into convenient categories: gamefish, panfish, and baitfish. Additionally, the inshore saltwater environs, like their freshwater counterparts, harbor numerous other organisms, many of which provide food for fish. Among them are several types of sea worms, crab, shrimp, and clams.

Where inshore salt water departs dramatically from fresh water in characteristics are in its vastness, its constant state of change, and, of course, its connection and relationships with the open seas.

In the United States we have 12,383 miles of general coastline. That's a lot of territory. But when we change our methods of measurement to include not only the outer coast but offshore islands, bays, sounds, estuaries, and tidal creeks and rivers upstream to the head of tidewater, our tidal-shoreline area swells to a staggering 88,633 miles. In evaluating any coastal state, then, in terms of its availability of inshore angling opportunities, its length of coastline is not a useful criterion; its overall tidal shoreline is the key. The state of Maryland, for example, has only 31 miles of general coastline, but a whopping 3,190 miles of tidal shoreline. Florida's Atlantic coastline is 580 miles long and its Gulf coast stretches some 770 miles, but its combined Atlantic and Gulf of Mexico tidal shoreline amounts to 8,426 miles. Our largest state, Alaska, has 5,580 miles of Pacific coastline and 1,060 miles of Arctic coastline, but 33,904 miles of tidal shoreline.

All of this vast area is affected by weather, the seasons, offshore currents (such as the Japanese Current in the Pacific and the Gulf Stream in the Atlantic), salinity levels, and by tides. While all of these play major roles in the presence and behavior of marine fishes and the tactics of marine anglers, the tides are probably the single most important influence on inshore species and angling.

Tides, the rising and falling of sea waters, are caused by the gravitational attraction of the sun and the moon, with the moon exerting the greatest tidal influence on the earth's oceans. The tides change completely twice every 24 hours and 51 minutes, or each lunar day. That is, there will be two high tides and two low tides on most days of the year.

The exchange of water, the difference between high and low tide, varies from month to month, day to day, tide to tide, and from one part of the coast to another. It is also influenced by geographical features, phases of the moon, and the alignment of the sun and moon relative to earth. In some areas, the differences between high and low tide are so small as to be virtually unnoticeable. In other areas, the differences are dramatic. In North America, tide changes can be so small as to create a difference of only a few inches between high and low tide, as is the case in the vicinity of New Orleans, Louisiana. Or, as at certain times of the year in the Bay of Fundy, Nova Scotia, high and low tides can differ by as much as 53 feet.

The incoming tide is known as the flood tide, and outgoing tide is an ebb tide. The unusually high tides that coincide with a new or full moon are called spring tides. The exceptionally low tides associated with the first and third quarters of the moon are called neap tides. Tides, or tides and currents, that run in opposite directions and usually create considerable turbulence are called tiderips or rips.

What all this has to do with you is that when you travel to the coast to fish unfamiliar waters, you'll need to concern yourself with tides. But since the tides vary so greatly from one part of the country to another (indeed, from one part of a bay to another) and since fish and fishing will be affected differently, you'll have to talk to local fishermen, bait-and-tackle-shop owners, marina operators, and fish-and-game agents to find out where, when, why, and how to fish the tides. You'll find, for example, that some species are best sought on a flood tide, while others are normally caught on the ebb tide. In some areas and with some species, you'll find slack water (high or low) the best part of the tide to fish, while other species are normally caught only in tidal flows. And you'll discover notable exceptions to most of the rules.

In the larger bays and estuaries, you might even find that at some locations a certain species of fish is normally caught on a flood tide, while elsewhere the same fish are caught on the ebb tide. And it's not really as daffy and difficult to reason out as it may at first seem.

For example, I live on a large bay where, from late winter to mid-summer, several species of surfperch are taken in good numbers. Although decent catches are made in the surf along open ocean beaches, the best catches are made in the bay, during the spring, when schools of perch come in on the flood tide to feed. In the upper bay, the best fishing is usually during the two hours before high slack tide. When the tide turns, it's possible to drive to several spots along the shore of the lower bay and intercept the schools as they head back out on the ebb tide. So you might talk to one fisherman who will swear that the perch hit best on an incoming tide, while another will try to convince you that you should always fish an outgoing tide. Nail down the spots where they're fishing, and you'll soon see a pattern developing—one that will put you on the fish.

Some marine species do show a marked preference for the flood tide when they cruise the inundated flats and grassbeds searching for food. Others will congregate in the channels on the ebb tide where they wait to ambush baitfishes forced off the flats and out of the grassbeds by receding waters.

On the whole, in the various places I've fished over the years, I've taken more fish on the flood tide than on the ebb. For that reason, when I'm fishing unfamiliar waters and haven't been able to gain any local intelligence or recommendations on which tides to fish, I'll fish the four hours around high slack tide—two hours before and two hours after high tide. In this way I have the chance to fish the flood and the ebb, and if I haven't found fish, I still have the opportunity to do a bit more prospecting on the outgoing tide. If I haven't connected with fish by low slack tide, the next time out I make it a point to be fishing four hours before high tide, reasoning that perhaps I arrived too late on the flood tide the first time.

Along the Atlantic, Gulf, and Pacific coasts, some of the most important sport species are the abundant marine panfish. You'll find most anglers going after them with live and cut baits that they fish on bottom, but many of these fish will readily take jigs. Bucktail and marabou jigs that are painted and dressed to simulate forage species in any particular area are always top producers. If you're unsure about local baitfishes, the so-called crappie jigs in white or yellow are good lures to prospect with. Small bucktail and marabou jigs in the same colors are also good in the same waters, and I've found that those dressed with a few strands of silver tinsel are the best in clear, inshore waters. I also like $1/16$-ounce and $1/8$-ounce jig heads dressed with pearl-white or black twist-tails. And the $1/8$-ounce pearl-white Wig-Wag Minno is always a top choice for the smaller marine species.

White is always my first choice of jig colors when I'm fishing unfamiliar inshore waters. You'll find yellow another standby and black a good third choice. But with some experimentation, you might find other colors to be even better at times. For example, by studying the stomach contents of surfperch for a couple of seasons, I found that while these fish fed on a great variety of marine organisms (including small crabs, ghost shrimp, and clam necks), the largest fish were invariably gorged with tiny, semitransparent pink fish that resemble killifish. One three-pound perch had 28 of these fish in its stomach. I had caught perch on small white jigs but always fared better with bait, namely, shrimp or nightcrawlers. I didn't start catching them consistently on jigs until I tried $1/8$-ounce, hot-pink Wig-Wag Minnos. As a bonus, I have also caught several small salmon and steelhead while fishing for perch with these jigs, which leads me to believe that I might do well to try them in the

Part of the inshore jig fisherman's arsenal of jig heads and plastic grub and shrimp tails. (*Photo by C. Boyd Pfeiffer.*)

tidewater stretches of our coastal rivers when the anadromous salmon and trout are making their spawning migrations.

Flounder and other flatfishes are also great targets for the jig fisherman. While a good many of these fish are taken by still-fishing with bait, the angler who keeps his bait moving will fare best. Flounder like to lie on the bottom where they can blend naturally into their environment and can ambush hapless forage species. A white bucktail, marabou, or twist-tail jig, worked slowly along the bottom is probably the best flounder lure there is. In roiled waters, I like a small white bucktail tipped with a small strip bait or piece of shrimp. On the flats, I prefer light tackle and light line that I can use to make long casts and work the jig slowly over the bottom. In deeper waters, I prefer to fish from a drifting boat where I jig vertically for flounder.

In addition to the plentiful panfish found in inshore salt water, the young of some larger gamefish are also present and can be seasonally abundant. The red drum (also known as redfish or channel bass) is an example. While large red drum are taken regularly on leadhead and diamond jigs fished in the surf (particularly at the northern reaches of their range, from the Carolinas to New Jersey) along the south Atlantic and Gulf coasts, so-called "puppy drum" are taken consistently with jigs in inshore waters. Your best bet for these fish, which run up to about 10 pounds, are jig heads and soft-plastic shrimp tails.

Although red drum of any size are tough and tenacious fighters, they tend to take a jig gently and mouth it before inhaling it. So when you feel a pickup, it's best to hesitate for a second before setting the hook.

Also of importance to the inshore jig fisherman are the members of the rather large jack family, which include the amberjacks, crevalle, yellowtail, runners, scads, permits, pompanos, lookdowns, leatherjackets, and various jacks. More than thirty species of jacks are known to occur in North American waters. Although most are considered tropical or subtropical fishes, some species range well up the east coast of the United States.

This diverse family of fishes includes some considered unfit for human consumption and others that are highly prized as table fare. Some will seldom exceed a pound in weight or one foot in length, while others may reach three or four feet in length and exceed 50 pounds. The greater amberjack has been reported to reach a maximum weight of 177 pounds, although fish of 10 to 15 pounds are probably nearer the average.

Most members of the family are superb gamefish. They are strong, fast, and dogged fighters. Although they aren't jumpers, their strikes are normally fast and hard. While amberjack and large permit call for substantial tackle and stout lines, most jacks can be pursued with light spinning tackle and lines of 6- and 15-pound test.

If you enjoy eating the fish you catch, you'll find the Florida pompano unexcelled in the culinary department. It is, as well, a superb gamefish on light tackle. So named because of the extensive commercial fishery in Florida, this species ranges as far up the east coast as Massachusetts, although it is more plentiful farther south, particularly along Florida's Atlantic coast.

Pompano are school fish that frequent sandy beach areas, inlets, and bays, often moving into shallow backwaters on the flood tide and heading out to open beach areas on the ebb tide. The angler equipped with small white jigs and light tackle who can intercept these feeding schools will usually outfish the bait fisherman, will find great sport, and will reap an epicurean delicacy in the process.

The crevalle (also known as jack crevalle, common jack, and horse crevalle, among others) is an often maligned fish, considered by some to be a nuisance. I'll admit that the sometimes large loose schools of crevalle on the prowl can get in the way of other fishing as they viciously slash and strike at everything you toss in the water, but I certainly can't fault them for it, especially when the target species might prove to be elusive or totally unavailable. Crevalle have certainly saved more than one otherwise fishless day for me and many other anglers as well.

They're not great on the table, although if dressed and bled soon after they're caught and then either canned or smoked they can be worth the trouble.

When you look at a crevalle (or most other jacks, for that matter), it's hard to believe that they can be so fast. A bonefish looks fast. A ladyfish looks fast. Barracuda, wahoo, king mackerel, and dolphin look fast. But a crevalle just looks tough and mean, which he is, too. The speed with with a crevalle can overtake a lure and the runs that follow are shocking to the angler new to jack fishing.

I remember one windy afternoon in southern Florida. I was walking a long, narrow spit and working a shallow bay area for barracuda. I had spotted several fair-size fish suspended just beneath the surface. On a calm day I could have easily reached them with the big Upperman jig dressed with white bucktail. My seven-foot, fast-taper rod and eight-pound-test line were perfect for making long casts to the basking barracuda, but stout crosswinds caused the jig to fall short by 20 feet or more on every cast. In several dozen tries, I hadn't once put the jig near enough to catch the attention of the big, lazy barracuda. I had attracted two hammerhandles and managed to catch and release one of them.

Trying to time my two-handed casts for the lulls between the gusts, I heaved once more with all my might. A wind that might well have been dubbed "Flora" or "Daniel" and put the entire south coast on storm watch nabbed my jig in mid-air and carried it up the spit, dropping it only a short distance beyond the edge of the spit in the small but growing combers. To retrieve my misplaced jig and keep it from snagging in the rip-rap along the spit, I held my rod tip high and cranked the reel handle as fast as I could. I could see my jig speeding toward me only inches beneath the surface, when suddenly in a blur of blue and flash of gold, it swapped directions, bent my rod double, and nearly yanked me from my precarious balance.

My drag complained in a long, high-pitched whine, as the fish made a headlong nonstop run, for which I would have been much better prepared had I been wading the bonefish flats. With line so taut that it sung in the wind, I managed to turn the fish before my reel spool came up bare black plastic. In the ensuing 15 minutes, I had to lean against a half-dozen similar runs, horse the fish away from the rip-rap, turn him out of grassy shallows, and coax him up when he sounded for bottom debris and coral heads that would part the light line on contact.

I had no idea of what I had tied into, but I knew it was no barracuda. Although it had all the speed and maneuverability of the blue runners I caught regularly in the same spot and on the same bucktail jigs, it was much larger and stronger than those small jacks that seldom exceeded two pounds and averaged closer to one.

When the fish finally but reluctantly admitted defeat, I kept my rod high and line taut and let it wash in on a small breaker. When I eased it up on the spit, I was shocked to see how small the crevalle was for all the fight it had given me; it couldn't have weight more than five or six pounds, but had fought longer and harder than many fish twice the size would have.

My next shock came when I reached down to remove my jig. He had swallowed it! Far back in the fish's throat I could see the nose of the jig and a few strands of white bucktail, but that was all. Remember, I was cranking that jig across the water as fast as I could possibly reel, yet this mighty fish was able not only to overtake it, but with sufficient speed to entirely engulf it.

Among the most fascinating and unusual inshore areas to fish are the flats found in southern Florida and elsewhere. Although they're often referred to as "bonefish flats," there are other species that frequent these broad expanses of shallow waters, and most can be taken on jigs. In fact, while fly fishing might rank as the most challenging way to take the bonefish, barracuda, permit, and other species that feed on the flats, I think jig fishing is probably the most efficient method.

Whether you're wading the flats or working from the casting platform of a flats skiff, this is sight angling that calls for peak alertness, good vision, polaroid sunglasses, total concentration, and the ability to make accurate casts.

Most bonefish anglers agree that presentation of the jig is more important than color and design, although white, yellow, and light-pink bucktail dressings are probably used more than any other colors. Head weights of ⅛ and ¼ ounce are standard, the smaller weight always preferable if it can be cast the required distance and put in the right spot. Lines of six- or eight-pound test are standard and should be spooled on reels capable of holding at least 200 yards, matched with medium-action rods of 6½ to 7 feet. The hooked bonefish is likely to make an initial run of 50 to 100 yards: hence, the need for plenty of line in reserve. The long rod held high will help keep the line from tangling in grasses or abrading on coral heads. It should go without saying that the reel should be in top form, with a smooth and well-oiled drag.

Bonefish generally move from deep channels onto the flats on the flood tide to feed on shrimp, crab, and other forage species found on the flats. They are bottom feeders that root in the sand and marl in a nose-down tail-up attitude. Feeding fish are often located in shallow waters when their caudal fins wag above the surface. These are known as "tailing" fish and are prime targets for the jig fisherman who tries to put his jig a yard or so in front of the fish.

In deeper waters, schools of bonefish are often located by the clouds of suspended sediment they create when feeding. These are known as "mudding" fish and are a bit more difficult to cast for, as individuals might be impossible to pick out in the cloudy waters, and jigs won't be as visible to the fish.

Cruising fish in clear waters are the most difficult of all to cast to, as the slightest movement detected by the school can send the fish scurrying off the flats for the safer haven of deep water. Casts should be made well ahead of these fish, as much as 20 feet, with the hope of intercepting the school and coaxing a strike.

Jigs are perhaps the best lures for pursuing bonefish on the flats. This one was taken by Bill Wilke of Baltimore, Maryland, while he was fishing the turtle grass flats of the Turniffe Islands off Belize in British Honduras. (*Photo by C. Boyd Pfeiffer.*)

No matter what situation you encounter, you should always try to make a careful approach and a bull's-eye cast. Then work your jig very slowly across the bottom, inching it along with light twitches of the rod. And when I say "inch it," I don't mean "foot it."

Bonefishing can be mighty frustrating, and unless you are on an extended trip with plenty of time to learn the flats and the fish, you would be well advised to hire a guide. A guide will put you onto many more fish than you'll ever find on your own. In fact, one day of fishing with a competent guide will teach you more about bonefishing than you'll learn on your own in a month.

Barracuda frequent the flats, and the smaller ones are generally easier to catch than bonefish. Big barracuda can be aloof and elusive at times, but the smaller ones are almost always willing to chase a well-placed jig, skittered through the clear, shallow water. They seem to prefer a bit of flash, so white or yellow bucktail jigs dressed with a few strands of tinsel or Mylar are your best bets. Although they'll readily take jig heads dressed with soft-plastic tails, their needle-sharp teeth will make short work of these. Even the tougher bucktails will succumb to repeated strikes by barracuda, so take along plenty of extra jigs.

The real brute of the flats is the permit, one of the larger members of the jack family. Although they are present in good numbers at times, they're tough to entice into striking. But patience and persistence can pay off in a spectacular battle with a fine gamefish.

Like bonefish, permit spend most of their time in the deeper channels and holes, but move onto the flats on a flood tide to feed. Since these deep-bodied fish require more water than bonefish do, they come in later on the tide and leave earlier than bonefish.

Permit are often sighted swimming the flats in search of food or are found feeding, during which their caudal and dorsal fins will break the surface. As with bonefishing, your casts should be accurate, and you may have to cast a number of times to any given fish if he is rooting for food on the bottom.

Most permit anglers use the same spinning gear as bonefishermen, either intentionally or because of the fact that permit might be taken incidentally to bonefishing. At any rate, a medium-action spinning outfit and eight-pound-test line should prove adequate for tossing ¼-ounce jigs, but be forewarned: you might end up doing battle with a fish of 20 pounds or more with all the speed and brute strength associated with this rugged family of gamefishes.

Bucktail jigs in white or yellow are the favored lures, and for added insurance you might try tipping yours with a piece of shrimp or a whole shrimp tail. Hooks should be sharp, and you'll need to set the hook several times to penetrate the permit's rubbery mouth beyond the barb.

Another southern Florida environment unlike anything else on earth is the Everglades, with its tangles of mangroves and its myriad creeks, channels, and backwaters. Since summer rains tend to freshen the waters and drive many marine species toward areas of higher salinity, and winter storms tend to muddy the waters and lower the temperatures below the tolerance level of many species, spring and fall are the times to fish the glades. Mild winters can produce some outstanding fishing, so don't pass the Everglades by if you're there then. And, to be sure, the veteran glades angler can find fish even during chilly snaps or stormy weather.

If you plan to venture into the inside waters of the Everglades, I recommend that you hire a guide for at least the first trip or two. After that, if you know how to handle a boat, can read a chart, and use a compass, you might want to go it on your own. But if you're unfamiliar with the glades, a guide will not only be more successful at finding fish, but he'll also keep you from getting lost in the maze of creeks, sloughs, ditches, and jungle that are the Everglades.

The outside waters of the glades, along the southwestern tip of Florida, are much easier to work, but even there you'd be well off to fish them with a guide the first time out. Depending on weather and season, you can expect to find bluefish, snook, tarpon, spotted seatrout, red drum, cobia, ladyfish, various jacks, grouper, snapper, and other species that will readily take your jigs.

For these waters, I would recommend a greater assortment of jigs than is required on the flats. Although the same bucktail jigs that you might use for bonefish and permit will certainly take most species here, you'll find others to be better producers of some gamefish. Jig heads dressed with plastic shrimp tails or grubs are best for spotted seatrout and red drum. Bucktail, marabou, or feather jigs, dressed with large pork-rind strips or Ripple Rinds are great for tarpon, and they'll hold up better than the soft plastics when used for the toothy species. A black weedless jig, dressed with a black plastic twist-tail or black pork-rind eel is deadly on snook and can be tossed right up into the aerial roots of the mangroves.

Of course, southern Florida isn't the only place for the inshore jig fisherman to find sport. All tidal shoreline areas in the United States harbor fish that will take jigs. Some will seasonally provide fishing every bit as good as, and at times even better than, you'll find in the abundant and productive waters of the Florida peninsula.

Although the diehard bluefish and seatrout fishermen might debate the point, most inshore anglers will agree that the striped bass is the king of inshore fishes, not only because the striper grows large and is great sport

Seatrout are among the most sought-after species by jig fishermen. Joel Arrington took this one with a jig head dressed with a plastic grub tail while fishing off North Carolina's Outer Banks. *(Photo by C. Boyd Pfeiffer.)*

and fine eating as well, but because it is available to sport fishermen in so many areas.

Old linesides is present in varying degrees of abundance along the Atlantic coast from northern Florida to the Gulf of St. Lawrence, with Atlantic concentrations apparent from South Carolina to Massachusetts. It is also found along the Gulf coasts of Florida and Louisiana.

Striped bass were introduced to the Pacific in 1879, but their range there is restricted to the northern California, Oregon, and southern Washington coasts. In California, stripers are mainly concentrated in San Francisco Bay, along nearby open ocean beaches, and in the river-delta areas of the upper bay. Along the Oregon and Washington coasts, stripers are found in several coastal bays and rivers, including the Columbia, but population concentrations are highest in Oregon in the Winchester Bay area and lower reaches of the Smith and Umpqua rivers as well as the Coos Bay area and lower reaches of the Coos and Millicoma (North Fork Coos) rivers.

Stripers are anadromous fish, seldom found far offshore. They like bays and estuaries and are often found in brackish and fresh water. Along the east coast, some populations migrate northward for some distance during the summer months and later return to their wintering grounds. They also make spawning migrations up coastal streams in late spring and early summer.

On the west coast, stripers are generally dispersed in the bays during the summer where they gorge themselves on abundant forage fishes. In the fall they migrate into the river delta areas, and many spend the winter in the rivers, moving farther upstream in the spring to spawn.

Just about anywhere and anytime they're available, stripers are prime targets for jig fishermen. In the surf, where stripers move right into the combers to feed on schooled baitfish, surf fishermen toss heavy leadheads and diamond jigs to the feeding fish.

In the bays and coastal rivers, jigs are cast and trolled, both for the large stripers that tend to be loners and for the smaller school fish.

Where stripers are concerned, it's best to go well prepared with a good variety of tackle and baits; when these fish show a preference for one particular food, they tend to shun all other offerings. Consequently, when my wife and I head out for a bout with striped bass, we have a tackle box full of lures and three rods and reels apiece, rigged and ready for whatever we might encounter. We each have a trolling outfit and two spinning rods and reels rigged for casting.

During the spring and summer on the rivers, our trolling rods are usually rigged with either Rebel Super Minnow lures or Bomber Water Dogs, trailed by white or yellow bucktail jigs. We alternate the jigs and usually dress them with four-inch pieces of plastic worms or four-inch twist-tails. In the fall, we usually troll with the same rigs and with Burke Jig-A-Do Eels as well.

During the summer on the bay, we sometimes troll with identical rigs, but we also use magnum-size Wig-Wag Minnos and Weber Hoochy Trolls as well. We generally tip the Hoochy Trolls with strips of herring or anchovy.

The spinning outfits we carry for casting are the same ones we use for freshwater largemouth-bass fishing. We each have a medium-action, fast-taper rod and reel spooled with 15-pound-test line, rigged with a 1/4-ounce to 1/2-ounce jig (usually a jig head and four-inch twist-tail), or a 3/8-ounce or 5/8-ounce Wig-Wag Minno. We also carry medium-action spinning rods with fairly stout tips. These outfits are rigged for surface-school action with a popping-type plug, usually trailed by a jig, popper/dropper style.

These are the rigs we start with and stay with if we get into fish. But if we need to prospect, we have plenty of backup tackle and bait along. We use a variety of jigs, but most are either dressed with bucktail or soft plastic. On slack tides, we also like to work eight-inch plastic worms or nine-inch plastic twist-tails on worming jig heads of 1/4 to 3/4 ounce, depending on depths and currents. These rigs are good for working cover and the flats on high slack tide. On low slack tide, we probe the pockets, pools, and channels with them. Occasionally, we drift them through the channels on an ebb tide. In weedy, rocky, or other snag-strewn waters, we often switch to a weedless jig and pork-rind eel.

When the stripers are showing a marked preference for bait and the still-fishermen are lining the banks of our coastal rivers and sloughs, we switch to bucktail jigs and strip baits. In clear water, we use either white or yellow jigs; in roiled waters, we use black. We rig our jigs with fillets cut from frozen herring or anchovies we buy, or sculpins we catch in the bay (on tiny jigs, of course). We cast from shore or from a boat, but we cover plenty of territory, reasoning that we're more likely to catch fish than the fisherman bound to a camp stool and bonfire. We might not be as cozy and comfortable, especially during blustery weather, but it's really surprising how a bent rod and the run of a powerful fish can warm you to the marrow.

There is a certain amount of seasonal overlapping of inshore and off-shore species along many stretches of United States coast. Although the pelagic species will range nearer to or farther from shore than normal with the drifts in currents, they are normally not available to the inshore angler. But a fair number of reef dwellers and bottom fishes will work into the bays and backwaters at times, and you should remain alert for such out-of-the-ordinary migrations; these fish are oriented toward bottom structure or cover, and jigs are the best lures to probe such areas.

On my own part of the coast, for example, there is some excellent offshore fishing for a fair variety of reef and bottom species. Some are found only a short distance offshore, while others are in honey holes well out and deep down. In the winter, though, some of these fish move into the lower reaches of the bay and concentrate in several depressions. I only discovered their presence last year and haven't yet figured why they come into the bay during the cold months, unless it's because the seasonal rains so drastically lower the salinity of the upper bay as to drive crab, shrimp, and forage fishes to the lower reaches of the bay where they are easy prey for these fish.

At any rate, there are a couple of holes just a short run from the launch ramp that are devoid of fish during the summer months, but which give up sizable catches in the winter. The technique is quite simple. We launch our boat, head for the hole, and shut down the outboard up current. Using medium-action spinning rods rigged with jig heads and four-inch, pearl-white twist-tails, we cast and let our rigs sink to the bottom. As the boat drifts over the hole, we keep a taut line and occasionally impart slight jigging action. It only takes a few minutes to drift the length of the hole, and rare is the drift that doesn't result in several strikes and a hookup or two. At the termination of the drift, I simply switch on the electric trolling motor, return the boat to its original position, shut the motor off, cast out, and make another drift which usually accounts for more strikes and another fish or two. Most are rockfish of one variety or another, but now and then we'll pull up a nice lingcod or cabezon. Later in the winter, we'll pick up a starry flounder or two.

If you live on or near the coast, you can find such spots the same way we did. We watched. On drives along the bay, we made it a point to keep a pair of binoculars in the pickup. When we saw several small boats working an area, we found a good spot to park and study the fishermen through the glasses. Sure enough, they were catching fish. We pinpointed their locations, watched their patterns, and duplicated their efforts.

One of the best ways to get onto the inshore action in any area is to talk to other fishermen, bait-shop owners, and marina operators. But if people tend to be closed-mouthed about angling prospects, just take matters into your own hands and spend a few days spying with binoculars. It really works, and it can put you onto the fish.

And have no qualms about your clandestine operations. More than once, my wife and I have caught others observing us from a distance with the aid of spy glasses. All's fair in love, war, and fishing.

Offshore Salt Water

Unless you own a boat suited to offshore travel and possess the necessary boat-handling skills and navigational abilities, you're going to have to rely on friends or charters for your offshore jig fishing. But you might have to educate your friends or charter-boat skippers on the qualities and fish-catching abilities of jigs. There are a lot of people who haven't caught on to the versatility and efficiency of jigs.

To be fair, plenty of offshore anglers and charter-boat skippers know what jigs can do, and they've done much to convince others that jigs are the most important of all artificial lures. But I have had to introduce a few

Various members of the jack family favor jigs above all other lures. Jackie Pfeiffer of Baltimore, Maryland, took this one while deep-water jigging with a bucktail off La Paz, Baja, Mexico. *(Photo by C. Boyd Pfeiffer.)*

friends to jigs and I've convinced more than one skipper, either verbally or by demonstration.

Among the most popular and effective methods for taking the deep-water denizens is vertical jigging. Both large leadhead and diamond jigs are employed and are sometimes dressed with strip baits, soft-plastic tails, or pork rinds.

Boyd Pfeiffer with king mackerel taken off North Carolina coast on casting tackle and vinyl-skirted leadhead. (*Photo courtesy C. Boyd Pfeiffer.*)

Deep-water jigging is most productive over reefs and wrecks, or near offshore oil-drilling rigs and other structure, both man-made and natural. The jig is allowed to sink to the bottom and is then worked vertically by jigging the rod. Although the jig is freespooled to the bottom, or allowed to fall to the bottom as some writers put it, it's important that you

Boyd Pfeiffer hoists a hefty cobia he took with a jig near an offshore oil rig in the Gulf of Mexico off the Louisiana coast. *(Photo by Jackie Pfeiffer.)*

maintain control of the jig on the descent. The term fall implies freefall. It's better to think in terms of a controlled descent, during which you keep the line taut against the jig's weight, while letting it drop toward the bottom at its own speed. Fish will often strike a descending jig, and if you are not exercising such control, you are apt to miss a lot of pickups. As soon as you detect a pickup—either by feel or by sight of the line moving off the vertical—you must engage the reel, take in any slack, and set the hook hard.

When you feel your jig touch bottom in deep water, reel up about a foot or so of line and begin jigging. Owing to the weight of the jig and length of line you'll have out in deep water, much of the jigging action you impart with the rod will be absorbed by line stretch as well as the rolling and pitching of the boat. Consequently, your jigging action must be exaggerated. Additionally, you must use a stiff rod that will not absorb the jig's action.

Jigs are also effective on pelagic species, and when these fish might be present in any waters where you are deep-jigging, you would do well to periodically bring your jig back to the surface with a jigging action. Near bottom it will attract the reef species; on the retrieve it might well take other gamefish that are cruising or suspended at mid-depths or near the surface.

Both leadhead and diamond jigs are used for trolling in offshore waters. They are also cast and retrieved to fish that are feeding on or near the surface. And sometimes an extremely fast retrieve will excite the fish into striking.

The method known as "speed squidding" was developed in the 1960s by charter-boat skippers in the east and is an effective way to take feeding bluefish. Diamond jigs are cast and retrieved so fast as to set up a rapid vibrating action. A reel with a high-speed retrieve ratio is essential for this kind of fishing, although the lures are sometimes trolled fast to accomplish the same results.

While bluefish are favorite species for speed squidding, other Atlantic gamefish are attracted to the fast-swimming, vibrating jigs. In the Pacific, the California yellowtail, a popular member of the jack family, is another fish that will readily attack a fast-moving jig.

One jig designed specifically, albeit accidentally, for rapid retrieve or fast trolling is the Wobble Eel, manufactured by Bead Chain Tackle Co. According to the company's sales manager, Pete Renkert, "We were drifting and jigging blues off of New Haven harbor when a tanker suddenly came into view heading straight for us. Our boat's captain started racing for safety before I could retrieve my jig—an old tin-squid type that Bridgeport Silverware started selling in the late '30s.

Diamond jig and head of little tunny it took off the North Carolina coast. (*Photo by C. Boyd Pfeiffer.*)

Speed squidding produced this little tunny for Boyd Pfeiffer, who notes that these fish are caught when they're breaking the surface, chasing bait. High-speed spinning reels and the fastest retrieves are essential. (*Photo courtesy C. Boyd Pfeiffer.*)

"As the boat picked up speed and I began reeling frantically, the jig started a crazy wobbling action that I felt all the way to the butt of the rod. Intrigued, I experimented with the jig at trolling speeds for the remainder of our trip. Several modifications later, the old jig became a

Partyboat anglers cast small bucktail jigs with light spinning tackle to schools of black rockfish roving near the surface off the Oregon coast.

highly successful casting and trolling lure. Perhaps because of its heritage, it still makes a fair jig, too."

Although plenty of Atlantic and Gulf anglers have discovered the merits of light-tackle and shallow-water offshore jig fishing, this is a technique too often overlooked by west-coast anglers, particularly along the northwest coast.

Most offshore fishing off the coast of northern California, Oregon, and Washington consists of trolling for salmon and occasionally for albacore when warm currents sweep near enough to shore for the charter boats to reach the small tuna. The predominant means of catching other abundant species is by anchoring near or drifting over reefs and bottom-fishing or deep-jigging for them with heavy boat tackle. From July through the middle of September, though, many of the so-called bottom fishes can be found in relatively shallow waters not far from shore, as well as in the beds of kelp that float on the surface. And there's no better way to catch them than with light spinning gear and jigs.

Several seasons ago, I was heading back to port aboard the 65-foot charter boat, *Sea Fury*. We had set out of Coos Bay about 11 P.M. the previous night and headed up the coast to Winchester Bay where we took on a supply of live herring. We then set a westerly course and fought rough seas until dawn when the deckhands put out the trolling lines and our search for tuna began. We ranged some 100 miles offshore, trolled for more than twelve hours, and managed to hook only one small albacore that was lost near the boat.

The dozen anglers on board got rain checks for bottom-fishing trips, but no one seemed too enthused after a long, tiring, and unsuccessful trip. I wasn't all that disappointed as I knew that tuna fishing can be feast or famine; this was just one of the lean trips.

After we crossed the Coos Bay bar and were on the last short leg of our trip, Jim Ray, the *Sea Fury's* skipper and a friend of mine, turned the wheel over to the mate and took a seat beside me on the sun deck.

"Come fishing with me tomorrow," he said, in a tone that suggested he had recently been let in on a secret about vast schools of migrating fish nearby.

"I don't know if I'm up to another tuna trip so soon," I begged off.

"Naw, not tuna. Bottom fish. I'm running out to the reef about noon tomorrow, and the boat's never crowded on afternoon trips."

"I don't know, Jim. . ."

After a half hour of casting jig heads dressed with plastic twist-tails, angler Jim Martin has a good start on his bottomfish limit with a large black rockfish, two lingcod, and a cabezon.

"Hey, man, we've got the wells full of live herring. And nothing beats live bait this time of the year. We'll anchor in shallow water just off Simpson's Reef and we'll catch all the fish you want."

The following afternoon, as we cruised toward the reef with a half-dozen fishermen aboard, I noticed the beds of kelp scattered along the calm surface. While the others readied their boat rods and rigged them with sinkers and hooks for live-bait fishing, I limbered up my medium-action spinning rod and tied a snap onto the 15-pound-test line. I searched through the box of jigs and settled on a 1¼-ounce, hot-pink Wig-Wag Minno.

Jim cut the *Sea Fury's* engines, dropped the anchor, and called down from the bridge that the graph was full of fish. As the deckhands helped others bait their hooks, I started casting my jig to the floating kelp beds off the port stern. Before anybody hauled a fish up from the bottom, I had three hefty black rockfish on the deck. As the boat swung on its anchor rode, away from the kelp beds I was working, I let the jig sink to the reef and retrieved it with a slow jigging and swimming action and was soon hard into a fish of some size.

When I called for a gaff and hauled the big lingcod aboard, Jim frowned down at me over the sundeck railing. "I bring you out here with the wells full of live herring and you use jigs?" he asked incredulously.

"Whatever works, Jim," I said with a grin, as I replaced my chewed-up jig with a fresh one.

Jim moved the boat to three different spots along the reef that afternoon to quell possible mutiny among the disgruntled bait fishermen. But nothing was about to keep those jigs of mine from catching fish. Whenever the boat swung toward the kelp beds, I caught black rockfish and kelp greenling. In the open waters, I fished the jig deep and brought up more black rockfish as well as China rockfish, barred rockfish, tambor rockfish, cabezon, and lingcod.

In all, I caught my limit of three lingcod that afternoon and filled out the rest of my twenty-five-fish limit with assorted reef species. Most fell for the hot-pink Wig-Wag Minno, although I caught several of the rockfish on a ⅜-ounce chartreuse Wig-Wag Minno and all the greenling on a ⅜-ounce white bucktail jig.

The largest catch made by one angler on live bait that day was twelve fish. Not only did the jigs outfish live herring, but they proved much more versatile by taking fish at all depths, from just beneath the surface to the bottom. They were certainly easier to cast and work, and I didn't have to rebait after each fish caught. Tantamount to the jig's ability to take offshore species, though, is the light tackle that can be used for greater sport.

If you aren't fishing with jigs by now, pardner, you just aren't catching all the fish you might. For my money, there's no better lure for fishing fresh or salt water. If you're about to make that discovery yourself, get braced for some real action, and plan for the best fishing season you've ever had.

Source Directory

Following are the names and addresses of sources of jigs, related tackle, and jig-making tools and materials mentioned in this book. If you are unable to locate any company's products locally, write the company for information and a copy of its latest catalog or brochure.

Tony Accetta & Son, Inc.
932 Avenue E
Riviera Beach, FL 33404

Jim Bagley Bait Co., Inc.
L.H. Recker Hwy.
P.O. Box 110
Winter Haven, FL 33880

Bead Chain Tackle Co.
241 Mountain Grove St.
Box K
Bridgeport, CT 06605

Blakemore Sales Corp.
P.O. Box 505
Branson, MO 65616

Bomber Bait Co.
326 Lindsay
P.O. Box 1058
Gainesville, TX 76240

Burke Fishing Lures
1969 So. Airport Rd.
Traverse City, MI 49684

Cordell Tackle
P.O. Box 1452
3601 Jenny Lind Rd.
Ft. Smith, AR 72902

Creme Lure Co.
P.O. Box 87
Tyler, TX 75710

Do-It Corporation
Hwy. 63 North
Denver, IA 50622

Flambeau Products Corp.
Middlefield, OH 44062

Fle-Fly Mfg., Inc.
9406 E. 38th St.
Tulsa, OK 74145

Gapen's World of Fishin', Inc.
Highway 10
Big Lake, MN 55309

Lee Precision, Inc.
4275 Highway U
Hartford, WI 53027

326

Limit Mfg. Corp.
Box 369
Richardson, TX 75080

Lyman Products Corp.
Rt. 147
Middlefield, CT 06455

M-F Mfg. Co., Inc.
P.O. Box 12442
Ft. Worth, TX 76118

Mann's Bait Co.
Box 604
Eufaula, AL 36027

Mister Twister
P.O. Drawer 996
Minden, LA 71055

O. Mustad & Son (USA), Inc.
Box 838
247-253 Grant Ave.
Auburn, NY 13021

Netcraft
2800 Tremainsville Rd.
Toledo, OH 43613

Orbex
620 So. 8th St.
Minneapolis, MN 55404

C. Palmer Mfg., Inc.
West Newton, PA 15089

Pfeiffer's Tackle Crafters, Inc.
14303 Robcaste Rd.
Phoenix, MD 21131

Plano Molding Co.
Plano, IL 60545

Plasti-Dip International
1458 West County Rd. C
St. Paul, MN 55113

Sweet's Molds
P.O. Box 127
Springville, NY 14141

Uncle Josh Bait Co.
Fort Atkinson, WI 53538

Weber
1039 Ellis St.
Stevens Point, WI 54481

Worth Co.
P.O. Box 88
Stevens Point, WI 54481

Wright & McGill Co.
4245 E. 46th Ave.
Denver, CO 80216

Yakima Bait Co.
Box 310
Granger, WA 98932

INDEX